Indigenous Peoples and the State

Indigenous Peoples and the State

THE STRUGGLE FOR NATIVE RIGHTS

Bradley Reed Howard

NORTHERN ILLINOIS UNIVERSITY PRESS

© 2003 by Northern Illinois University Press

Published by the Northern Illinois University Press, DeKalb, Illinois 60115

Manufactured in the United States using acid-free paper

All Rights Reserved

Design by Julia Fauci

Library of Congress Cataloging-in-Publication Data

Howard, Bradley Reed.

Indigenous peoples and the state : the struggle for native rights /
Bradley Reed Howard.

   p.   cm.

Includes bibliographical references and index.

ISBN 0-87580-290-7 (alk. paper)

  1. Indigenous peoples. 2. Human rights. 3. Self-determination, National.
4. Racism. 5. Globalization. I. Title.

GN380 .H68 2002

323.1'1—dc21

2001051411

CONTENTS

Indigenous Peoples and the State

Chapter One

INDIGENOUS PEOPLES AND THE ANTHROPOLOGY OF DOMINATION

◆ Parading down a technoconsumer superhighway into the new millennium, we are unintentional witnesses to an extraordinary event: a resurgence of activism among indigenous peoples, energetically asserting their international rights not only as individual human beings but as self-determining peoples, unique and independent cultures. Long simply dismissed as relics and metaphors of times lost, their concerns confined to shadowy domains of national governmental administrations and regional economic development programs, indigenous peoples and indigenous political organizations now reach out to the international community and international law and demand the promotion and protection of their rights as "peoples," as nations.

Indigenous peoples are articulating their conception of their unique rights, a perceptive conception distinct from that originating in national governments and in larger, urban and industrial societies. They are insisting on collective rights as peoples, as proper subjects of international law, a position that is generally antagonistic to the perceptions and decisions of political and judicial institutions worldwide. They are proclaiming and protesting numerous historical and contemporary violations of their right to self-determination. A vocal portion of indigenous spokespersons and organizations demand the reinstitution of the treaty process as the preferred form of negotiation and agreement between states and indigenous nations. Until recently, neither national laws nor international law has been receptive to the exceptional political arguments and entreaties of indigenous peoples, who have characteristically been legally and scientifically designated as aboriginals and as ethnic minorities.

Because anthropologists are preoccupied with indigenous peoples and have intimate contact with them, and because they have personal and professional connections with former and contemporary colonial powers, legal systems, and cultural ideologies, they often advance and endorse misrepresentations of the colonization and assimilation of indigenous peoples, and of the aspirations of indigenous peoples, historically and presently, for self-determination. They advance these misrepresentations, whether consciously or unconsciously, deliberately or unintentionally, through ethnographic depictions, theoretical positions, and personal actions.

These longstanding political and economic relationships and anthropologists' power to create or accommodate perceptions of social identity and history—sometimes in response to, but often regardless of the criticisms and objections of indigenous peoples—suggest certain questions concerning the anthropological program: first, what perceptions of indigenous political entities, indigenous sovereignty and self-determination, and indigenous political history have anthropologists fostered? Second, what impact have anthropologists had on the creation of national and international laws in the past, and what kinds of actions are they currently taking with respect to the international movement for the rights of indigenous peoples? In other words, in what ways is it true that anthropologists have both consciously and unconsciously participated in the colonization of indigenous peoples? And now that contemporary anthropologists know that acts of colonialism and genocide violate international law and that the self-determination of peoples represents a fundamental principle of that law, how might they consider and promote both the concept and the process of the liberation of indigenous peoples?

Statecentric people characteristically define indigenous societies as *prestate* or *stateless* societies, terms that suggest an inherent deficiency and therefore influence indigenous peoples' status as proper subjects of international law. When statecentric people identify indigenous tribal organizations and communities of bands as corporate groups, they are better able to deliberately effect the legal and social transformation of indigenous organizations into actual corporate organizations, thus opening otherwise inalienable lands to market forces. This occurred with the Indian republics known collectively as the Five Civilized Tribes (Choctaw, Chickasaw, Cherokee, Creek, and Seminole) through the Dawes Severalty Act of 1887 and the Curtis Act of 1898 (Debo 1940; Debo 1970), with Alaskan natives through the Alaskan Native Claims Settlement Act of 1971 (Anders 1990; Berger 1995; Bowen 1991), and with the Passamaquoddy, Penobscot and Mashpee through the Maine Indian Land Claims Settlement Act of 1980 (Brodeur 1985; Clinton and Hotopp 1979; Kent 1982; Vollman 1979). This process of conceptualization may also stimulate our present ability to equate indigenous self-government with "self-management." Kinship studies that emphasize or exclusively concentrate on systems of consanguinity and affinity may devalue indigenous claims to kin relations with animals and places, as animism and totemism have not been dislodged, in our "modern" perception, from their places at the lower, primitive end of an evolutionary scale. Statecentric peoples recognize state claims to inviolable sovereignty over land and resources occupied and governed by indigenous nations that have since time immemorial interacted with other indigenous nations in identifiable forms of foreign political relations; statecentric peoples thus impose an ethnocentric artificial reality, an ideological construct, an arbitrary authority.

One may contend that statecentric peoples continue to evaluate nonstate peoples, at least in relation to their authenticity as independent and sovereign political entities, in much the same way that earnest scholars in the nineteenth and early twentieth centuries appraised the so-called races of mankind, as depicted in Gould's classic of intellectual and social history, *The Mismeasure of Man* (1992) and earlier in Stanton's *The Leopard's Spots* (1960). In the present era of the United Nations–sponsored "New Partnership" between states and indigenous peoples (United Nations 1992a; Barsh 1993b), an era brought about largely by indigenous peoples themselves after five hundred years of dispossession, forced assimilation, and genocide, cultural and political appraisals of indigenous cultures and their natural ecosystems may yet be transformed. Hopefully it will be an intellectual, structural, and historical transformation similar in degree to, but opposite in content from that which emerged from the Age of Discovery.

CULTURAL ANTHROPOLOGY AND THE EXPERIENCE OF INDIGENOUS PEOPLES

Indigenous peoples are extremely articulate on issues of their international political history and identity, and an enlightened transformation of international law demands their continued participation in the unmasking of a wide variety of fundamental misconceptions. Meanwhile, a growing number of anthropologists are critically examining their profession and realizing that it is the progeny of imperialism, that it has links with colonialism and has participated in the continuing transformation of and assimilation of indigenous cultures and peoples. Despite these associations, anthropologists have recognized the existence and operation of indigenous political, legal, and religious systems and are evolving intellectually through close contact with indigenous peoples. They have also contributed to the progressive transformation of national and international law, and are questioning the necessity and logic of the destruction of indigenous peoples' cultures and natural habitats. At present, indigenous peoples are contributing to the transformation of anthropology, law, and other fields in a process of international legal evolution taking place in the United Nations, a process that exposes the longstanding essential interrelatedness of anthropology, indigenous cultures, and law.

"Into each life . . . some rain must fall. Some people have bad horoscopes. . . . Indians have anthropologists," writes distinguished Native American legal scholar and activist Vine Deloria Jr., in his insightful critique *Custer Died for Your Sins* (Deloria 1969:78). Anthropologists have often reacted defensively and even bitterly to Deloria's criticisms, viewing themselves as the non-Indians most supportive of indigenous ceremonies, rituals, and beliefs (Oswalt 1973:595). Although not absolving humanistic anthropologists, Deloria takes particular issue with the anthropological concept of cultural evolution that is popularly depicted by Peter Farb in *Man's Rise to Civilization* (1968). Deloria writes:

> Farb's basic assumption is that somehow Indians have risen to civilized heights by being the victims of four centuries of systematic genocide. . . . The implications of Farb's book are . . . frightening. Indians, people will feel, weren't really as good as we thought, therefore we must hurry them on their way to civilization. Indians weren't conservationists, therefore all this business about them having an attachment to their lands is bunk. Why not, therefore, go ahead with the plan for wholesale mortgage of Indian lands; they aren't using them anyhow. (Deloria 1969:97)

Deloria argues that Farb's book reinforces an anti-Indian, anti-indigenous picture and disregards issues of Indian culture and of colonialism, racism, and genocide. Therefore, Deloria continues, the "white man will continue to take Indian land because he will feel that he is HELPING to bring civilization to the poor savages" (Deloria 1969:99).

Russel Lawrence Barsh, a Native American legal scholar and activist who was trained as an anthropologist and who coauthored *The Road: Indian Tribes and Political Liberties* (Barsh and Henderson, 1980), echoes many of Deloria's criticisms in his essay "Are Anthropologists Hazardous to Indians' Health?" (Barsh 1988). For Barsh, a manifest distinction separates humanistic or philosophical anthropology from scientific anthropology. The philosophical anthropologists reject the concept of cultural evolution and the primacy of Western civilization and thereby promote the concept of the equal value of cultures. Scientific anthropologists, on the other hand, have "often helped to justify the manipulation of indigenous cultures." Barsh contends that as an investigative strategy and as an ideology science has been detrimental both for anthropology and for American Indians. Unfortunately, though, it is science that receives the applause and financial support, while progressive thought is ridiculed (Barsh 1988:1).

This emergent critique of anthropology as a science and as a humanistic discipline is offered not only by Native American writers. In one of the most important United Nations studies concerning the situation of indigenous peoples, the "Study on Treaties, Agreements and Other Constructive Arrangements between States and Indigenous Populations" (United Nations 1992e), Special Rapporteur Miguel Alfonso Martínez deliberates over the contributions that anthropological theory can make to illuminating the history of political relations between states and indigenous peoples, as revealed through treaties and agreements and the cultural practices they involve. Martínez believes it is incumbent upon him, and imperative for the thorough comprehension of the significance of the treaties, to reveal indigenous peoples' perspectives on the content and status of those treaties as binding instruments of international law. In his second progress report, Martínez offers a harsh characterization of cultural anthropology, of its value to his study, and of its general contribution to the historical existential and contemporary political situation of indigenous peoples.

Martínez argues that while cultural anthropology, like history, is absolutely necessary to his study, it has not yet removed itself from the colonialist ideology or mentality that has for so long enveloped it. This ideology obscures or obstructs a more thorough investigation of indigenous cultures. It tends to warrant the use of economistic models that inherently place consumer or market-oriented economies in a superior evolutionary position and thus justify the hegemony of global capitalism's sociopolitical domination in a new world order. According to Martínez, cultural anthropology is bound within the essentially racist and xenophobic society from which it arises, and it cannot fairly represent the claims of indigenous peoples regarding treaty rights and obligations.

Martínez's assessment of cultural anthropology is severe, but that severity might be mitigated by the fact that the primary target of his criticism seems to be the theories and practices of a previous generation of anthropologists. Martínez does praise ethnohistory as the key to his own research method, the methodological cornerstones of which are cultural relativism, structural-functionalism, and postmodern anthropology, in which ethnocentrism is recognized as both problematic and inescapable.

Recent developments in international human rights standards, in the current emphasis in anthropology on human rights, and in the participation of indigenous peoples in defining those rights have begun to expose the legacy of genocide and the justification of the deliberate destruction of indigenous peoples that until now has apparently been intrinsic to state-centric forms of thought. In recognition of that legacy, and as one significant step toward addressing criticisms such as those of Deloria, Barsh, and Martínez, the study of human rights in general and indigenous rights in particular should be institutionalized as a fundamental field of study in academic and professional anthropology programs. Then anthropologists should vigilantly guard against the circumstance portrayed by Akwesasne spokesman Jerry Gambill in his satirical essay "On the Art of Stealing Human Rights," wherein concerned and outraged profession-als "hold a conference on human rights, have everyone blow off steam and tension, and go home feeling that things are well in hand" (Gambill [1969] 1983:162).

CULTURAL ANTHROPOLOGY AND AN ARCHAEOLOGY OF KNOWLEDGE

A human rights concentration in anthropology that would elevate the aims and perspectives of indigenous peoples concerning their own human rights and self-determination to the level of serious inquiry should be distinguished as a separate field from scientific anthropology and ap-plied economic anthropology, as well as separate from the more general advocacy of participation in social welfare programs. An anthropologi-cal approach focused on human rights, indigenous rights, and indige-nous political histories would be required to include the examination of the intellectual history, theoretical constructs, and sponsorships of which cultural anthropology is composed: in essence, an intellectual and existential archaeology.

Elaborating on the works of Marx and Freud, his contemporaries Merleau-Ponty and Althusser, and especially the philosopher Nietzsche, Michel Fou-cault posits that within given time periods of Western civilization, *épistèmes*, or fundamental discursive rationalities, constructed their objects and sub-jects, as well as social rules of cohesion. Foucault maintains two basic premises. The first, derived from Nietzsche, is that every human situation, belief, or institution is a product of history: it is a contingent rather than a natural fact, no matter how convinced one may be of its immutability. Be-cause we are convinced of the truth and certainty of our beliefs and of the necessity and rationality of our institutions, we do not recognize their contingency. The second premise constitutes a demand for a "relentless suspicion of progress." For example, in *Madness and Civilization* (1965), his study of the transformation of the treatment of the insane from prisonlike confinement to humanitarianism, especially in the work of Samuel Tuke, Foucault argues that:

> liberation of the insane, abolition of punishment, constitution of a human milieu—these are only justifications. The real operations were different. In fact, Tuke created an asylum where he substituted for the free terror of mad-ness the stifling anguish of responsibility; fear no longer reigned on the other side of the prison gates, it now raged under the seals of conscience. (Fou-cault, quoted in Nehamas 1993:28)

In Foucault's analysis, leg irons and the bonds of conscience are essentially one and the same; individuals and their groups or organizations are components of "a vast network of meaning and control over which they were powerless." Foucault attempts to describe this network historically and to demonstrate its self-perpetuating quality (Nehamas 1993:28).

In *The Order of Things,* a study of the development of West European thought from the seventeenth century to the present, Foucault argues that bourgeois capitalist economics and Marxism were essentially inseparable, both products of a nineteenth century a priori *épistème* that is now coming to an end, as is the *épistème*'s creation: "economic man." This position bears an unmistakable resemblance to the view advanced by American Indian activist and former American Indian Movement spokesperson Russell Means, who argues that for indigenous peoples both capitalism and communism are "the same old song and dance," both intending to liberate indigenous peoples from their "ignorance" and their territories, an "inevitability" deemed necessary for the advance of human progress and the benefit of humankind (Means 1983).

In *Discipline and Punish* Foucault argues, on the basis of the transformation of European prisons from places of torture and terror to institutions of reform, that the

> mechanisms used to understand and to control marginalized and ostracized groups were also essential to the understanding and control—indeed to the constitution—of "normal" individuals. Thus, the constant surveillance of prisoners that replaced physical torture as a result of penal reform came to be applied also to schoolchildren, to factory workers, to whole populations (and, we might add, to average citizens, whose police records, medical reports and credit ratings are even today becoming more available and more detailed). (Nehamas 1993:30–31)

Foucault contends that the "subject" is the construction, the product, of these practices and methods of control, of the exercise of power. For Foucault, "Power produces knowledge . . . power and knowledge directly imply one another . . . there is no power relation without the correlative constitution of a field of knowledge, nor any knowledge that does not presuppose and constitute at the same time power relations" (Foucault, quoted in Nehamas 1993:31). The study of power and knowledge, then, are inseparable. With the birth of the reform prison and of contemporary European society, the expression of power has become cloaked in humanism and humanitarian ideals that veil the presence of power and worsen the conditions of oppression by appearing to incorporate or assimilate the principles essential to resistance, thus rendering resistance enigmatic.

As an archaeologist Foucault seeks to undermine the human sciences' claims to objectivity and independent truth and to expose them as techniques for the deliberate creation and control of the human subject. As a genealogist he attempts to demonstrate that what is accepted without question as the organized and the rational is actually the product of domination and subjugation (Foucault 1977b; Nehamas 1993:31–32). Alexander Nehamas, a professor of philosophy who specializes in the works of Nietzsche and Foucault, explains that Foucault's position at the time of *Discipline and Punish* recognizes that

> power is a productive force. It is not exercised by subjects, it creates them. Power is exercised through individuals, but it is not often under those individuals' control. On the contrary, established relationships of power, despite the intentions of those who try to modify them, reassert themselves in constantly changing forms. Efforts to humanize power, to rationalize it, even to renounce it result only in another exercise of power—in the creation of new ways of knowing what individuals or "subjects" are, indeed, of new individuals or "subjects." People who are subject to the sovereign's absolute and total vengeance are essentially different from people whose every movement is observed and catalogued by minor functionaries, who are themselves observed by someone else. (Nehamas 1993:32)

Although *Discipline and Punish* is perhaps Foucault's greatest work and his analyses of institutions devastating, his theoretical position at this stage was uncompromisingly nihilistic. Literary theorist and international political activist Edward W. Said describes this as the inexorable paradox of Foucault's position: that his analysis brilliantly reveals the cruelty and injustice of power, but his theoretical position quiescently allowed this cruelty and injustice to prevail (Said 1986:152).

Said, the intellectual architect of postcolonial studies primarily by means of his classic critique *Orientalism* (1979), argues that Foucault has demonstrated that discourse not only is the translation of political struggles or of systems of domination, but also is that for which people engage in struggle: "What [Foucault] seemed not quite willing to grant is, in fact, the relative success of these counter-discursive attempts to show, in Fanon's words, the violence done to psychically and politically repressed inferiors in the name of an advanced culture, and then afterwards to begin the difficult, if not always tragically flawed, project of formulating the discourse of liberation" (Said 1986:153). Toward the premature end of his career, Foucault seeks in the article "What is Enlightenment?" (1984) to stimulate through his genealogical critique the separation of ourselves from the selves created by our contingencies so we can pursue, in Foucault's words, the "undefined work of freedom" (Foucault 1984; Nehamas 1993:33).

In his essay in *Conquest of America: The Question of the Other* (1984) exposing the source of European intellectual interest in indigenous cultures, literary theorist and historian Tzvetan Todorov posits that a great change occurred in European civilization at the dawn of the sixteenth century after the arrival of Columbus in the New World and prior to Cortéz's bloody conquests. Europeans began to believe in the superiority of Europe and that the physical destruction and assimilation of the exterior alterity was necessary or inevitable; the destruction or assimilation was achieved through an ability to understand the "other." Todorov writes that Cortéz offers an unusually clear example of this proposition:

> [Cortéz] was conscious of the degree to which the art of adaptation and of improvisation governed his behavior. Schematically this behavior is organized into two phases. The first is that of interest in the other, at the cost of a certain empathy or temporary identification. Cortéz slips into the other's skin, but in a metaphoric and no longer a literal fashion: the difference is considerable. Thereby he ensures himself an understanding of the other's language and a knowledge of the other's political organization (whence his interest in the Aztecs' internal dissension, and he even masters the emission of messages in an appropriate code: hence he manages to pass himself off as Quetzalcoatl returned to earth). But in so doing he has never abandoned his feeling of superiority; it is even his very capacity to understand the other that confirms him in that feeling. Then comes the second phase, during which he is not content to reassert his own identity (which he has never really abandoned), but proceeds to assimilate the Indians to his own world. In the same way . . . the Franciscan monks adopted the Indians' ways (clothes, food) to convert them more effectively to the Christian religion. (Todorov 1984:248)

Todorov contends that as a result of Europe's belief in its own superiority and its success in obliterating colonized peoples, Western civilization has lost the capacity to communicate with other cultures.

However, according to Todorov, since the discovery of the dark soul of the unconscious, of the Other within, European civilization has begun to lose its sense of superiority. Recent emphasis upon equality and difference in the late twentieth century may bring the era of European cultural imperialism to a close; this suggests the possibility of an intellectual transformation that would permit a more profound comprehension and appreciation of the indigenous Other. For Todorov there exists both the necessity of "seeking the truth" and the "obligation of making it known." Father Bartolomé de Las Casas represents the realization of this moral and intellectual edict, but ethnology, "at once the child of colonialism and the proof of [colonialism's] death throes" (Todorov 1984:250), represents the possibility of a dialogue among cultures as equals and without a last word, insofar as ethnologists choose to follow in the footsteps of Las Casas.

Johannes Fabian, in his renowned book *Time and the Other: How Anthropology Makes Its Object* (1983), argues that contemporary ethnology is marred by a deliberate form of bias called *allochronism*, the denial of the coevalness of the Other, the anthropological object. But the colonialist enterprise involves movements and relations not only in space but also in time. Like Foucault, Fabian asserts that knowledge is power and that the application of and belief in the appropriateness of descriptive terms such as *savage, primitive,* or *ahistorical* in relation to indigenous peoples and indigenous societies constitutes a political act of alienation and domination that represents the construction of the object, rather than the apprehension of the Other. With the nineteenth-century adoption of the cultural evolutionary scheme in anthropology, the most obvious act of allochronism appears with the invocation of the various stages of "progress." Fabian argues that this fundamental denial of coevalness continues in contemporary forms of neo-evolutionism, cultural materialism, and scientific objectivism.

The identification of allochronism in cultural relativism, structural-functionalism, structuralism, and symbolic anthropology is more problematic, but it appears through the isolation of indigenous societies in a separate time, or in ahistoricism, and through an emphasis on the priority of social institutions and cultural symbols separate from lived lives. This gives rise to a "hall of mirrors" effect, because it reflects the anthropologists' preconceptions rather than communication with indigenous cultures. The one historical development that prevented anthropology from being nothing more than a vast collection of hallucinations, Fabian contends, was the integration of fieldwork into anthropological practice. Communication during fieldwork requires intersubjectivity and intersocietal contemporaneity—in other words, shared time. But the information gathered and the experience gained then undergoes the transformation of anthropological professionalization, a process that both separates theoretical discourse from empirical research and regards the ethnographic experience as the prelude to entry into the profession, a ritual initiation. Fabian concludes that both strategies are nothing more than a cover-up of the denial of coevalness. And worse, Fabian adds,

> they obstruct critical insight into the possibility that those ritually repetitive confrontations with the Other which we call fieldwork may be but special instances of the general struggle between the West and the Other. A persistent myth shared by imperialists and many (Western) critics of imperialism alike has been that of a single, decisive conquista, occupation, or establishment of colonial power, a myth which has its complement in similar notions of sudden decolonization and accession to independence. Both have worked against giving proper theoretical importance to overwhelming evidence for *repeated* acts of oppression, campaigns of pacification, and suppression of rebellions, no matter whether these were carried out by military means, by religious and educational indoctrination, by administrative measures, or, as is common now, by intricate monetary and economic manipulations under the cover of foreign aid. The ideological function of schemes promoting progress, advancement, and development hide the temporal contingency of imperialist expansion. We cannot exclude the possibility, to say the very

least, that repetitive enactment of field research by thousands of aspiring and established practitioners of anthropology has been part of a sustained effort to maintain a certain type of relation between the West and its Other. To *maintain* and *renew* these relations has always required coeval recognition of the Other as the object of power and/or knowledge; to rationalize and ideologically justify these relations has always needed schemes of allochronic distancing. (Fabian 1983:149)

Allochronism in anthropology and elsewhere is expressive of a political cosmology, a myth, and thereby tends to "establish a total grip on our discourse" (Fabian 1983:152). Therefore, the opposition to this imperialism of the mind, through a struggle for the recognition of contemporaneity and equality between dissimilar cultures and peoples, must likewise be as comprehensive. This theory of coevalness must not be appropriated in order to constitute a further absorption or assimilation that would justify total domination by the capitalist world system (Fabian 1983:152–54).

Taking the analysis of anthropological theory and method a step further in *A Critique of the Study of Kinship* (1984), David M. Schneider looks back critically on his own ethnographic and theoretical research and that of other leading figures in the area of kinship studies, and calls into question both that research and the concept of kinship itself. Schneider suggests that anthropology begins with the proposition that all human beings act in ways related to their culture, and that a culture consists of shared perceptions or beliefs concerning the nature of the world, the structure of existence, and the ways persons should act in the world. Culture is a shared system of symbols and meanings, categories and concepts, a specific way of organizing conceptions of reality or realities.

The prerequisite step for the anthropologist, then, is to comprehend the symbols and meanings of the culture under study, as well as their particular configuration. Schneider contends, however, this rarely occurs:

My difficulty with the study of kinship can be summed up simply: the assumptions and presuppositions which the anthropologist brings to the process of understanding the particular culture he is studying are imposed on the situation blindly and with unflagging loyalty to those assumptions and little flexible appreciation of how the other culture is constituted, and with it a rigid refusal to attempt to understand what may be going on between them. The anthropologist has, as part of his culture, his conceptual scheme, a way of ordering his experience of another culture, a way of constructing the reality he believes he is encountering, and he is not easily shaken loose from that secure, reassuring, comfortable, well-worn common language to which he is committed and shares with his community of anthropologists, and which helps to define his place in that community. (Schneider 1984:196–97)

One of the most basic fallacies to which anthropologists cling, Schneider maintains, is the functional division of society into the institutional worlds of kinship, economics, politics, and religion. Another fallacy is that kinship basically deals with biological reproduction. By preconstructing the indigenous world in this manner, anthropologists have taken back from the ethnographic field the information, the analytic construct, that they first brought with them. There has been no communication between anthropologists and indigenous peoples, or the Other.

THE HISTORY OF ANTHROPOLOGY AS AN ANTHROPOLOGICAL PROBLEM

Anthony F. C. Wallace persuasively argues that Lewis Cass deserves recognition as the progenitor of American anthropology and as the principal source of dominant trends in cultural anthropology that prevailed well into the twentieth century (Wallace 1993). As President Andrew Jackson's Secretary of War, Cass institutionalized the utilization of ethnological theory and practice in support of the U.S. government's expansionist policies. Recognized as the leading American authority on Indian languages and cultures at the time, Cass classified all Indians as culturally fixated in a "nomadic hunter stage" and therefore incapable of progress, and he disregarded substantial indisputable evidence to the contrary (Wallace 1993:41–44). In his article "Removal of the Indians" (1830), Cass explains that the Indian mind is shaped by the Indians' mythological tales, supernatural beliefs, sorcery, heroism, and duplicity, and is therefore immutable to the civilizing impulse (Cass 1830; Bieder 1986:153). This classification and characterization was used as justification for Indian removal west of the Mississippi to "liberate" indigenous lands for progress and order. Following arguments then dominant among philosophies of natural law, Cass contended that there could be no justification for "that system of legal metaphysics, which would give to a few naked and wandering savages, a perpetual title to an immense continent" (Cass, quoted in Wallace 1993:45). In fact, Cass considered Indian removal economically, legally, and morally justified, necessary for the survival of the Indian race (Wallace 1993:42) until the Indian mind had been altered and made accessible to civilization (Bieder 1986:155). As Secretary of War, Cass supervised numerous Indian land cessions and the removal of nearly all of the Eastern Indians to west of the Mississippi River.

Cass used questionnaires to study Indian languages, and he was committed to the proposition that "language constrains and reveals the thought processes of its speakers." His studies suggested to him that American Indians were incapable of distinguishing the abstract from the concrete and were thus unable to reason logically (Bieder 1986:152; Wallace 1993:43). Furthermore, as hunters, aboriginals first existed in a stable state of hunting and warfare, but with the arrival of the Europeans and the introduction of the fur trade, the Indians depleted their game reserves and increasingly engaged in intertribal warfare, fought with settlers, participated in European conflicts, and sold their land. Finally, according to Cass's theory, after the Indians' defeat, submission, and confinement to reservations, the hunter stage descends into "a degenerate condition of squalid poverty, marked by drunkenness, murder and mayhem, disease, and general corruption by vices introduced by unscrupulous whiskey traders and squatters," and, in Cass's words, a state of "want and imbecility" (Wallace 1993:43, 45). Deliberately disregarding prevalent Eastern Indian horticultural practices, Cass saw no possibility of Indian redemption through reform under the conditions of the now debased hunter stage. For their own benefit Indians must be removed westward. Cass defended American policy as one of extending care and patronage over the Indian tribes. For those who discerned value in Indian culture, the reward was Cass's unmitigated criticism and contempt (Berkhofer 1979:94; Bieder 1986:152–53; Prucha 1967; Wallace 1993:45–47). It is worth noting that the historian Francis Paul Prucha (1967:16–17) considers the possibility that Cass later revised his personal opinion on U.S. Indian removal policy although long after he had left his position of political power.

Ethnologist and Cass protégé Henry Rowe Schoolcraft endorses Indian removal in his article "Our Indian Policy" (1844), in which he argues for the obvious inferiority of the Indians on the basis of their barbarism (Schoolcraft 1844; Bieder 1986:174–75). Schoolcraft had earlier opposed removal, and his change of heart is directly attributable to his esteem for Cass (Bieder 1986:173–74). Cass's influence by way of Schoolcraft on physician and phrenologist Samuel G. Morton and ethnologist and archaeologist Ephraim G. Squire was also profound and consequential. In the mid–nineteenth century both Morton and Squire advanced influential polygenist biological and ethnological theories "confirming" the inferiority of Indians and sub-Saharan Africans. These theories, now recognized as scientific racism, supported U.S. government policies of Indian removal and slavery (Berkhofer 1979:58–59; Bieder 1986:66–94; Wallace 1993:112–13); in essence, science condemned certain races and peoples to extinction.

Cass's influence was also apparent in the work of influential nineteenth-century historian Francis Parkman, who was a friend of Squire (Bieder 1986:102). Parkman's *History of the Conspiracy of Pontiac* (1851) and later works utilized Cass's unpublished notes. Parkman's works, like those of Cass, celebrate the demise of the deceitful and savage Red Race at the hands of the advancing White Race (Parkman 1851; Berkhofer 1979:95; Wallace 1993:113). Parkman embraces the polygenist view of the inherent inferiority of American Indians and of their destiny of imminent extinction as a race (Bieder 1986:102; Wallace 1993:113).

Manifest Destiny was an ideological euphemism that glorified and rendered inevitable American expansionist military aggression, legal duplicity against independent indigenous nations, and the enslavement and extermination of nonwhite peoples, all accomplished for the advancement of democracy, self-determination, free enterprise, and the fulfillment of religious destiny (Drinnon 1980; Hietala 1990; Stephanson 1995). A Government-sponsored pseudoscience of society and its research strategies played a role in support of Manifest Destiny. For example, the annexation of Texas was democratically legislated partially as a result of the use of social scientific data, and the 1840 Census of the Insane statistically demonstrated that Northern free blacks were far more likely to be impoverished, criminal, insane, or physically infirm than blacks living in slavery: "freedom degenerated blacks, whereas slavery uplifted them" (Hietala 1990:27–28). By this logic, a free, abolitionist Texas would have threatened the Northern U.S. and the well-being of all blacks. Many of the census statistics had clearly been fabricated, and although the census was later exposed as fraud, the perception that it helped to create predominated (Hietala 1990:26–32).

Lawyer and anthropologist Lewis Henry Morgan is traditionally recognized as the father of American anthropology. He was influenced in part by Schoolcraft and thus indirectly by Cass, although, significantly, neither Schoolcraft nor Morgan accepted polygenist explanations of Indian inferiority. In the work for which he is most remembered, *Ancient Society, or Researches in the Lines of Human Progress from Savagery through Barbarism to Civilization* (1877), Morgan argues for the efficacy of the theory of social evolution, of the idea that progress in history is the elemental force of social or human transformation. Morgan classifies human societies according to three ascending stages: savagery, barbarism, and civilization. Each stage is elaborated into three substages, and each stage and substage represents a certain level of technological innovation and economic progress. Morgan, who had obvious respect for American Indian culture and achievement, especially that of the Iroquois, placed aboriginal Americans in the stage of barbarism. Morgan concluded his popular magnum opus by calling for the creation of an anthropological salvage operation that would collect information about the indigenous tribes before America's Red Race, one of the last great specimens of barbarism, died out completely.

John Wesley Powell, director of the Smithsonian Institution's Bureau of American Ethnology, established in 1879, considered Morgan's *Ancient Society* so invaluable that it was required reading for all ethnologists on his staff (Bieder 1986:243). According to Curtis M. Hinsley, "Powell wanted to do for the science of man what Darwin had done for biology: formulate a powerful guiding theory of (human) evolution buttressed by an unassailable mountain of empiricism" (Hinsley 1994:136). Powell's theoretical perspective, as well as that of his bureau protégé W J McGee, continued to promote the distinction between savagery and civilization: "The age of savagery is the age of the kinship clan, when maternal kinship is held most sacred; the age of barbarism is the age of kinship tribes, when paternal kinship is held most sacred; the age of civilization is the age of nations, when territorial boundaries are held most sacred" (Powell 1888:12). Powell's perspective betrays a reluctance to grant nation status and to recognize national territories for indigenous peoples, a position that was conceded in the Bureau of Indian Affairs document "Indian Land Cessions in the United States" (Royce 1899). By that time, however, the U.S. government had, for all practical purposes, annexed all indigenous territories on the mainland.

Late-nineteenth-century anthropological research was often brilliant, but it was also acquiescent and, perhaps unwittingly, promoted the destiny that American society prepared for its indigenous peoples. Anthropologists' advocacy of assimilation policy provides one telling example: the Five Civilized Tribes, removed from their traditional territories by President Andrew Jackson and Secretary of War Lewis Cass in direct violation of U.S. law, were given tribal autonomy and perpetual title to their new lands (Debo 1940:5). These nations formed self-governing republics that flourished economically and culturally. Although the nations were largely Christianized and engaged in agricultural pursuits, they owned resources tribally and maintained traditional communal social obligations (Debo 1940:14–15). The subsequent illegal influx of whites into Indian lands led to conflicts that necessitated, according to U.S. policymakers, further Indian pacification. The illegal settlers rapidly became the majority population in Indian territories, and consequently they claimed the "democratic" right to impose their anti-Indian values (Debo 1940:21).

Toward the end of the nineteenth century, a self-professed humanitarian movement ascended to the forefront of the American political scene. Some of the Indians had successfully reserved through treaties and other agreements substantial tracts of their former territories and some elements of political independence, and the "humanitarian" movement purported to save the Indians from their own folly. These friends of the Indian viewed tribal culture as an impediment to Indian progress toward civilization: lacking selfishness and greed, Indians had no propensity for progress (Debo 1940:21–22). A program was created to encourage or enforce private property on the Indians, a program that would displace the Five Civilized Tribes and the Western Indian nations from the large blocks of land guaranteed them by treaties and federal statutes. Federal allotment policy, which legally dismembered tribal territories, received the outspoken support of leading anthropologists, including those of the Bureau of American Ethnology.

Alice Fletcher, distinguished Bureau of American Ethnology anthropologist and occasional agent of the Bureau of Indian Affairs, best known for her classic ethnography "The Omaha Tribe" (1911), freely expressed her opinion that allotment policy was, for the Indian, "educational . . . a most important step in the process of leading the natives to abandon the hunter stage and to depend for their subsistence on agriculture and home industries" (Wallace 1993:116; Otis 1973:66; Lurie 1966a, 1966b). In 1882 Fletcher testified in Washington, D.C., to urge the passage of the Omaha Allotment Act, which would guarantee the Omaha Indians, the subjects of her research, their land through individual title; Fletcher was later directed by the U.S. Indian commissioner to oversee the Omaha Indian land allotment (Mark 1980:67). The final form of the Dawes Severalty Act of 1887, the major piece of legislation calling for the allotment of Indians' tribal territories, was the result more of Alice Fletcher's work than that of any other person, according to Fletcher's biographer, anthropologist Joan Mark (Mark 1988:119). Mark offers an explanation for Fletcher's position on Indian allotment:

> First, . . . Alice Fletcher had adopted the point of view of the first Indians she met, the La Flesche family, whose views were not shared even by a majority of the Omahas. Joseph La Flesche, the half French, half Indian leader of the Omahas, . . . saw allotment policy as a way of preventing "removal." La Flesche also thought that the Indian way of life was a thing of the past. . . . He believed the tribal system was an obstacle to the advancement of his people. . . . Second, . . . Fletcher worked out in the field where she felt the political heat of the white man's desire for Indian land. She knew that it was hardly a question of preserving the reservations. . . . The question was whether the Indians would get allotments of land or no land at all. . . . Finally, . . . Fletcher went west much influenced by the latest scientific thinking in anthropology, the ideas of Lewis Henry Morgan. If the Indians were truly at the stages of Upper Savagery and Lower and Middle Barbarism, as Morgan had suggested, then the solution to their current troubles was for them to move as rapidly as possible up the ladder to Civilization. (Mark 1980:71–72)

Recognizing the dismal failure of the allotment program, with which even its namesake, Senator Dawes, would later disavow any personal connection, Fletcher reversed her position on Indian assimilation, but she never made a public admission to that effect (Mark 1988:267–70). Several years later, in the classic work *The Changing Culture of an Indian Tribe* (1932), Margaret Mead would probe the disastrous effects of allotment policy on the Omaha Indians and examine their unique cultural adaptations to forced assimilation.

Fletcher presented a paper on the Ghost Dance to the American Folklore Society in 1890, one month prior to the infamous massacre at Wounded Knee. In this paper, Fletcher advances an insightful interpretation of the Ghost Dance, relating it to social causes and characterizing it, in her biographer's words, as "the result of a crisis situation where the Indians had been crowded off coveted lands onto tracts of barren soil; their livelihood—the buffalo and other game—had been killed off, and their children were being educated in a new language with new ideas" (Mark 1980:74). The Indians found hope in the supernatural and in the expectation of the coming of an Indian messiah to deliver them from their misery. Franz Boas, whose anthropological work is generally acknowledged as the intellectual source of the theory of cultural relativism, disagreed with Fletcher's interpretation. Boas, like many other theorists, claimed that deranged movements such as the Ghost Dance have more to do with "nervous diseases" than with political movements (Mark 1980:74).

Not all minds were closed to Fletcher's interpretation. Bureau of American Ethnology anthropologist James Mooney apparently adopted aspects of Fletcher's paper in his masterpiece *The Ghost-Dance Religion and the Sioux Outbreak of 1890* (1896). Mooney claimed that the Ghost Dance had been seriously misrepresented by the Bureau of Indian Affairs and by the national media. It was presented as a preparation for war or as evidence of the Indians' fixation at a lower stage of social evolution. The Ghost Dance, Mooney argued, possessed historically and culturally significant characteristics. His extensive field research, including a meeting with Wovoka, the Paiute prophet, indicated to him that the dance was "a ceremony of peace and brotherhood, a movement of cultural revitalization among desperately poor, nearly hopeless peoples" rather than some sort of organized and armed Indian rebellion or a manifestation of the outbreak of a nervous disease (Hinsley 1994:216).

Mooney characterized the Ghost Dance as a religion that contained basic elements found in every religion, including Christianity, a religion in which the Indian tribes shared a belief in a coming messiah who would deliver them from their "insufferable oppression" (Mooney, quoted in Hinsley 1994:216). Mooney's comparison of the Ghost Dance religion with Christianity generated consternation among his superiors at the Bureau of American Ethnology, who included "an elaborate caveat" as a preface to Mooney's text (Moses 1984:91). Mooney notes Bureau of Indian Affairs agents' inconceivable ignorance and unconscionable corruption in dealing with the Ghost Dance movement. Mooney's criticism of the BIA agents and of the unnecessarily provocative actions of the U.S. military engendered antagonism against the Bureau of American Ethnology. Barsh suggests that Mooney's work, which dramatically breaks away from the rigid social evolutionism of Powell and toward cultural history and humanism, represents a reformation of anthropology into a science of the oppressed (Barsh 1988:4–5). Anthropologist Nancy Lurie recognizes Mooney, along with Frank Hamilton Cushing, as one of the first anthropologists "who actively championed the Indians and fought abrogation of their communal rights" (Lurie 1988:549).

Concerning the U.S. Army's massacre of Big Foot and his people at Wounded Knee, however, Mooney concludes "that the first shot was fired by an Indian, and that the Indians were responsible for the engagement;

that the answering volley and attack by the troops was right and justifiable, but that the wholesale slaughter of women and children was unnecessary and inexcusable" (Mooney 1896:870). Mooney's justifications for the attack on the Sioux have been discredited by historians and anthropologists alike (for example, Utley 1963; DeMallie, ed., 1984; Kehoe 1989). Despite his defense of the actions of the U.S. military and his stance in support of assimilation, however, Mooney became a political target because he appreciated traditional Indian culture and especially because he defended the Indians' religious use of peyote. Mooney described American antagonism toward peyote religion as being "based upon our prevailing ignorance and intolerance of Indian custom and feeling." As a consequence, Mooney suffered increasing criticism, isolation, and alienation both within and outside the Bureau of American Ethnology (Hinsley 1994:218–20; Moses 1984:179–205).

Anthropologist E. Adamson Hoebel apparently acquiesces to the American and anthropological tradition of quietism in the context of U.S. expansionism, exonerating past U.S. military incursions and pacification of autonomous Native American nations in his classic ethnography, *The Cheyennes: Indians of the Great Plains* (1978). Following his revealing discussion of the formation and existence of the legally recognized, independent Southern Cheyenne-Arapaho territory established by the Fort Laramie Treaty of 1851, Hoebel goes on to write:

> Much is made these days of the "Trail of Broken Treaties." In fact, every treaty between the Cheyenne-Arapaho and the United States was invalidated by circumstances within months of its signing. Neither the United States Government nor the leaders of the Indian tribes were capable of controlling the actions of their own people. In international law, a treaty which is broken by one party or the other is automatically invalidated. Both the Cheyennes and the United States broke their treaty commitments. Which party defaulted first is not always clear. (Hoebel 1978:115)

Even if Hoebel is correct that both sides equally violated their commitments, in international law the fact of broken treaties does not authorize the invasion, annexation, or enforced assimilation of one of the treating parties by the other.

In a somewhat more complex fashion, British anthropologist E. E. Evans-Pritchard, in *The Sanusi of Cyrenaica* (1949), excuses the extension of British authority over Libya. He voices strong opposition to and abhorrence for Italian colonialism in North Africa and expresses straightforward sympathy and support for the indigenous anticolonial resistance led by Omar El-Mukhtar, which suffered the loss of approximately one million individuals during its war against Italy. As an anthropological investigation of the history of an indigenous rebellion against European colonialism, *The Sanusi of Cyrenaica* must be recognized as an outstanding and groundbreaking achievement, which apparently it rarely is. Nevertheless, Evans-Pritchard's case study can be read equally well as an endorsement of British neocolonialism: he approves of Britain's attempt to act in a politically clever and anthropologically informed manner by setting up the nonindigenous Idris as a dependent Sanusi king.

The contributions of anthropology, or of any other academic field, to the historical justification of the loss of indigenous people's lives and tribal self-determination, and to the exoneration of the perpetrators of those losses, are perhaps unexceptional. As yet another example, Marvin Harris proposes a cultural materialist alternative explanation of the depopulation of the indigenous Americas. He argues that depopulation was fundamentally an unintended consequence of European contact and that charges of a genocidal holocaust in the Americas, such as that leveled by historian David Stannard in *American Holocaust: The Conquest of the New World* (1992), have been greatly exaggerated (Harris 1991:584). Harris's position stands in opposition to numerous accounts of genocide against indigenous peoples of the Americas and throughout the world, especially that of Las Casas (1992 [1552]). It is reasonable—indeed, fundamentally anthropological—to suggest that human beings are social beings, members of complex communities, and that consequently they may be compelled through various forms of underexamined or unforeseen social controls to survive and function economically, intellectually, and spiritually within their own cultural or sociopolitical totality in a way that demands a certain amount of allegiance to various shared concepts, visions, or necessary illusions. They may be constrained, for example, to act in a particular way to keep the wheels of progress turning. Thus the anthropologist as interlocutor may represent the colonized and still remain, in Edward Said's phrase, a "partner in domination and hegemony" (Said 1989:225).

Barsh considers anthropologists partners in domination and hegemony because they supported John Collier's Indian New Deal, the Indian Reorganization Act of 1934, and Collier's belief in the efficacy of the "scientific control of social forces" (Barsh 1988). He contends that the Indian Reorganization Act was a continuation of, rather than a break away from, the scientific evolutionism of the late nineteenth century embodied in the Dawes Severalty Act (Barsh 1991). According to Barsh, as President Franklin Roosevelt's Commissioner of Indian Affairs, Collier believed that allotment of Indian lands and individualizing property rights had undermined Indian initiative. The "Indian New Deal" instead encouraged elected tribal councils and the collectivization of remaining lands. As Barsh notes, many Indians opposed the new policy, so Collier engaged anthropologists to carry out the Reorganization Act, and they soon replaced missionaries as the most important influence on the Indian bureau. As government anthropologist Scudder Mekeel explained to his colleagues, although the Indian Reorganization Act "closely resembles the British policy of indirect rule in that the native political and social organization is strengthened by utilizing it for administrative purposes," in this case the policy is justified because "the objective is humane—rehabilitation of broken, pauperized, and demoralized Indian groups" (Mekeel 1944:209). Collier was so pleased with the success of his experiment that by 1945 he suggested that anthropologists should administer all non-white ethnic groups. Barsh continues,

> So powerful was Collier's vision that it blinded him completely to reality. He refused to believe any evidence that Indians had survived and adapted despite the allotment program, insisting upon characterizing his predecessors' policies as an unmitigated disaster. This led him to persist in collectivizing individual Indian landholdings to the point of stripping many reservations of the last vestiges of self-sufficiency (Barsh 1987b).

Many new opportunities were created for anthropologists, applying social science experimentally in the area of ethnic relations. Enthusiastic and concerned professionals, these anthropologists could speak out in the interests of the Indians. But as Barsh points out, "to speak for them—however benevolently—is to deny them that free will which Boas considered so essential to the dynamics of human progress" (Barsh 1988: 7–9). To Barsh, anthropologists are technomissionaries of a new, benevolent colonial order. As a notable legal scholar of American Indian origin who has an academic background in anthropology, he merits an audience among anthropologists.

Barsh is equally critical of American anthropologists' involvement in the Indian Claims Commission's determination of Indian legal claims to land, which originated with the Indian Claims Commission Act of 1946. Native American scholar and activist Ward Churchill, incidentally, describes the Indian Claims Commission as "a subterfuge designed to cast an undeserved mantle of humanitarianism and legitimacy over U.S. territorial integrity, [which] inadvertently served indigenous interests as well" (Churchill 1992:147). The commission was required to resolve several ethnohistorical issues in every land-claim case: (1) whether the Indian claimants constituted a "tribe, band or other identifiable group"; (2) whether the claimants were the descendants of the original indigenous occupants; (3) the extent of the territory originally occupied and used by the Indian group; and (4) the type of aboriginal use of the land and its economic value (Barsh 1988:14). Indian testimony, largely oral history presented by Indian elders, received less judicial weight than the scientific testimony anthropologists gave as expert witnesses (Lurie 1955).

Barsh observes that scholarly honesty in many of the Indian claimant situations required admission that ethnohistorical data was insufficient, but equivocating anthropologists were viewed by the commission's judges as less competent, less substantial witnesses than those who expressed assurance, however incorrect their individual points of view may have been (Barsh 1988:14–15). He criticizes the profession of anthropology for not having opposed or attempted to change an incompetent system that ultimately found that one-third of the contiguous United States had no aboriginal owners. Anthropologists continue to participate in similar legal deliberations with regard to fishing rights in "usual and accustomed areas" with Indian land claims where tribal identities are in question, such as with the Mashpee in eastern Massachusetts, and especially where there are questions of Indian religious freedom and of tribal identity in the federal acknowledgment process (Barsh 1988:14–17). Barsh charges that rather than opposing legal processes that deny Indian tribes federal recognition and that underrate the knowledge of traditional Indian religious and political leaders, the anthropological profession hails the opportunity for employment. Furthermore, once an anthropologist is inside the system, continued employment may depend on the position the anthropologist takes on an Indian tribe's claim for federal acknowledgment (Barsh 1988:18–20).

Deloria likewise bitterly admonishes and denounces the entire community of American scholars, claiming that "during the crucial days of 1954, when the Senate was pushing for termination of all Indian rights, not one single scholar, anthropologist, sociologist, historian, or economist came forward to support the tribes against the detrimental policy" (Deloria 1969:94). The termination policies of 1954 were designed to destroy tribalism among those groups of people known in the United States as tribal Indians, once again in the name of assimilation and progress. About this period of time, Lurie writes that:

> as a matter of record, individual anthropologists had opposed termination strenuously in regard to particular tribes with which they were familiar and in support of Indian-rights organizations that led the fight against termination in general (for example, Ostrom and Stern 1959; Stewart 1948). The views of at least two anthropologists were brought to the attention of Congress (Sturtevant 1954; Tax 1957). (Lurie 1988:552)

Lurie acknowledges Deloria's contention that the anthropological profession should have made a deliberate and organized effort to oppose termination sentiment and policy; but Lurie counters that faced with the ruinous threat of McCarthyism at the time, it is surprising that any American anthropologists spoke out against U.S. termination policy (Lurie 1988:552).

The fundamental beliefs or assumptions underlying indigenous assimilation and termination policies continue to be expressed in theoretical and applied anthropology in various guises. Social evolutionist Richard N. Adams, in *Energy and Structure* (1975), predicts the gradual but ultimate incorporation of peoples and ecosystems into increasingly centralized regionally and globally integrated "modern" cultural and economic systems. Contemporary social evolutionists characteristically argue that as a scientific and mathematical principle of social evolution, population increase results in increasing hierarchicalization, pressing the system to maximum inequality with shifts in wealth and power to a numerically decreasing elite, while ultimately, "the ideological component of the system and people's values, beliefs, choices, and so-called moral imperatives will come to conform in general fashion to the material organization that results from these structural shifts" (Segraves 1982:297). In *People and the State: An Anthropology of Planned Development* (1984), British anthropologist A. F. Robertson demonstrates that development anthropology has actively promoted the centralization of state power and control, and the assimilation of indigenous peoples and their territories into state political and economic systems, a position also more recently explored by poststructuralist anthropologist Arturo Escobar (1995). Laura Nader discusses contemporary development policy and Indians in Mexico, where the state attempts to deliberately assimilate "marginalized" peoples into the national politics and economy and consequently renders them entirely dependent upon the state system. She reveals a mental process that she identifies as "mind colonization," or "a situation under which individuals do not link 'progress' with a way of life that destroys the environment, community, nations and globe for fear of being luddites, . . . or . . . environmentalists" (Nader 1994:102–3). Finally, political anthropologist Ted Lewellen, in *The Anthropology of Globalization: Cultural Anthropology Enters the 21st Century,* notes that "a great deal of anthropological data suggests that unimpeded neoliberal capitalism increases inequality, destroys indigenous cultures, promotes rampant consumerism, commodifies everything, transfers wealth from the poor to the rich, eviscerates the environment, and disempowers the weak while further empowering the strong" (2002:192).

A HUMAN RIGHTS AND INDIGENOUS RIGHTS ORIENTATION IN CULTURAL ANTHROPOLOGY

In his groundbreaking ethnological work *The League of the Ho-de-no-sau-nee* (1851), in which he appreciates the Seneca in their own terms, Lewis Henry Morgan reveals the essential humanity of America's aboriginal peoples. Later, in *Ancient Society* (1877), Morgan argues that progress, or the civilization of "advanced technology," is not necessarily a question of race, but one of culture and its evolution. Unlike many of his colleagues, Morgan contended that Indians could adapt and, eventually, fully participate in American society (Eggan 1975:288–91). Although Morgan did attribute Indians' lack of progress to a "barbarism" from which they would gradually evolve, he placed responsibility for their misery on misguided, cruel federal programs and the unscrupulous actions of federal Indian agents, the American Fur Company, and religious missions (Bieder 1986:240; Eggan 1975:291).

Moreover, Morgan resisted prevailing opinion by defending the actions of the Sioux and Cheyenne, whose confederation had annihilated Custer's Seventh Cavalry, as reasonable and warranted by self-defense and self-preservation. Morgan criticized U.S. Indian policy for being wrong in its expansionist war against the Indians and for the "absence of intelligence and judgment in [its] management of Indian affairs." Morgan was opposed to Indian removal policy, the reservation system, the various methods of enforced assimilation, and the growing sentiment that would result in allotment legislation; he regarded these policies as unjust, coercive, and disgraceful (Morgan 1876a, 1876b, 1878; Bieder 1986:239–41; Wallace 1993:115). In his letter to President Abraham Lincoln, written in 1862, Morgan advocated Indian states (Kosok, ed., 1951).

As a lawyer in the 1840s, Morgan defended the land rights of the Senecas, violated by the fraudulent Treaty of Buffalo Creek; Morgan voiced opposition to the U.S. government's position on the treaty (Bieder 1986:240; Wallace 1993:109–10). Later Morgan would suggest that a legal convention, something like an Indian constitution, created by the Indians would go further toward stimulating the progressive evolutionary development of Indian cultures than could U.S. federal policies. Morgan proposed that the end result of the evolutionary cultural path would be the re-achievement, on a "higher level," of the "liberty, equality and fraternity" of the Indian tribes. Although the progressive foresight and anthropological insight in many of his political assessments on indigenous issues are now apparent, Morgan's persistent attempts to influence U.S. Indian policy proved futile, and his contemporaries reproved his views on policy (Bieder 1986:243).

Like James Mooney, Frank Hamilton Cushing, the enigmatic golden boy and young genius of the Bureau of American Ethnology, was changed by his personal contact with American Indians during his field experience of several years among the Zuñi. Cushing possessed "a gift that was rare in his (or any) time: a tentativeness toward truth, values, and mores" (Hinsley 1994:193); in other words, he had an uncommonly open, genuine, and imaginative mind. During his unexpectedly lengthy stay among the Zuñi, Cushing became known in the media as the "White Indian," and his moral state was questioned; he was rumored to have descended into the aboriginal state of mind (Hinsley 1994:195). By using a research method of "unfeigned reverence" for the Zuñi ceremonies and practices, Cushing developed a deep appreciation for Zuñi culture. Although Hinsley suggests that Cushing's evaluation of his acceptance among the Zuñi may have been exaggerated, Cushing was admitted into the sacred Zuñi Order of Priests of the Bow, and was given a Zuñi name that translates as "Medicine

Flower," a designation related to the use of some medicines that Cushing had brought with him (Mark 1980:101–2). Deeply absorbed in Zuñi culture, language, and history, and as a Zuñi assistant chief, Cushing aligned himself with the traditional tribal leadership in opposition to other Zuñi families and "progressive" forces such as missionaries, entrepreneurs, U.S. politicians, and the U.S. military (Hinsley 1994:196). Cushing published his research on the Zuñi in a series of articles that appeared in the popular journal *Century Magazine* under the title "My Adventures in Zuñi" (1882–1883) and in the annual reports of the Bureau of American Ethnology.

In 1882, Cushing led a successful Zuñi fight to retain traditional land claimed by the son-in-law of a U.S. Senator. In retaliation, the enraged senator launched a personal and professional attack against Cushing, accusing him of fraud and of moral degradation resulting from prolonged exposure to the Zuñi Indians (Hinsley 1994:196–97). Cushing defended himself and his actions as moral, correct, and self-respecting, but the senator also threatened the Bureau of American Ethnology, and Cushing was recalled by the Bureau to Washington, D.C., in 1884 (Hinsley 1994:197).

Cushing did return to Zuñi in 1886 to pursue his historical and archaeological interests rather than his ethnological ones. Unfortunately, Cushing's "flash[es] of brilliance, promising insight, [and] far-reaching theory" were never fully realized in publication. However, his theoretical formulations on the concept of culture, or of cultures as integrated totalities, plural and relative, preceded those of Boas's students, and Lévi-Strauss saw in his work an intuitive precursor to structuralism. Cushing's deep appreciation of Zuñi culture and his commitment to the protection of Zuñi rights, including land rights and the right to practice their traditional culture, represent much more than a footnote in the association of cultural anthropology with the promotion of the rights of indigenous peoples.

Franz Boas, traditionally recognized as a leading proponent of intensive anthropological field research, or participant observation, and of the systematic study of indigenous cultural traits, openly rejects Morgan's evolutionary perspective, finding in its cultural ranking a different type of scientific racism: ethnocentrism. Introducing Boas's scientific and social endeavors, biographer Marshall Hyatt writes:

> As an intellectual, Boas attacked the misusers of science who promulgated theories of racial inferiority based on alleged mental differences between ethnic groups. As a scientist, he directed the professionalization of the field of anthropology, overseeing its evolution from an amateur hobby to its maturity as a rigorous academic discipline. As a social activist, he strove to eradicate prejudice and bigotry from American society, in an effort to ensure that the premise of American democracy was articulated in reality and practice. (Hyatt 1990:xi)

In *The Mind of Primitive Man* ([1911] 1938), Boas rejects all forms of intolerance and proposes that the study of particular histories of unique cultures is more enlightening than combining the stories of all peoples into the movement of a single, transcendent history. Boas transformed the nature of anthropological research by stressing cultural relativism (Stocking 1968; Stocking, ed., 1974), an idea that was not foreign to Morgan: anthropologist Fred Eggan suggests that "see[ing] the problems of the Indian from their point of view" is one of the truly original aspects of Morgan's work (Eggan 1975:291). Like Morgan, Boas did not hesitate to soundly criticize U.S. foreign policy or the participation of anthropologists in undercover political missions, as he did in his editorial "Scientists as Spies" (1919).

Edward Sapir, Ruth Benedict, Margaret Mead, Benjamin Whorf, and other students of Boas expanded on the concept of culture, the holistic configuration of cultures, cultural pluralism, and cultural relativism. Ruth Benedict, most famous for her depiction of the holistic nature of Zuñi, Sioux, Kwakiutl, and Dobu cultures in *Patterns of Culture* (1934), now recognized as a precursor to postmodernism, took the emerging anthropological stance on moral behavior championed by Boas to a more manifest level in *Race: Science and Politics* ([1940] 1962), published as *Race and Racism* ([1942] 1983) in England; to the resource unit for teachers *Race and Cultural Relations* (1942), cowritten with high school teacher Mildred Ellis; and to the widely distributed pamphlet *The Races of Mankind* (1943), cowritten with Gene Weltfish and published by the Public Affairs Committee. In *Race: Science and Politics,* Benedict identifies colonialism and nationalism as historical and contemporary sources of racism, which must, as a result of its origins, be recognized as neither predetermined nor an immutable human characteristic. In these works Benedict outspokenly advocates the elimination of racism and the recognition and appreciation of cultural differences. She offers implied if not active support for universal respect for the human rights established in the United Nations Universal Declaration of Human Rights (1948) and the Charter of the United Nations (1945) and promotes concerted efforts to identify and condemn all forms of racism through the intervention of international law. Nevertheless, during the year following Benedict's resignation as president of the American Anthropological Association, the executive board of the association criticized the Declaration of Human Rights in the pages of the *American Anthropologist,* exposing the conflict between cultural relativism and the notion of universal rights (Messer 1983:240).

French anthropologist Claude Lévi-Strauss, in the UNESCO publication *Race and History* (1952), notably advances an anthropologically derived position similar to that of Benedict. Together Benedict and Lévi-Strauss represent the source of an anthropological tradition that seeks to promote, through lectures, seminars, publications, action anthropology and applied anthropology, and participation in international forums, respect for the rights of individuals and of peoples, including indigenous peoples. Anthropologists such as Ashley Montagu and Paul Radin conspicuously encourage the practice of an anthropology that is integrally opposed to racism. This is particularly evident in Montagu's recently updated classic *Man's Most Dangerous Myth* ([1942] 1997). "Modernization" itself has increasingly attracted the arrows of anthropological criticism: in works such as *The Dehumanization of Man* (1983), Montagu and Floyd Matson attempt to identify technological, economic, and cultural sources and symptoms of alienation and of the degradation of the integrity and dignity of the individual in the contemporary United States. The act of addressing issues of dehumanization expands the overall humanistic approach in anthropology, including the human rights orientation, but it does not necessarily address the specific issues associated with indigenous peoples' historical and contemporary anticolonial struggles for existence.

Lévi-Strauss brilliantly explores the issues of modernization and human degradation peculiar to indigenous peoples and to the outer limits of the third world in *Tristes Tropiques* (1955). Clifford Geertz describes *Tristes Tropiques* as travelogue, ethnography, philosophical text, reformist tract, and the key to all of Lévi-Strauss's later works:

> There has been an enormous number of indictments by now of the West for its impact on the non-West, but there are few, no matter how radical their authors, with the devastating bitterness and power of Lévi-Strauss's *Tristes Tropiques*. He makes Franz Fanon sound positively congenial.
>
> The passages are famous. The descriptions of the dilapidated "former savages" spoiling the view around São Paolo; the diatribes about the empty beer bottles and discarded tin cans; and the intense hatred for industrial civilization that keeps breaking through. . . .
>
> And the crime, of course, is that it is we who have done this, whether out of greed and pétulante activité or mere fits of absentmindedness and callousness— we who have thrown, as he says somewhere in *Tristes Tropiques*, our filth in the faces of the rest of the world, which now proceeds to throw it back in ours. (Geertz 1988:39–41)

Despite its penetrating illumination of the impact of colonialism on indigenous societies, *Tristes tropiques* remains, as Geertz describes, and in contrast with the thought and actions of Lévi-Strauss's intellectual rival Jean-Paul Sartre, an apolitical expression of "aesthetic repugnance" rather than a Fanon-like revelation of the re-emergence of indigenous peoples' political and cultural self-determination.

Moving toward the aim of indigenous self-determination, the controversial Indian Reorganization Act of 1934 and its implementation allowed and encouraged Indian tribes to operate as tribes as they engaged with the federal government in the assertion of their new rights of sovereignty.

Lurie suggests that the greatest contribution of anthropologists of this era may have been their inadvertent advancement of Indian political and legal education (Lurie 1988:552). The National Congress of American Indians was formed in 1944 with two objectives: to lobby for legislation in Indians' interests, and to provide information and expertise in implementing the Indian Reorganization Act (Lurie 1988:552). Anthropologists became directly involved in the indigenous movement for self-determination when in 1960 Sol Tax, an anthropologist "vitally concerned with the future of the American Indian," was invited to speak to the annual convention of the National Congress of American Indians. In his address Tax "proposed a plan whereby Indians could mobilize as a highly visible pressure group, publicizing their problems and making the nature of their aspirations known before the government and general public" (Lurie 1961:481; 1988:554).

Tax's proposal culminated in the American Indian Chicago Conference of 1961, organized by Tax and the University of Chicago Department of Anthropology. Four hundred and sixty-seven Indians representing ninety tribes and bands participated in the conference, and 145 non-Indians, including anthropologists and lawyers, attended as observers (Lurie 1961:489, 496). The participants produced a document titled "Declaration of Indian Purpose," in which they affirmed their right to their own spiritual and cultural values, presented their views on problems confronting them, promoted Indian participation in economic and social ventures that affect them, and demanded the abandonment of termination policy (Josephy, ed., 1971; Lurie 1961; Washburn 1995:229). As a result of Tax's efforts and his "action anthropology," Indians were inspired to create a more far-reaching and united Indian movement, which in turn resulted in the creation of the National Indian Youth Council, an activist organization that has moved far beyond the principles of the Declaration of Indian Purpose; it has engaged in numerous protest demonstrations and has been instrumental in the internationalization of indigenous issues (Lurie 1988:554).

One issue consistently expressed in contemporary international forums that is of fundamental importance for North American Indians and other indigenous peoples is their exceptional spiritual and ecological relationship to their natural territories. In *Pigs for the Ancestors* (1984), Roy Rappaport demonstrates the *ecological logos,* or integrated internal natural/cultural logic, of the Tsembaga Maring, an indigenous people of the Papua New Guinea highlands. His research represents a scientific recognition of the unique value of indigenous cultures and knowledge. Rappaport discovers that the ritual system of the Tsembaga, set in motion by the cyclic movement of the village and the planting of the *rumbim,* coordinates the dietary utilization of pig protein, the *kaiko* festival, the establishment of political and social alliances, the manageable size of pig herds, limitations on warfare, and the ecological utilization of the ecosystem through swidden agriculture. Rappaport's assessment of the perpetual sustainability of the Tsembaga's traditional cultural practices is a position that indigenous peoples, indigenous rights advocates, and scholars have successfully presented in international arenas as a fundamental characteristic of essentially all traditional indigenous societies.

For Rappaport, the Tsembaga represent successful cultural adaptation to the environment in an evolutionary sense. Turning the theory of social evolution on its head through the analysis of the alternative concept of "Maladaptation in Social Systems" (1977), and employing cybernetic-social-system concepts such as oversegregation, overcentralization, and usurpation or overspecification, Rappaport describes the deleterious impact that monetization and commercialization, industrialization and technologization based on fossil fuels, and the rise of an oligarchic elite have on natural ecosystems and indigenous cultures. As the simpleminded and selfish interests of these subsystems subvert the interests of the social system as a whole, and endow themselves with a sense of sacredness, the results are bound to be "stupid, brutal and . . . destructive" (Rappaport 1977:61-66). Rappaport's criticisms of the assimilationist and destructive tendencies of international corporate capitalism and of state capitalism that is partially veiled behind the facade of socialism anticipate the general conclusions of the United Nations study "Discrimination Against Indigenous People: Transnational Investments and Operations on the Lands of Indigenous Peoples" (United Nations 1994c) and those of related recent conferences, seminars, and declarations sponsored by the United Nations and other international organizations.

Contemporary indigenous spiritual and ecological issues are inseparable from larger, perhaps more controversial, political issues. In the Declaration of Barbados: For the Liberation of the Indians (1971), a handful of North American and South American anthropologists announce the continuation of colonialism, ethnocide, and genocide in the Americas with respect to its indigenous inhabitants and within a general system of the domination of the South American states by external metropolitan powers (reprinted in Dostal, ed., 1972:376–84; in Bodley 1990:211–16). The declaration was written following the Symposium on Inter-Ethnic Conflict in South America, convened January 25–30, 1971, in Barbados and sponsored jointly by the Programme to Combat Racism and the World Council of Churches. On the basis of expert testimony, it explores the sociopolitical situations of Indian tribes in Venezuela, Colombia, Ecuador, Peru, Bolivia, Paraguay, Argentina, Brazil, and the Guianas.

The authors of the Declaration of Barbados condemn the concept of *terra nullius* and the practice of internal colonialism; recommend to states and religious missions specific actions of redress and reconciliation, including immediate cessation of practices constituting genocide and ethnocide and of all forms of denial of indigenous peoples' fundamental freedoms and the right to self-determination; and propose a liberation anthropology that seeks to unmask colonialism and its ideological structures while denouncing ethnocide and genocide in all their manifestations. They believe that anthropologists in particular "must assume the unavoidable responsibilities for immediate action to halt this aggression and contribute significantly to the process of Indian liberation."

The authors of the declaration contend that anthropology was formed as an instrument of colonial domination and that anthropologists continue to rationalize colonial domination of indigenous peoples in scientific language and to supply knowledge of indigenous peoples that is useful for maintaining and disguising colonial relations. Rather than confronting these issues, the authors argue, anthropologists have adopted:

1. A *scientism* [that] negates any relationship between academic research and the future of those peoples who form the object of such investigation, thus eschewing political responsibility which the relation contains and implies;

2. A *hypocrisy* manifest in the rhetorical protestation based on first principles which skillfully avoids any commitment in a concrete situation;

3. An *opportunism* that although it may recognize the present painful situation of the Indian, at the same time rejects any possibility of transforming action by proposing the need "to do something" within the established order. This latter position, of course, only reaffirms and continues the system.

The authors affirm that the anthropology needed today is one that recognizes the colonial situation and is committed to the struggle for the liberation of Indian peoples. Anthropologists must take advantage of all opportunities to act on behalf of Indian peoples, must condemn all acts of genocide and all practices contributing to ethnocide, and must generate new concepts that overcome the subordinate position of Indians in anthropological research and discourse. Indians must lead their own liberation movement and must be supported in their experiments with the development of their own forms of self-government and self-development.

Several of the anthropologists who composed the Declaration of Barbados also served on the jury of the independent and populist Fourth Russell Tribunal, which convened in 1980 to adjudicate American Indians' claims that multinational corporations, states, and citizens of states had violated their rights as individuals and as peoples in international law. The jurors heard the testimony of witnesses, and documentation was presented, then the tribunal utilized the instruments of international law to render nonbinding judgments on the cases before them. For example, representatives of the Hopi Nation accused its own Hopi Tribal Council and the government of the United States, in association with energy corporations and Christian churches, of genocide, of imposing on the Hopi people an alien form of government, and of exploitation of natural resources on Hopi land against the wishes of the Hopi people, which resulted in deterioration of the environment and of Hopi quality of life. The Hopi Nation also accused the government of the United States of deliberately manipulating the legal system to prevent the return of ancestral land to the Hopi people. The Fourth Russell Tribunal determined that the U.S. government had violated the Hopi people's right to self-determination as protected by the Charter of the United Nations and additional United Nations conventions, declarations, and resolutions: the theft of Hopi lands violated rights protected by the Universal Declaration of Human Rights, the American Convention on Human Rights (1969) and other instruments; the unilateral imposition of certain forms of economic development upon the Hopi violated rights protected by numerous United Nations conventions, declarations, and resolutions, including the Declaration on the Granting of Independence to Colonial Countries and Peoples (1960); and the removal of Hopi children from their families constitutes genocide under the terms of the Convention on the Prevention and Punishment of the Crime of Genocide (1948) (Russell Tribunal 1980:11–12).

ANTHROPOLOGY AND THE SELF-DETERMINATION OF INDIGENOUS PEOPLES

In his article "The Russell Tribunal: Who Speaks for Indian Tribes?" (1981), historian Wilcomb E. Washburn, an expert on U.S. federal Indian law, and then Director of the Office of American Studies at the Smithsonian Institution, contends that the Fourth Russell Tribunal was a travesty, a mockery of justice, an injustice to the United States, and ultimately counterproductive to the cause of Indian self-government. Washburn charges that "none of the entities bringing charges against the United States in behalf of tribal groups was an official tribal body, none was designated by tribal governments to represent them, and none was elected by their tribal members to represent them" (Washburn 1981:8). Washburn asserts that American Indian radicals have trivialized the horrendous conditions and true injustices suffered by Indians in Central and South America by placing the government of the United States on the same level as the Latin American governments through the propagation of inaccuracies and pure inventions. In the Hopi case, according to Washburn, over 52 percent of eligible Hopi voters participated in the vote to accept or reject the Indian Reorganization Act of 1934, which created the Hopi Tribal Council (Washburn 1981:8). According to Washburn:

The Fourth Russell Tribunal provided a stage for another form of ideological warfare against the United States. Almost no press coverage was given this "tribunal," which was recognized by the news media as a performance in the continuing international "theatre of the absurd" in which the United States is beaten over the head by its ideological enemies around the world for the various "crimes" of "colonialism," "imperialism," "racism," "oppression," "economic hegemonism," etc., etc. . . . It is too bad that financial "angels" cannot be found to finance European trips for Indian leaders who truly represent their tribes. (Washburn 1981:14)

Washburn predicts that the result of these attacks will be the erosion of the Indian tribal governments on which any hope of Indian self-government and the improvement of Indian conditions of life on the reservations depends.

Since the early 1970s, anthropologists have been visibly engaged in the recognition and appreciation of cultural diversity and in the struggle for the survival of minorities and indigenous peoples, for the protection of their human rights, and for the promotion of their interests against encroaching settlement, ecological transformation, state-supported violence, and invasive transnational economic policies. These human rights–oriented commitments and the internationalization of anthropological research and theory are reflected in the formation and actions of the American Anthropological Association's Commission on Human Rights and Cultural Survival, including the publication of *Cultural Survival Quarterly*. Nevertheless, as Washburn's argument sufficiently demonstrates, some scholars may steadfastly and vigorously oppose racism, promote respect for national and international law and for human rights, and genuinely recognize past injustices, yet foster a political view far different from the views of those who are sympathetic to and supportive of an anthropology of liberation or self-determination for indigenous peoples as proposed by the authors of the Declaration of Barbados and by that hero of Todorov's history, Las Casas. When we acknowledge the positions of anthropologists and others in opposition to or in elision or evasion of the liberation of indigenous peoples, particularly as proclaimed in the United Nations draft Declaration of the Rights of Indigenous Peoples, we illuminate the sometimes subtle nature of the grievances and protests of indigenous peoples.

Chapter Two

INDIGENOUS CULTURES

AND THE LAW IN NORTH AMERICA

We true Hopi are obligated to the Great Spirit never to cut up our land, nor sell it. For this reason we have never signed any treaty or other document releasing this land. . . . We Hopi are an independent sovereign nation, by the law of the Great Spirit, but the United States Government does not want to recognize the aboriginal leaders of this land. Instead, he recognizes only what he himself has created out of today's children in order to carry out his scheme to claim all of our land.

—Dan Katchongva, Hopi Sun Clan leader

Indian land claims cases are, by and large, the backwash of a great national experiment in dictatorship and racial extermination.

—Felix Cohen, *The Legal Conscience*

✦ In *Welcome of Tears* (1977), an ethnography described by Claude Lévi-Strauss as "a masterly analysis," anthropologist Charles Wagley examines the culture and history of the Tapirapé Indians of central Brazil; their relationship with their voluntary guardians, the Little Sisters of Jesus; and his own relationship with the Tapirapé as an anthropologist. Wagley vibrantly demonstrates the humanity of the Tapirapé while discussing their bird societies and feast groups, the arrival of the *anchunga* spirits, the use of elaborate *upé* masks, rituals of reciprocity such as the *kawió* ceremony, shamanism, their sexual relations, and their methods of preserving social order. Wagley provides an important analysis of the ecological impact of slash-and-burn agriculture when people are compelled by outside forces to subsist on an ever smaller land base. Wagley situates Tapirapé history and culture change within the larger context of colonialism, particularly Brazilian authoritarianism; paternalism; and corruption. Wagley speaks out against both social Darwinism and the form of romanticism that regards the Indians as children and leads to the establishment of paternalistic policies and to the absence of Indian self-determination (Wagley 1977:301–2).

Wagley seeks to use anthropology not as a means of social control, but as a means of improving the lives of indigenous peoples. He argues that "one cannot be sympathetic to [Brazilian] national development at the expense of native Brazilian tribesmen" (Wagley 1977:299). Finally, Wagley argues against policies of total assimilation of indigenous peoples into Brazilian national society; he encourages the effective participation of tribal Indians in Brazilian society in a way that enables them to retain their culture and their ethnic identity (Wagley 1977:303).

Wagley's masterpiece is a compelling appeal for the survival of the Tapirapé in a world that wants, if not demands, their remaining territory and that seems to have no use for the Tapirapé as a people or a culture. Early in the narrative, he strangely adopts a melancholy myth that echoes throughout anthropological and documentary films and essays on contemporary indigenous peoples. In 1939 and 1940, when Wagley began his research among the Tapirapé, he found them living closer to an aboriginal state than most Indian groups; they were not yet "a dispirited or disorganized people." Nevertheless, for Wagley "it was obvious that the Tapirapé, without being aware of it, were doomed to extinction as a people and as a functioning society. That they have escaped such a fate seems a miracle to me" (Wagley 1977:39). Earlier, in a work that presaged the academic popularity of the concepts of ethnic groups and ethnic identity in anthropology, Wagley and Marvin Harris defined the indigenous peoples of Central and South America as "minorities" rather than as distinct, self-governing peoples occupying traditional territories and struggling under conditions of colonialism (Wagley and Harris 1958). Indians in the Americas were legally minorities, except perhaps in the United States where Indian governments were recognized as possessing some elements of sovereignty, but the period during which Wagley and Harris wrote was an era of "termination" of tribal status in the United States.

These two concepts, or interpretive strategies, (1) that aboriginal peoples and cultures are destined (or predestined) either for disappearance or for assimilation, and (2) the recognition of colonized peoples as minorities or ethnic groups equivalent to various immigrant groups, arise in anthropological thought and practice from the long history of the subjugation of indigenous peoples in international and domestic law. Anthropologists have often, perhaps unwittingly, played significant roles in this continuing process of alienation and assimilation, as they did in the case of the Dawes Act. On the other hand, anthropologists such as Wagley have played remarkable roles in raising the awareness of scholars who were entrapped behind opaque, rather than rose-colored, glasses. A growing number of contemporary historians, legal theorists, native scholars, and anthropologists offer accomplished and acclaimed analyses of the history of political and legal relations between North American Indians and the colonial European powers—and subsequently the United States and Canada—and of the near total annihilation of North America's indigenous peoples. These analyses expose conventional history as a myth, as the result of a political exercise of power and domination that has colored the perceptions of anthropologists and other scholars, past and present, through whose research the myth has been scientifically consecrated.

THE EUROPEAN AGE OF DISCOVERY

In 1492 Columbus's three-ship expedition sailed across the Atlantic for the New World bequeathed with a value system that originated in the medieval Crusades for the Holy Land. The Catholic Church dominated the European political arenas of the time, and the pope's spiritual jurisdiction was regarded as extending over all of the world's peoples; his dominion was global. This jurisdiction was considered to be the principle behind the Crusades, which respected no non-Christian people's rights to either land or liberty. Pope Innocent IV, a thirteenth-century lawyer, answered the question of whether it is proper to invade territories in the possession of infidels by arguing that all infidels, as a result of their violation of Christian "natural law," should fall under the jurisdiction of the pope, whose authority in all moral matters was imperative (Getches, Wilkinson, Williams 1993:42–44).

In 1436, the pope issued the papal bull *Romanus Pontifex,* which granted Portugal all rights to the Canary Islands and Africa. Upon the return of Columbus in 1493, the pope issued the *Inter Caetera,* which authorized Spain to take responsibility for the conversion of the Indians of the Americas, a responsibility that the Spaniards interpreted in an unorthodox manner (Washburn 1995:5): the method they used to carry out the *Inter Caetera* came to be known as the "Black Legend." The Treaty of Tordesillas (1494) further established the boundaries distinguishing Spanish and Portuguese colonial territories. When the Spanish arrived in a new territory or among a new people, they read aloud to the indigenous inhabitants the Spanish *Requerimiento,* a legal device rendered by lawyers and intended as a charter of conquest.

Spain's expanding empire in the Americas generated considerable thought and discussion in Spanish universities on the nature of the rights of aboriginal peoples. In 1532 Franciscus de Vitoria, theologian, jurist, professor, and founder of modern international law, authored "On the Indians Lately Discovered," in which he set out three basic propositions that subsequently influenced the developing law of nations:

1. The inhabitants of the Americas possessed natural legal rights as free and rational people.

2. Any Spanish claims to title to the Americas on the basis of "discovery" or papal grant were illegitimate and could not affect the inherent rights of the Indian inhabitants.

3. Transgressions of the universally binding norms of the Law of Nations by the Indians might serve to justify a Christian nation's conquest and colonial empire in the Americas. (Getches, Wilkinson, and Williams 1993:50–51)

According to Vitoria's reasoning, Indian peoples possessed ownership of their territories in law, and therefore the Spaniards' assertion of "title by discovery" would obtain only in unoccupied lands and could not justify seizure of Indian territories. Furthermore, Vitoria claimed that the pope possessed no power over the Indians and thus any Spanish assertions of dominion or seizure of property on the basis of papal grant or the reading of the *Requerimiento* were likewise invalid.

According to Vitoria, however, the law of nations did guarantee the Spaniards' right to travel through Indian territories and to economically exploit the Indians, regardless of Indian laws or preferences. The Indians, who were bound by the law of nations but ignorant of it, should therefore be placed under a form of guardianship for their own protection (Getches, Wilkinson, and Williams 1993:51–53; Todorov 1984:147–50; Washburn 1995:9–12; R. Williams 1990a). Although the requirement of guardianship carries with it racist overtones (R. Williams 1991; Todorov 1984:150), Felix Cohen, perhaps the most influential figure in twentieth-century U.S. Indian law, argues that Vitoria's writings continue to provide the foundation for humane and rational treatment of American Indians under U.S. law (Cohen 1942).

The Spanish conquistadors continued to mete out destruction on the Indian peoples despite Vitoria's celebrated musings. During Pizarro's predatory conquest of Peru, Father Bernardino de Minaya left Peru for Rome, where he pled with the pope to protect the Indians from Pizarro, who had received authorization only to save Indian souls. As a result of Minaya's entreaties, Pope Paul III issued the bull *Sublimis Deus* (1537), which declared that Indians are humans and have rights in liberty and property that are not to be deprived, and that all actions to the contrary are "null and of no effect." The Emperor Charles, however, ignored the bull, and his emissaries confiscated copies of the pope's edict. Charles urged the pope to change his opinion and ultimately prevailed. Minaya was subsequently thrown into prison by the Dominican order (Washburn 1995:12–13). The historian Oviedo would later write: "God is going to destroy them soon. . . . Satan has now been expelled from the island [Española]; his influence has disappeared now that most of the Indians are dead. . . . Who can deny that the use of gunpowder against pagans is the burning of incense to Our Lord" (Oviedo, quoted in Todorov 1984:151).

Bartolomé de Las Casas persistently urged the Spanish Crown to intervene on behalf of the rights of the Indians, and the king eventually ordered a conference of jurists, scholars, and theologians to convene at Valladolid in 1550 and 1551 to hear the issues. The principal antagonists in the debate before a jury of intellectuals and officials were theologian, historian, and eyewitness Las Casas and Spanish "humanist scholar" Juan Ginés de Sepúlveda, an acknowledged authority on Aristotle. Sepúlveda's request to publish a treatise on the just cause of war against the Indians had been denied, and for him the debate represented something of an appeal. He argued that the Aristotelian hierarchy is the natural state of being among humankind: there are those who are born to rule, and those who are born to serve; those who are masters and those who are slaves. As for the Indians, Sepúlveda argued, "In wisdom, skill, virtue and humanity, these people are as inferior to the Spaniards as children are to adults and women to men; there is as great a difference between them as there is between savagery and forbearance, between violence and moderation, almost—I am inclined to say—as between monkeys and men" (Sepúlveda, quoted in Todorov 1984:153).

After presenting his thesis on the inherent differences among people, Sepúlveda continued by elaborating a political philosophy concerning the conquest of the Americas:

1. To subject by force of arms men whose natural condition is such that they should obey others, if they refuse such obedience and no other course remains.

2. To banish the portentous crime of eating human flesh, which is a special offense to nature, and to stop the worship of demons instead of God, which above all else provokes His wrath, together with the monstrous rite of sacrificing men.

3. To save from grave perils the numerous innocent mortals whom these barbarians immolated every year placating their gods with human hearts.

4. War on the infidels is justified because it opens the way to the propagation of Christian religion and eases the task of the missionaries. (Todorov 1984:154)

Sepúlveda's moral imperative of imposing "good" on others includes the Spaniards' obligation to use military power to support the oppressed Indian masses by overthrowing tyrannical Indian regimes.

Las Casas argued, on the other hand, that Spanish jurisdiction in the New World was spiritual only. Under the grants of the papal bulls, actions involving force were justified only when the Indians refused to hear the Christian message. Furthermore, Las Casas insisted, the Christian salvation of one Indian life could not justify the destruction of thousands or millions of lives, for the salvation of one cannot justify the death of even a single other. Possessing no coercive authority over the Indians, the pope could not confer such authority on the Spanish. Las Casas contended that the king should evict the Spaniards from the New World because they had violated the terms of their grant and that all property seized should be restored to the Indians. In essence, Las Casas argued for the equality of Spaniard and Indian on the basis of the words of Jesus of Nazareth: "You must love your neighbor as yourself" (Washburn 1995:14; Todorov 1984:160–67). At this stage of his intellectual evolution Las Casas advocated equality through assimilation by conversion to Christianity, a form of colonialism that Todorov finds little different from that of Cortéz, but Las Casas would later champion both cultural relativism and Indian self-determination (Todorov 1984:191–93). The jury at Valladolid rendered no decision; Sepúlveda's appeal was not granted.

COLONIZATION AND GENOCIDE IN THE AMERICAS

By 1509, on the islands of Puerto Rico and Jamaica, "lands flowing with milk and honey," approximately six hundred thousand to one million indigenous people had been slain by the Spaniards, leaving fewer than two hundred aboriginals living in the land (Las Casas [1552]1992:26). The indigenous inhabitants of Española (Haiti and the Dominican Republic), nearly a quarter of a million people at contact in 1494, were virtually, if not completely, extinct by the early 1500s (Rouse 1992; Debo 1970:20). Even at this early time, colonization eliminated entire nations of peoples: in less than a decade the pattern of the events resulting from European contact with the indigenous peoples of the Americas had become obvious and inescapable.

Estimates vary concerning the total scope of American Indian depopulation, but anthropologist Russell Thornton suggests an overall 90 to 95 percent reduction in the number of indigenous inhabitants of the Americas that was largely due to continuous epidemics of European-introduced diseases. Thornton, a Native American, argues that the pre-1492 Indian population in the Americas stood at over 70 million and that in the following four centuries, as the result of introduced diseases, warfare against

European colonialists, genocide at the hands of the Europeans, and the ensuing near-total breakdown of traditional Indian lifestyles, the total aboriginal population plunged to between 4 and 4.5 million, a 94 percent reduction. In the United States alone, the pre-1492 population of over 2 million Indians bottomed out at about 125,000 by the early twentieth century, a 93 percent reduction (Thornton 1987).

Thornton's population analysis is distinguished by the fact that he includes genocide as one significant factor in the numerical reduction of Indian tribes. The works of Las Casas ([1552] 1992), historians David Stannard (1992) and Kirkpatrick Sale (1990), and Ward Churchill (1997) graphically document the genocidal acts, ambitions, and ideologies of European nations and their representatives in the New World and their consequences for aboriginal peoples throughout the Americas. If epidemics generally result from more than one cause, then economic and cultural warfare, deliberate biological warfare, slavery and other forms of forced labor, political deception and fraud, and outright extermination all contributed to the "disease-related" genocide of the Indians.

England asserted sovereignty over the East Coast of North America by virtue of John Cabot's "discovery" of Newfoundland in 1497. The English inherited the Spanish belief that the spread of Christianity throughout the world was predestined, and that consequently "heathen" lands were theirs to seize by claim of divine right and the "moral good." Declarations of sovereignty justified by the Doctrine of Discovery and occupation served to distinguish which Christian nations were in possession of which territories.

Francis Jennings suggests that the Indian population of North America may have been reduced by approximately 90 percent immediately upon contact with Europeans as a result of European-introduced diseases; some areas may then have been "widowed" lands, rather than territories that otherwise would have fallen under the designation of *terra nullius,* or unpopulated lands (Jennings 1975:27–29). Nevertheless, the English colonists' survival at first depended largely upon the assistance of the Indians, who shared their knowledge of indigenous flora and fauna, particularly of the value of maize, and who also donated agricultural surpluses to needy colonists (Jennings 1975:40, 66). In North America both English and French colonists and traders coexisted amicably with Indians over the first several decades of contact, despite the fact that the ultimate goals of all the European powers were conquest and exploitation, goals that were graphically illustrated by the expeditions of Cortéz, Coronado, and Pizarro.

Indian attacks upon European colonists usually constituted reprisals for unprovoked assaults. With the single-minded ruthlessness behind European colonialist expansion exposed, the notorious reference among the English to the "Indian Menace," an ideological device sanctifying European colonial practices of enslavement, annihilation, and extermination, is perhaps better understood as a mask for the "European Menace" in the

Americas (Jennings 1975:36–37). Europeans often praised the Indians' "humanity," their generosity and honesty; "nothing is so frequently recorded in the earliest chronicles as the warmth of the reception accorded the first colonists" (Washburn 1995:33). When expedient, however, these same voices concocted a mythical characterization of the Indians as treacherous savages and barbarians, devil-worshipping heathens, wild beasts, irrational and warlike people, filthy and sinful creatures, murderous brutes, and red pagans whose race and culture was infinitely inferior to that of the civilized Christians (Berkhofer 1979; Jennings 1975:43–57).

The colonists engaged in political relations and economic trade with Indian tribes or nations and survived at times on Indian agricultural surpluses, but when it was expedient, the Europeans uniformly viewed the Indians as "nomadic" peoples with no recognizable form of government or land ownership. Under the popular form of Anglo-American political philosophy expressed in the writings of John Locke, Indians possessed no legal or moral claim to any land they occupied. The land could be considered vacant; it was *terra nullius,* and European claims to sovereignty over the Americas via the Doctrine of Discovery were thus justified (Deloria 1985:88–90).

AMERICAN INDIANS IN EARLY INTERNATIONAL LAW

The English expansionist discourse, a malleable system of ideas drawn from the eras of the Holy Crusades and the conquest of Ireland, underscored that popular principle of English law that neither recognized nor protected the Indians' tribal ownership of land, particularly those hunting and agricultural reserves necessary for slash-and-burn cultivation. Thus the colonists' increasing encroachment upon "unoccupied" or "legally vacant" Indian land was not considered immoral, although European governments sought to maintain control by purchasing land and establishing verifiable political and legal sovereignty over it. With the endorsement of their religious leaders, European Kings, including the English Kings, laid claim to the Americas in the name of Christianity; the claim of discovery was endorsed by the "necessity" of converting savage souls to the doctrines of the Church, which gave supermoral authority and urgency to political and economic exploitation.

Because the Indians were considered "demonic infidels," the Europeans did not consider their enslavement and execution a crime. Nevertheless, and in direct contradiction to these deeply held beliefs, Europeans participated in a dynamic economic trade with the Indians for agricultural products and furs; European governments made treaties with Indian nations and purchased land from them, made political and economic alliances with Indian nations, and engaged Indian nations in wars against rival European powers. These contradictory beliefs or policies, which could be molded and adapted as seen fit, as Jennings argues in *The Invasion of America* (1975), combined to form a more expansive European ideology, an "ideology of power."

The English, however, limited the powers of the Doctrine of Discovery by disavowing Spanish claims to the East Coast of North America, claims that were not supported by continuous occupation and colonial settlement. In a further limitation on the doctrine, the English followed Dutch and Swedish practice based on the Roman and medieval doctrine of immemorial possession and entered into treaties with the indigenous nations, thereby acknowledging the absolute territorial and national sovereignty of the indigenous nations through acts of international law. The English entered into these treaties with the intention of upholding their colonial claims to the exclusive right of purchase against the competing European powers, but without divesting indigenous nations of their territorial sovereignty or aboriginal title (Morris 1987:288–89; Newton 1980; Berman 1978). Aboriginal title could be extinguished through purchase, conquest through legitimate war, and voluntary abandonment of the land by the aboriginal inhabitants (Clinton 1989:332–33).

Although local colonial authorities possessed substantial autonomy in the management of local affairs, the British Crown retained the right to govern all land transactions between Indians and colonial authorities and settlers. In 1664, following complaints by Indian tribes to King Charles II and the appointment of a royal commissioner to investigate the complaints, the English Crown declared through its commission that colonial authorities could not confiscate Indian lands through conquest unless that conquest was "just," or in other words, occurred in the course of defensive actions, and unless the territories in question were included in the colonial charter. The commissioners also declared that the confiscation of Indian hunting grounds as vacant waste was illegal, because these territories were the sovereign property of the Indian tribes (Clinton 1989:334).

Mohegan Indians v. Connecticut, the first formal litigation of Indian rights, was brought before the Queen in Council in 1703 and subsequently before numerous royal commissions, through 1773. The Mohegans claimed that the colonists had violated a series of treaties and agreements entered into between 1659 and 1681 and that these treaties gave the colony of Connecticut only the right of first purchase. Connecticut argued for the transfer of sovereignty to themselves, through which it had parceled out the territory in question for colonial settlement. Although the decision deprived the Mohegans of most of the land that they did not actually occupy, it also established two fundamental principles of Indian law: "(1) the central government (then in the form of the British Crown government in London), rather than local colonial authorities, ultimately controlled Indian policy; and (2) the Indian tribes were separate sovereign nations not controlled by local laws of the colony" (Clinton 1989:335).

In 1743 the Connecticut colonists disputed the authority of the royal commission to intervene in their affairs, claiming that the Mohegans were subject to the laws of Connecticut and that Connecticut courts maintained jurisdiction over the case. The royal commission held that the Indian tribes were distinct peoples not subject to the laws of England or of its colonial courts, and that land disputes between such distinct peoples and English subjects represented an international dispute, subject to the laws of nations; the disputes were therefore the province of royal commissions (Clinton 1989:335–36).

When Indians attacked colonists to defend their sovereignty against illegal colonialist encroachment and usurpation, as when Powhatan and the confederated tribes of Virginia carried out the massacre of 1622, the colonists used the attacks to justify wars of conquest against the Indian tribes. After first pacifying the Indians with a peace treaty that raised their false belief that their legitimate complaints had been resolved, the governor and the council of Virginia, in association with the Virginia Company, ordered a war of enslavement and extermination of the Indians in the Virginia colony. When questioned about their deceit, the Virginia council defended it as an entirely moral act, as would be any act of liquidation of the Indians, in their estimation, including poisoning the wine that agents of the government of Virginia gave to the Indians following the signing of the peace treaty (Washburn 1995:35–37).

INDIAN NATIONS AND EUROPEAN STRUGGLES FOR SUPREMACY

Trade with the Europeans, no matter how peaceful the relations and how equitable the transactions, consistently led to the decline of Indian autonomy and sovereignty. The sale of land, for example, moved in only one direction, from Indian to European, the territory from Indian political authority to European political authority. Early on, the lucrative fur trade fueled the Industrial Revolution, but the sale of pelts to Europeans ultimately led to the decline of animal populations, to economic wars between Indian tribes as they fought for access to European markets and for control of hunting grounds, and to disruption of traditional Indian values and culture (Jennings 1975:85–105). Indians quickly became dependent upon the firearms, textiles, and metal tools and utensils that they received in exchange from Europeans, and as a consequence they apparently lost both appreciation for much of their traditional material culture and the knowledge needed for its manufacture. The Indians also received alcohol in exchange for their products, and alcoholism immediately became the severe problem that it continues to be to this day. The Europeans consciously targeted the shaman, a central figure of Indian traditional culture, for elimination, and they created or co-opted Indian leaders in order to undermine cultural independence. But the attack upon Indian culture and autonomy by means of economic intrusion was no less effective than those strategies.

Indians who were economically allied with one of the competing European powers would fight on the side of their trading partner against the rival colonial power, or against the rival's indigenous allies in a battle for supremacy among subordinates (Jennings 1975:102). The French and Indian War (1754–1763) is an example: the Great Lakes Indian nations and their trading ally, France, fought the Iroquois nations that were on the side of the British (Jennings 1988; Debo 1970:71, 78–81). The Europeans did not always return such fidelity to the Indians. The French governor of Louisiana, for example, expressed his lack of concern for the well-being of the French colonists' Indian allies when he wrote about the result of the French and Indian War for the Choctaw and Chickasaw Indians in the South:

> The Choctaws . . . have raised about four hundred scalps and made one hundred prisoners. . . . [This] is a most important advantage which we have obtained, the more so, that it has not cost one drop of French blood, through the care I took of opposing the barbarians to one another. Their self-destruction in this manner is the sole efficacious way of ensuring tranquility in the colony. (quoted in Wilson 1986:12)

The British, similarly, maneuvered to splinter the French-allied Choctaw nation by inducing elements of the Choctaws to take a pro-British stance, in effect generating a Choctaw civil war.

Following the British victory over the French in the war for regional domination and the cession of French colonial territories to England under the 1763 Treaty of Paris, several Great Lakes Indian nations and the Seneca nation of the Iroquois united under the political leadership of Pontiac of the Ottawas and the spiritual vision of the Delaware prophet Neolin and engaged in a war for liberation from British domination (Dowd 1992:33–36; Debo 1970:78–81). These Indians feared the expansion of the rebellious British colonies. The British, fearing their own colonists' expansion into more secure Canadian territory and into the territories won from the French, issued the Royal Proclamation of 1763, which contained three key elements for Indian affairs:

> (1) centralization of the management of land cessions, diplomatic and other relations, and trade with the Indian tribes in British agents and officials responsible to the central government in London, coupled with the diminution or elimination of all local authority over such matters; (2) long-term, effective guarantees to Indian tribes of their lands and resources, including their hunting and fishing rights; and (3) protection of Indian autonomy and sovereignty, separated and protected from local colonial authority, even in areas in close geographic proximity to non-Indian settlements. (Clinton 1989:357–58)

The Royal Proclamation also recognized an independent Indian Territory west of the Appalachians that would serve as a buffer state between the rebellious and aggressive American colonies and the more secure British territories in the Great Lakes region and Canada. According to the Royal Proclamation, any purchase of Indian lands in this territory would be illegal; Indian sovereignty and title to possessions in the region would be secure.

But the Royal Proclamation of 1763 could not halt the tidal wave of colonists pouring into the region, so it was disregarded by colonial authorities. In the Declaration of Independence, Thomas Jefferson, writing for the new nation of Americans now united against the British in a war for liberation, claimed the right to make war upon the "savages" incited against them by the king of England. The Anglo-American colonists and their governments continued to view Indian lands as untilled waste in the Lockean sense, and hence they considered the Royal Proclamation of 1763 as a violation of natural law and as another illegitimate, tyrannical action committed against them by the British Crown. The Royal Proclamation was one of the reasons for the Revolutionary War.

The American Revolution again divided the Indians. Declared neutrals, such as the Abenaki Confederacy, were not tolerated. The most powerful Eastern and Central nations either fought their own wars of liberation or sided with the British, who had recognized Indian autonomy and sovereignty and had guaranteed protection of Indian land rights through several treaties in addition to the Royal Proclamation of 1763. Several other Indian nations, such as the Oneida and the Tuscarora of the Iroquois Confederacy, a number of the tribes of Maine, and the Mahicans of Massachusetts, sided with the Americans (Calloway 1995). The war left formerly formidable Indian nations and confederations, such as the Iroquois Confederacy, internally divided, militarily weakened, and irresolute. At roughly the same time, Spain invaded California, subdued a majority of the Indians there and hunted the "wild" Indians with the same maniacal cruelty as the early conquistadors (Wilson 1986:12).

INDIAN NATIONS AND THE UNITED STATES OF AMERICA

Following the conclusion of the War for Independence, the United States immediately entered into treaties with several powerful Indian nations, including the Cherokees, Creeks, and Choctaws, whose territories were located on the borders of the Spanish empire. The Treaty of Hopewell with the Cherokees (1785) carried the promise of territorial integrity and apparently of eventual statehood in the United States. Historian Angie Debo argues that the invitation to the Cherokees in Article XII of the treaty to send a "deputy" to the Congress of the Articles of Confederation (1777) constituted, in the language of the time, an offer of statehood

(Debo 1970:89); others have argued that this deputy might have been little more than an observer. However, in Article VI of the Delaware Indian Treaty of 1778, the first U.S. treaty with the Indians, the United States explicitly offers the formation of an Indian state composed of a confederation of friendly Indian nations, including the Shawnee. The Delaware Indians would head this confederation and represent it in the U.S. Congress. Previously a similar attempt was made to invite the Iroquois Confederacy to join the Continental Congress as "free, sovereign, and independent states," but that treaty mission failed (Washburn, ed., 1973:2263).

The Treaty of Paris of 1783, which officially ended the Revolutionary War, did not end the war between the United States and the Indian tribes. In the first treaties after the Revolutionary War, the Treaty of Fort Stanwix (1784) with the Iroquois, the Treaty of Fort McIntosh (1785) with the Delaware, Wyandot, Chippewa, and Ottawa, and the Treaty of Fort Finney (1786) with the Shawnee, vast territories were ceded to the United States in exchange for smaller, delineated territories and peace. Despite Congress's outspoken affirmation of the U.S. commitment to the humane and liberal treatment of the Indians, U.S. agents drew up these treaties unilaterally, treated the Indians as conquered nations, and made no compensation for ceded territories (Prucha 1984, 1:44–45). When the Indians were made aware of the treaty conditions, they objected to this singular arrogance, and they insisted that they were neither conquered peoples nor peoples who had asked for peace (Mohr 1933:93–138; Prucha 1984, 1:45).

In 1787 the Confederation Congress, which had no genuine political control over the territory in question, declared in the Northwest Ordinance that the peoples of the independent Indian Territory would be treated with "the utmost good faith," that their properties, rights, and liberties would never be seized or abolished without their consent except through "just and lawful" acts of Congress, and that settlement of lands in the Ohio area would be orderly and regulated. Nevertheless, Indian territorial title that was established by the Royal Proclamation of 1763 would, with the exception of those areas expressly stipulated by treaties, be extinguished by the Northwest Ordinance. The former Indian Territory would now be recognized by the United States as U.S. colonial territories, until such time as these territories would become states (Berkhofer 1979:140–41; Jones 1982:163–65).

The constitutional Congress enacted a series of trade and intercourse acts during the late eighteenth and early nineteenth centuries that were influential in asserting congressional authority to regulate commerce with the Indian tribes, but that also sought to protect treaty promises and to punish settler or state infringement on Indian lands or treaty violations (Newton 1984:201; Prucha 1970:44–49). Like the British Crown before them, however, the new U.S. government, which preferred a "humane policy" of territorial expansion (Debo 1970:90), was unable to slow and regulate the rapid, disorderly, and often violent influx of colonial immigrants into the Ohio River region. These settlements were established in violation of the Northwest Ordinance and international treaties with the Indian tribes, and they often came under Indian attack.

By the end of the 1780s, the Ohio frontier was embroiled in battles between Indian tribes residing in territories guaranteed them and American settlers who refused to respect the Northwest Ordinance of 1787 (Prucha 1984, 1:62). In 1790 and 1791 the powerful Miami Confederacy, under the political leadership of Little Turtle, inflicted several crushing defeats on military expeditions sent into the region by President Washington. The Miami Confederacy refused to recognize the treaties of Fort McIntosh and Fort Finney because they had not been party to them, and they insisted that all such partially signed treaties were null and void. The Miami did not consider themselves to have been defeated along with the British in the Revolutionary War (Prucha 1984, 1:62). The Miami Confederacy united Indian nations in the West, the South, and Canada in an agreement that the Ohio River would remain the boundary between Indian land and the United States (Debo 1970:90–91; Prucha 1984, 1:62–63). The British again offered their support to the Indians in maintaining and securing this boundary line. But warriors from several Indian nations under the leadership of Shawnee warrior Blue Jacket found the gates of British Fort Miami closed and locked when they sought entrance as they retreated following a failed attempt to halt the advance of General "Mad" Anthony Wayne at the Battle of Fallen Timbers (Debo 1970:92–93). With this Indian military alliance defeated, Wayne's forces destroyed every Indian village he could find and dictated the 1795 Treaty of Greenville, which forced the Indians to surrender nearly all of present-day Ohio and parts of Indiana, Michigan, and Illinois.

In the South, American settlers directly violated the Treaty of Hopewell by committing what amounted to unprovoked acts of war against the Cherokee nation. The Cherokees petitioned the U.S. government for assistance, but it reacted as if it were powerless to prevent the settlers' incursions (Prucha 1984, 1:48–54). The Creeks, militarily the strongest and most organized of the southern Indian nations, likewise suffered infringements upon their sovereignty. In violation of the established principle of the U.S. government's exclusive authority to enter into negotiations with the Indian tribes, the state of Georgia had concluded land cession treaties with a few Creek chiefs. The Creek confederacy denied the validity of these treaties. The U.S. government, under the personal direction of President Washington and with prior consultation with the U.S. Senate, intervened by negotiating the Treaty of New York (1790) with the Creeks, which ceded only those lands actually occupied by Georgia's settlers in return for a small annuity, recognition of U.S. protection, and a guarantee that the United States would respect Creek sovereignty over their remaining territory (Prucha 1984, 1:54–56). Spanish and British representatives observed this treaty process, apparently in support of the Creeks. Later treaty negotiations followed the procedure used for dealing with other independent nations, with the executive branch under the authority of the president negotiating and signing the treaties, then sending them to the Senate for ratification.

Article IX of the original Articles of Confederation had granted the federal government a general power over Indian affairs (Clinton and Hotopp 1979; Newton 1984:199; Prucha 1970:28–31). Article 1, Section 8, of the U.S. Constitution, on the other hand, grants only the power to regulate trade with the Indian tribes, because its framers regarded the Indian tribes as sovereign nations. President George Washington and Secretary of War Henry Knox continued the British policy of treating the tribes as sovereign nations, if only to avoid devastating wars with the still militarily powerful Indian peoples. They both advocated a policy that called for respect for existing treaty promises and for the negotiation of new treaties with the Indian tribes. The new agreements would include promises, in exchange for land cessions, to protect Indian lands and peoples against settler intrusion and violence. That policy remained in effect at least until 1871 (Newton 1984:200).

Nevertheless, the new American system of justice provided little legal relief for the Indians. In addition to losing lands in violation of agreements and treaties, Indians were hunted, robbed, and murdered by American settlers, who carried out these criminal acts with near impunity. William Henry Harrison, governor of Indiana Territory, claimed that he could do nothing to stop the carnage, commenting that "a great many Inhabitants of the Fronteers [sic] consider the murdering of Indians in the highest degree meritorious" (Harrison, quoted in Edmunds 1983:5). Indians, on the other hand, received the most severe penalties for similar crimes, and when they retaliated against settlers for their unwarranted and unjust violence, their actions enhanced the image of vicious, murderous savages threatening to overwhelm the achievements of hard-working and God-fearing American pioneers.

Following in the tradition of Neolin and other Indian prophets before him, the Shawnee prophet Tenskwatawa, or "The Open Door," professed a religious vision that entailed concepts of pan-Indian brotherhood, the liberation of Indian lands, the revitalization of traditional Indian culture and a return to ecological prosperity, and the identification of the white man as the offspring of the Evil Spirit. Tenskwatawa performed miracles and won many new converts from among disparate Indian nations. In response to the Treaty of Fort Wayne (1809), Tenskwatawa's brother, Tecumseh, who had participated in Blue Jacket's expeditions and who refused to recognize the involuntary cessions under the Treaty of Greenville, combined religious unity and vision with political unity and military action in the tradition of Pontiac. The emerging confederacy of Indian nations built upon the visions of Tenskwatawa and Tecumseh died with Tecumseh on a battlefield in Canada. The Indians had been betrayed once again by their British allies during the War of 1812 (Edmunds 1983; Dowd 1992:136–47; Horsman 1967:152–53, 166–67). Tenskwatawa first remained in Canada in exile, but he became infuriated with the level of white immigration into the region. Later, following the counsel of Lewis Cass, he would return to Ohio, champion U.S. Indian removal policy among the Indians, and move with the Shawnee to a reservation in Kansas (Edmunds 1983:165–90).

The Creek Confederacy, with which Tecumseh and his Shawnee brothers maintained close contact, rose in similar rebellion in the south with the support of the Spanish. The war was a response to both continued encroachment of settlers into Creek territories, and corruption among the U.S. government agencies and their Creek allies. On the latter issue, historian Gregory Evans Dowd notes:

> As in the North, the successful American infiltration of Indian government rested, in part, upon the annuity system, which its opponents charged was a system of bribery clothed in the mantle of payments for lands. Treaties promised annuities both to the entire Creek nation and to individual chiefs, but the broader distribution benefited some Creeks greatly and others not at all. For Americans paid the stipends only to Creek "agents" appointed by each town. These Creek leaders, who were not expected to distribute the goods evenly, gained a control over the annuity that would permit them "to do justice to those who faithfully exerted themselves for the honor and interest of their country." In other words, federally recognized leaders, the government chiefs, were to reward their followers. Indian annuities throughout the borderlands did not simply pay for land (a task for which they were woefully inadequate); they advanced American interests among factions of Indian leadership. (Dowd 1992:149–50)

The Treaty of Fort Wilkinson (1802) and the Treaty of Washington (1805) exemplify an American technique that historian Reginald Horsman has called "judicious bribery," a promise to pay off Creek chiefs in personal annuities for signing the treaties of cession (Horsman 1967:130–33). With the spiritual guidance of the Creek prophet Francis and in alliance with the Seminoles, who followed their own nativist prophet, militant Creek nativists attempted in 1812 to overthrow the pro-U.S. Creek National Council in the Creek Civil War (Dowd 1992:170–72).

That war and Creek nativist participation on the side of Tecumseh's forces in the War of 1812 brought the U.S. military into the conflict in 1813 on the side of the Creek National Council. Andrew Jackson, commander of the Tennessee militia, and his Creek and Cherokee allies turned northern Creek country into a slaughterhouse. They defeated the defiant nativists in the Battle of Horseshoe Bend in 1814, killing roughly eight hundred of the one thousand Creek warriors (Dowd 1992:185–86; Prucha 1984, 1:79–80). Many of the survivors, including the prophet Francis and escaped black slaves who had fought on the side of the Creek nativists, eluded the U.S. Army and its Indian allies and joined the Seminoles in Florida. Through the Treaty of Fort Jackson (1814), which was drawn up by Jackson and officially ended the Creek War, the Creek accommodationists who had sided with Jackson against the nativists were forced to cede large portions of their territory to the United States, much to their disappointment (Dowd 1992:188–89).

Although Congress pronounced fairness and justice in U.S. relations with the Indians in the Northwest Ordinance of 1787 and in treaties that guaranteed Indians' legal rights to their territories, the actual source and authority of U.S. Indian law remained ambiguous. According to historian Joseph C. Burke:

> In theory, the Government treated with the tribes as sovereign nations, purchasing only the lands they chose to sell and guaranteeing forever their title to the lands they chose to keep. In practice, the constant encroachment of white settlers, which the state governments would not and the federal governments could not prevent, made a mockery of Indian sovereignty by forcing tribes to sell lands they wanted but could not peacefully keep. Written treaties that spoke of Indian nations, Indian boundaries, and Indian political rights remained on file, while time and the lack of records concealed the bribery, threats, and force that so often preceded their signing. (Burke 1969:501)

All of the land east of the Mississippi River was perceived as integral to the American nation by those who had votes and political power. Despite U.S. treaties with the southern Indians, in his Indian Removal Act of 1830 President Jackson forced the Five Civilized Tribes to comply with the demands of states, relinquish what remained of their ancestral homelands, and settle in Indian Territory west of the Mississippi. Indian removal violated the sovereignty guaranteed in treaties and inflicted tragic suffering and loss, but Indians were promised perpetual, patented title to Indian Territory in return. The Cherokees, however, refused to leave. They fought Jackson's policies in U.S. federal courts, forcing these courts to give permanent shape to an equivocal U.S. Indian policy and law.

The U.S. Constitution guarantees that treaties, which can only be entered into with foreign nations, are the supreme law of the land and are thus as legally binding as the Constitution unless Congress specifically overturns them. In 1821 and 1828 U.S. Attorney General William Wirt issued two opinions on the question of treaties with Indian nations that represented the policy of the U.S. government. He affirmed both the treaties' nation-to-nation nature and U.S. recognition of the sovereignty of the Indian tribes in international law. In the 1821 opinion the attorney general stated: "So long as a tribe exists and remains in possession of its lands, its title and possession are sovereign and exclusive. We treat with them as separate sovereignties, and while an Indian nation continues to exist within its acknowledged limits, we have no more right to enter upon their territory than we have to enter upon the territory of a foreign prince" (Wirt, quoted in Morris 1987:291). And in the 1828 opinion the attorney general elaborated:

> Like all other independent nations, they are governed solely by their own laws. Like all other independent nations, their territories are inviolable by any other sovereignty. . . . As a nation, they are still free and independent. They are entirely self-governed and self-directed. They treat, or refuse to treat, at their pleasure; and there is no human power which can rightfully control them in the exercise of their discretion in this respect. (Wirt, quoted in Morris 1987:291)

The position of the attorney general appears to be unambiguous. It constitutes a federal recognition, in the context of U.S. and international law, of Indian tribal governments, Indian tribal law, and Indian tribal independence and self-determination.

When he wrote the decisions of two Cherokee Nation cases, *Cherokee Nation v. State of Georgia* (1831) and *Worcester v. State of Georgia* (1832), Chief Justice of the United States John Marshall established legal principles that continue to guide U.S. relations with Indian nations. The Cherokee Nation cases followed two previous Marshall Court decisions concerning the rights of Indian tribes. The decision in *Fletcher v. Peck* (1810) held that states retain rights of *seisin in fee* in, or legal possession of, unceded Indian territories. It characterized the Indians as perpetual lessees even on land they had possessed since time immemorial and thus rendered superficial the concept of aboriginal title. In *Johnson and Graham's Lessee v. McIntosh* (1823) the Court determined that the ultimate sovereignty over Indian land in the New World and the sole right to acquire that land, which were claimed by England, France, and Spain through the Doctrine of Discovery and the derivative Rights of Conquest, had transferred to the U.S. federal government via succession. At the same time Indians possessed aboriginal title as developed in *Fletcher,* and that title was sacrosanct until extinguished by the United States, essentially at will and without compensation (Berman 1978:644–45; Burke 1969:502–3; Henderson 1977; Wilkinson 1987:39). Although the decision speaks of absolute U.S. dominion and ultimate title, the definitive, narrow holding in *Johnson and Graham's Lessee v. McIntosh* established the exclusive right of the United States to acquire Indian lands via purchase or conquest (Newton 1984:209).

The Marshall Court's decisions were pragmatic. The Court's characterization of Indian tribes and territories represents judicial invention because the territories in question were neither vacant, which is necessary for implementation of the Doctrine of Discovery, nor spoils of a just war, which was necessary for the application of the Rights of Conquest (Clinebell and Thomson 1978). Finally, as the long history of political alliances, treaty relations, agricultural trade, and even Christian conversion clearly attests, the Indians could not truthfully be considered anarchic savages. Legal scholar Robert A. Williams Jr., a Native American, distinguishes *McIntosh* as the case that established in U.S. law on Indian rights and status the medievally derived racist belief that "normatively divergent 'savage' peoples could be denied rights and status equal to those accorded to the civilized nations of Europe." This later provided a rational, legal foundation for genocide (R. Williams 1990a:317).

Acting as lawyer for the Cherokees, former attorney general William Wirt brought *Cherokee Nation* before the Supreme Court. The case was dismissed when the Court ruled in an irreconcilably divided opinion that it possessed no jurisdiction because the Cherokees were neither U.S. citizens nor a foreign nation under Article III, Section 2, of the U.S. Constitution. In *Cherokee Nation* the Court issued a legally nonbinding dictum reiterating positions put forward in *Fletcher* and *McIntosh*. These positions asserted U.S. sovereignty not only over the territories of the nascent Cherokee republic, but over all Indian territories. The dictum, which proved instrumental in deciding future cases, declared that when the U.S. Constitution, in Article I, Section 8, empowers Congress to "regulate commerce with foreign nations, and among the several states, and with the Indian tribes," it identifies Indian tribes as neither foreign nations nor states. Marshall laid the foundation for federal trusteeship over Indian affairs when he developed the concept of Indian tribes as dependent domestic nations, designated their current state as one of pupilage, made an offhand remark that their relationship with the United States resembled that of a ward to a guardian, and claimed that the Indian tribes look to the United States for protection and benevolence (Clinton, Newton, Price 1991:15).

With the assistance of National Republican vice presidential nominee John Sergeant, Wirt represented the plaintiffs again in *Worcester v. Georgia*. In his opinion in *Worcester*, Chief Justice Marshall attempted to forge a compromise between the overwhelmingly popular position of President Jackson and the position of several Supreme Court justices who viewed the Indians as legally independent foreign nations. Marshall once again described Indian nations as dependent domestic nations possessing rights of self-government and legal title to their lands as nonforeign states that are not subject to the laws of other states, such as Georgia (Burke 1969:522). Marshall determined that the Indian tribes had not yielded their sovereignty in treaties with the United States, had never been conquered by European powers (apparently overturning his own holding in *McIntosh*), and were regarded as nations by the government of the United States, which used the term in the same manner with Indian tribes as it did with all other nations. Indian sovereignty and self-government predated the Constitution, and relations between the United States and the Indian tribes were therefore governed by principles of both international law and constitutional law (Newton 1984:202). The only limitations on Indian sovereignty under the treaties were that the Indians were not to enter into treaty relations with other foreign nations (Burke 1969:522) and that the United States had preemptive privilege or exclusive right of purchase of Indian lands when Indians consented to sell (Newton 1984:209).

Marshall's position on Indian independence in *Worcester* resembles Justice Thompson's dissent in *Cherokee Nation,* in which Thompson argues that the Cherokee Nation constitutes a foreign state, except that Marshall maintains the dependent domestic nation distinction for Indian tribes. This status, relying on the statements of Vattel on feudatory states, does not diminish the Indian tribes' sovereignty, but places the tribes in association with and under the political protection of the United States. The Constitution and the trade and intercourse acts vest in Congress the power to regulate intercourse with the Indian tribes, a power that, Marshall notes, gives effect to the treaties. In ruling that Georgia's state laws carry no legal force over the Cherokees, Marshall's position is ultimately one of defending federal authority over the tribes against state authority. It subjugated Indian sovereignty to the power of Congress, which subsequently and inappropriately seized upon the use of the last-in-time rule, which was relevant to international treaties, in abrogating Indian treaties (Newton 1984:202).

President Jackson refused to recognize and execute the ruling of the Supreme Court, and the Cherokees were convinced only by relentless persecution by the state of Georgia, the intervention of the U.S. Army, and promises in a fraudulent treaty, to leave their ancestral homelands for Indian Territory. Article 5 of the otherwise "malodorous" Treaty of New Echota (1835), which the Cherokees overwhelmingly rejected, guaranteed their new territories to them forever through a patent grant of fee simple title (Debo 1970:123–24; Newton 1984:210–11). Later, in *United States v. Rogers* (1846), the Supreme Court would misinterpret the decisions of the Marshall Court, including *United States v. Mitchel* (1835), which recognizes U.S. interest in Indian land as an ultimate fee that is subject to the right of Indian possession and takes effect only after Indian abandonment or cession to the United States. In *Rogers* the Court adopted an erroneous interpretation of the Doctrine of Discovery that negated Indian ownership of their lands and subjected the tribes to the authority of the U.S. government (Newton 1984:209–10). The *Rogers* decision would not bind the U.S. to the treaties with the Indians, including the Cherokees' guarantee of fee simple title, allowed race-based legislation, and imposed upon the Court the limitation of the political question doctrine, which prevents the Court from interfering in the foreign politics of the United States (Newton 1984:210–11).

The Cherokee Trail of Tears was one more brutal episode of the removal policy, although many Cherokees slipped away into the hills of North Carolina rather than leave their homeland forever (Foreman 1953; Strickland 1975; for opposing interpretations of U.S. Indian removal policy, see Prucha 1969; Satz 1975; Wallace 1993; Washburn 1965). With Indian removal and the defeat of the Sauk and Fox rebellion led by Black Hawk and the nativist Winnebago prophet Wabokieshiek in 1832 in the Black Hawk War—or "ten weeks of dire suffering among vastly outnumbered, outgunned, and starving Native American families fleeing for their lives" (Dowd 1992:193)—the pacification of the Indian tribes in all lands east of the Mississippi was complete. The Shawnee, Miami, Delaware, and other nations were also relocated west of the Mississippi onto tracts of land guaranteed to them in perpetuity. Later, when Missouri and Kansas became states, they were transferred to Indian Territory, which eventually became Oklahoma. A large number of Florida's Seminoles, under the leadership of Osceola, refused to relocate. The ensuing Second Seminole War (1835–1842) was the United States' most costly Indian war in terms of both dollars and lives. The war ended in a stalemate and therefore was a victory for the Seminoles, who remain a nation living in the Florida Everglades (Debo 1970:125–26).

MANIFEST DESTINY AND U.S. INDIAN LAW

The discovery of gold in California, now owned by the United States as a result of the Treaty of Guadelupe Hidalgo (1848), led to the great genocidal migration westward to the Pacific Ocean. The westward expansion was rationalized during the second half of the nineteenth century by the ideology of Manifest Destiny. Historian and journalist Dee Brown describes this expansionist ideology in political terms:

> To justify the breaches of "permanent Indian frontier," the policy makers in Washington invented Manifest Destiny, a term which lifted land hunger to a lofty plane. The Europeans and their descendants were ordained by destiny to rule all of America. They were the dominant race and therefore responsible for the Indians—along with their lands, their forests and their mineral wealth. Only the New Englanders, who had destroyed or driven out all their Indians, spoke against Manifest Destiny. (D. Brown [1970] 1991:8)

In 1870 the members of the Big Horn Association, a mining interest group of frontiersmen organized to extinguish Indian treaties, explained why the Sioux must inevitably relinquish their tribal claims to land and sovereignty:

The rich and beautiful valleys of Wyoming are destined for the occupancy and sustenance of the Anglo-Saxon race. The wealth that for untold ages has lain hidden beneath the snow-capped summits of our mountains has been placed there by Providence to reward the brave spirits whose lot it is to compose the advance-guard of civilization. The Indians must stand aside or be overwhelmed by the ever advancing and ever increasing tide of emigration. The destiny of the aborigines is written in characters not to be mistaken. The same inscrutable Arbiter that decreed the downfall of Rome has pronounced the doom of extinction upon the red men of America. (quoted in D. Brown [1970] 1991:184)

Armed with the logic of an evolutionary and divine American destiny, and possessing overwhelmingly superior population, weapons, and wealth, the U.S. concluded the infamous Indian Wars by the end of the 1880s and resettled the western Indians on militarily secure reservations (Drinnon 1980; Hietala 1990; Stephanson 1995.

While Indian reservations were sometimes enormous areas of land, these remnants of the Indian territories established by treaties between Indian nations and the United States were often too small and too infertile to support their Indian residents (Getches, Wilkinson, and Williams 1993:163). Treaties with Indian nations originally did not grant entitlements to land given by the United States to the Indians, but constituted U.S. recognition of preexisting Indian sovereignty, the establishment of a trust relationship between Indian nations and the United States, and the grant of land rights to the United States by the Indian nations (Kickingbird, Kickingbird, Skibine, and Chibitty 1980). Because the treaties were often negotiated in Indian languages but involved Anglo-American legal terminology and were always written in English, the language barrier inevitably led to problems in interpreting treaty provisions (Wilkinson and Volkman 1975). During the process of congressional ratification the treaties themselves were unilaterally transformed from the terms to which the Indians, or some form of Indian representation, had agreed, albeit sometimes involuntarily and sometimes without authorization. Later agreements intransigently replaced previously signed treaties—treaties between independent nations—that had been violated by illegal incursions on Indian lands that had been guaranteed sovereignty (Wilkinson and Volkman 1975).

Cohen ([1940] 1988) and others point out that much of the land taken from the Indians by the United States was not acquired through outright theft, but was purchased, generally via treaties, for an entire sum of approximately $800 million. These transactions, however, involved fraud and coercion in the agreement and corruption in the implementation (Washburn 1995:109–10). Without a declaration of war, and in violation of treaties of peace and cooperation between nations, the unprovoked massacres of Indian peoples on their own sovereign territories, the unwarranted political and genocidal destruction of Indian nations, the intentional slaughter of the buffalo upon which the Plains Indian lifestyle depended, the breaking of sacred promises, and the expansionist appropriation of an entire continent ended a way of life.

With the Indian Department Appropriations Act of March 3, 1871, Congress passed into law a new policy terminating the treaty-making arrangement with American Indians. It essentially determined that Indian peoples are neither foreign nations nor independent nations nor entities possessing a sovereign form of government capable of entering into treaties with the United States. Although the status of prior treaties was unaffected, the constitutionality of this implementation of congressional plenary power over Indian affairs remains dubious (Canby 1988:17; for a legal debate on that plenary power see Laurence 1988a, 1988b; R. Williams 1988). Furthermore, while Indian nations may have recognized dependence on the United States to the exclusion of all other foreign powers in matters of trade and political alliance, they arguably did not agree to the termination of their own independent, treaty-making status or of their jurisdictional sovereignty over remaining Indian territories. Nevertheless, under the policy orientation of the late nineteenth century, U.S. agents regulated Indian behavior on the reservations, and the federal Courts of Indian Offenses implemented legal and behavioral codes that outlawed Indian religious dances and other customary practices. When the Supreme Court ruled in *Ex parte Crow Dog* (1883) that the murder of one Indian by another on an Indian treaty reservation that legally retained its juridical sovereignty was not subject to federal jurisdiction, Congress continued to advance its plenary and assimilationist policy by immediately responding with the Major Crimes Act of 1885, declaring murder and other serious crimes committed on Indian reservations federal offenses (Harring 1994).

Even though the Confederation Congress declared in the Northwest Ordinance the enduring position of the U.S. government on relations with Indian nations as "articles of compact" (Deloria 1989:220–22), and the Marshall Court's ruling in *Worcester* on the status of Indian nations remains in effect today, the focus of the United States in the late nineteenth century was one of "civilizing" the Indians and breaking up what remained of Indian territories. This mission of detribalization was legally justified by reliance upon the illustration presented in Marshall's nonbinding dictum in *Cherokee Nation* that the Indians' relationship with the United States as dependent, domestic nations resembles that of guardian and ward. Although the suggestion implies eventual independence for the Indian nations rather than dissipation, Congress seized upon the guardian relationship as one giving Congress permanent plenary power over Indian nations, another constitutionally suspect act allowing Congress to dispose of Indian property (Deloria 1985:134).

In the earliest treaties Indian nations did not dispossess themselves of their status as independent, sovereign nations, but in later treaties and agreements Congress gave themselves powers over Indian tribes that were then interpreted as plenary (Prucha 1994:5–11, 61–62) even though the Indian nations apparently neither consented to nor ever intended to consent to congressional plenary power over them. Supreme Court submission to the plenary power of Congress is most evident in its ruling in *United States v. Kagama* (1886), which legally recognized the diminution of Indian tribal sovereignty and Congress's "incontrovertible right" to express its authority through the Major Crimes Act, and which characterized Indian people as "helpless 'wards' under the legislative control of Congress and daily bureaucratic supervision of the reservation by the [Bureau of Indian Affairs]" (Getches, Wilkinson, and Williams 1993:187) and as ignorant, degraded savages (Carter 1976; Harvey 1982). The Court reasoned that the power of Congress over the Indians in Indian country resided in U.S. ownership of the territories via the Doctrine of Discovery as expressed in *Rogers,* that the 1871 statute ending treaty making with the Indians indicated that Congress would now govern the tribes by statute, and that such power had always been exercised and never denied (Newton 1984:215, 222).

This new congressional plenary power was expressed in the General Allotment Act of 1887, or Dawes Severalty Act, which provided for the partitioning of Indian territories, the allotting of a certain amount of land to each Indian on the reservation, and sale of the "surplus" to the federal government, which would then sell or give this land to American settlers. The ideological rationale, honestly intended by Senator Dawes and other supporters of the policy, who were sympathetic to the welfare or guardianship of the Indians, was that tribal or communal ownership of property impeded progress and that private property would be the stimulus for Indians to participate in private enterprise and the mainstream of American life. On the other hand, there were those who saw the Dawes Act as the pulverizing instrument that would finally and forever eliminate the great tribal landmass.

A minority of the U.S. House of Representatives Indian Committee were sincerely troubled by the bill and went on record with their concern:

> The real aim of this bill is to get at the Indian lands and open them up to settlement. The provisions for the apparent benefit of the Indian are but the pretext to get at his lands and occupy them. . . . If this were done in the name of greed, it would be bad enough; but to do it in the name of humanity, and under the cloak of an ardent desire to promote the Indian's welfare by making him like ourselves, whether he will or not, is infinitely worse. (House Report No. 1576, May 28, 1880, quoted in Cohen [1940] 1988:209)

The form of self-proclaimed humanitarian concern for the progress of indigenous peoples expressed by supporters of the Dawes Act, combined with the greed of the land grabbers, constitutes the essence of assimilation policy. The Dawes Act was supposed to be implemented when the tribes indicated they were ready to disestablish tribalism, but the Bureau of Indian Affairs interpreted the act as an exploitative device at their disposal and forced many tribes into allotment by threatening dire consequences. The Supreme Court had tied its own hands by recognizing in *Kagama* the political question doctrine and the guardianship power of Congress (Newton 1984:222–23).

In the beginning, the Five Civilized Tribes were exempt from allotment. They had received, as one of the favorable conditions of removal, fee simple title to their lands, which were guaranteed never to be taken from them by congressional act or any other means; only if the Indians abandoned them or became extinct would the lands revert back to federal ownership. Most Indians of the Five Civilized Tribes had adopted Christianity and modern agricultural methods, had established their own schools, which were superior to those of the Americans in the region, and had established recognized Indian republics. They had successfully adapted to Euro-American civilization without completely relinquishing their Indian identity. Furthermore, these Indians, especially the more assimilated mixed bloods, were wealthy and well educated. Other Indian nations looked to the Five Civilized Tribes for guidance (Debo 1934; Debo 1940; Foreman 1934).

In 1861, following the secession of the Southern states, the Indian republics, essentially abandoned by the Union and facing coercive pressure from neighboring states, sided politically with the Confederacy—although they were internally divided on the issue—and signed several treaties of allegiance and military alliance. Sympathetic Indians fought tenaciously for the South, but the Confederacy failed in its treaty obligations to protect the Indian republics, and the Indians suffered utter devastation once again during the war and the political chaos afterward (Hauptman 1993; Prucha 1984, 1:415–27). Even though the Five Civilized Tribes were not the aggressors in the Civil War, it was the Indian republics and not the states of the Confederacy that were eventually dismantled.

Immediately after the Civil War, the United States imposed new treaties on the republics of the Five Civilized Tribes that obliged them to assist the United States in pacifying the Western tribes, to abolish slavery and incorporate their former slaves as members of the tribes, to set aside portions of their land for the removal of tribes in Kansas and elsewhere, to agree to a consolidation of the Indian republics into one Indian Territory if the United States should so decide, and to prevent whites from residing in the Indian republics unless they were incorporated into the tribe in some manner (Prucha 1984, 1:431–32). But without the assistance of the U.S.

government, the Five Civilized Tribes were unable to prevent the illegal and overwhelming postwar flood of American settlers from streaming into their territories. Antagonistic to Indian authority over them, these settlers petitioned sympathetic figures in the federal government, asking that they be given democratic representation in the government rather than having to profess allegiance to Indian governments. Many Northerners, including some who were friends of the Indians, considered the Five Civilized Tribes to have forfeited their treaty rights with the United States by siding with the Confederacy, and to have therefore lost their right to national autonomy. This sentiment intensified after the end of the war. Congressional implementation of the Curtis Act in 1898 terminated the Indian republics, allotted their lands, and dismantled their excellent educational system and placed it in the hands of the Bureau of Indian Affairs. Much of the republics' wealth was confiscated by the federal government then used to settle what became the state of Oklahoma in 1907 (Debo 1940; Debo 1970; Prucha 1984, 2:743–57). The enormous clouds of dust raised by the great Oklahoma land rushes buried formerly sacrosanct Indian territories.

Many Indians resisted allotment, but they were no match for an opponent that held all the cards. Full-blood Indians often used threats to try to prevent other Indians from receiving their allotments; some hid in order to avoid being forcibly given the allotments but were hunted down by the civil agents. The Indians were often assigned the worst land available. (In a strange twist of fate, some of the apparently worthless Indian land has been found to contain substantial reservoirs of oil; other reservation lands are coveted today for their water and for their mineral, especially uranium, deposits [Guerrero 1992].) While tribal land could not be sold to private individuals, private allotments were easily sold and swindled. Some reservations, such as the small Miami reservation in Indiana, the last remnant of the great Miami Confederacy in its ancestral territories, were simply sold out of existence (Winger 1935). The great scheme of social engineering known as the Dawes Act resulted in the loss of over ninety million acres of land and incalculable Indian suffering. It was the "beginning of the end of the Indian problem," even though in a strict legal sense treaties with the Indian tribes remained "the supreme law of the land" (Hoxie 1984; McDonnell 1991; Otis 1973).

Congress's capacity to abrogate treaty provisions by statute according to the last-in-time rule while leaving the remainder of the treaty intact was upheld by the Supreme Court in *Lone Wolf v. Hitchcock* (1903), in which the Court declared that Congress, as guardian, had always held plenary power over the Indian tribes, and that it therefore could allot Indian land even in violation of treaty terms (Newton 1984:221–22). In *United States v. Winans* (1905), however, the Court held that unless Congress suspended a treaty or an Indian tribe relinquished specific rights or powers in the treaty, those rights and powers are presumed to remain with the Indian nation (Deloria 1995:145). Continuing the policy of federal authority over the Indian tribes, the reserved rights cases of 1905–1908 and *Winters v. United States* (1908) protected against state usurpation Indian treaty rights and sovereignty over resources that had not yet been removed by an act of Congress. Assimilation and incorporation of the Indian nations were legally complete when Indians were unilaterally bestowed with American citizenship under the Indian Citizenship Act (1924), a move that several Indian nations, including the Onondaga and Hopi, as sovereign peoples, refused to acknowledge (Churchill and Morris 1992:15).

In 1928, Lewis Meriam's objective study of U.S. federal Indian policy, prepared under the direction of the U.S. Secretary of the Interior, revealed the deplorable social conditions of Indians and the failures of allotment policy, of the Bureau of Indian Affairs, and of the tragic policy of removing Indian children from their families in order to educate them in boarding schools where they were taught to despise their Indian heritage (Deloria 1985:191–92; Meriam 1928). Although President Hoover ignored Meriam's recommendations, his work stimulated a growing concern for the welfare of the Indians. In 1932, John Collier, President Franklin Roosevelt's Commissioner of Indian Affairs, initiated several new investigations as follow-ups to the Meriam Report. Among these was an inquiry into the legal status of Indians conducted by attorney Felix Cohen, who concluded that Justice Marshall's determination that within the ultimate sovereignty of the United States Indian nations were "distinct, independent political communities retaining their original natural rights," first expressed in *Worcester,* remained in force (Cohen [1940] 1988:123). On this issue, Cohen wrote explicitly: "the most basic principle of Indian law, supported by a host of decisions, . . . is the principle that *those powers which are lawfully vested in an Indian tribe are not, in general, delegated powers granted by express acts of Congress, but rather inherent powers of a limited sovereignty which has never been extinguished"* (Cohen [1940] 1988:122). Adherence to this fundamental principle of tribal sovereignty distinguished Collier's tenure as Commissioner of Indian Affairs from those of his predecessors and colleagues, and perhaps of his successors.

Collier was devoted to the preservation of traditional Indian culture and to Indian legal rights, including their group self-determination. He commissioned investigations and made farsighted proposals regarding the signification and implementation of Indian rights. His work ultimately resulted in the Indian Reorganization (Wheeler-Howard) Act of 1934. Although it fell far short of Collier's original proposals, the act as passed by Congress empowered tribal sovereignty by endorsing self-government based on newly adopted tribal constitutions, allowed tribes administrative and fiscal control over the reservation, established tribal courts and enforced tribal legal jurisdiction on reservations, provided for an annual appropriation of federal money to assist in developing these organizations, overturned allotment and permitted tribal or communal land ownership, allowed the Secretary of the Interior to purchase former Indian lands or return them to the reservations and to acquire water rights and surface rights for the Indians, and ruled that formerly extinguished Indian tribes and reservations could be resurrected and recognized (Deloria and Lytle 1984:140–53; Taylor 1980; Washburn 1984; Prucha 1984, 2:940–1012). The Bureau of Indian Affairs was given enhanced power to regulate tribal constitutional development, elections, and outside contacts, and to promote Indian welfare, education, housing, and development.

Some Indian critics of the Indian Reorganization Act contend that puppet governments run by lackeys of the U.S. government were imposed upon the Indian nations and that these governments were not consistent with traditional Indian governmental structure and practice (Barsh 1982b). Others, such as Matthew K. Sniffen, who wrote in the periodical *Indian Truth* in 1934, were opposed to retribalization both because it perpetuated segregation and because it had the potential to place individual Indian ownership rights in jeopardy (Prucha 1984, 2:960). Washburn argues, on the other hand, that the Indian Reorganization Act preserved at least some form of tribal sovereignty in the face of complete annihilation (Washburn 1984:279). Prior to the Indian Reorganization Act the superintendent of the Indian Bureau had handpicked certain pliant Indians to act as legal representatives of the tribe in order to aid mining enterprises in gaining access to tribal territories. The act allowed a more representative form of Indian government, which diminished the control of the superintendent of the Indian Bureau, the Department of the Interior, and the Office of Indian Affairs (Deloria and Lytle 1983; Spicer 1962:352).

Both Felix Cohen and Interior Department Solicitor Nathan Margold interpreted the Indian Reorganization Act as empowering Indian tribes' self-government, subject to the discretion of Congress as expressed through legislation or treaty abrogation; hence the act boldly strengthened the notion of congressional plenary power over the Indian nations (Cohen [1940] 1988:122–23). Barsh argues that Cohen and Margold's formulation is an "extremist" one that relies on a notion of conquest that was explicitly overturned in *United States v. Mitchel,* the case in which the Marshall Court ruled that European treaties with Indian tribes preclude the Rights of Conquest. Cohen and Margold's position distorts the Court's holding, and it is a fabrication that has been seized upon by Congress and the judiciary, especially as is apparent in later cases, such as *United States v. Wheeler* (1978) and *Oliphant v. Suquamish Tribe* (1978) (Barsh 1983:105–10; Barsh and Henderson 1979). At its inception the Indian Reorganization Act applied only to federally recognized tribes. It left the Five Civilized Tribes and Alaskan natives, among others, out of the picture, although these groups were eventually given legal status as native corporations.

None of the tribes that had been extinguished before the passage of the Indian Reorganization Act were resurrected and federally recognized as sovereign Indian tribes as provided for in the act.

In 1946 Congress passed the Indian Claims Commission Act, which was intended to settle with finality, through monetary payment, the claims of Indian tribes and bands to territories that had been expropriated illegally, and by consequence to affirm U.S. title to Indian lands. This was the first time that Indian tribes and bands could sue the United States, which had formerly been protected by the sovereign immunities doctrine, for treaty violations without first having to individually obtain a specific grant of Congress. Restoration of territories to the Indians was not an option, despite expressed Indian aspirations. Award payments were generally limited to the value of the land at the time that it was illegally taken, minus various amounts of financial aid and other forms of assistance that had been paid to Indian tribes by the United States during the ensuing years. This minimized U.S. expenses and rendered the amounts actually received by the Indians insufficient for their losses. In Indian legal cases against the United States, little attention was given to Indian perspectives, and attorneys for the Indians possessed an interest in accepting the financial awards of the Indian Claims Commission, which amounted to over $818 million, and, eventually, the settlements of other U.S. courts (Barsh 1982c; Lurie 1978; Tullberg and Coulter 1991). Although the commission's decisions could be appealed to the U.S. Court of Claims and its life span was extended from its initial ten-year period of operation to 1978, its work was substantially a failure; it brought neither justice nor finality to Indian claims against the United States (Prucha 1984, 2:1020–23).

Traditional Indians objected to the Indian Reorganization Act, arguing that it violated Indian sovereignty because it allowed a statutory interpretation that recognized congressional plenary power over the Indians and imposed upon them foreign political and legal institutions. Today that interpretation divides Indian reservations between "traditionals" and "progressives" (Deloria and Lytle 1983:15). Non-Indians' reaction against the act, based on the contention that it gave too much to the Indians, led Congress to utilize its self-designated and Court-supported plenary power to enact statutes, including House Concurrent Resolution no. 108 (1953) and Public Law 280 (1953), that were designed to overrule parts of the act. These statutes ended Indian wardship; terminated separate, tribal status; and abolished oversight of the Bureau of Indian Affairs for those Indian tribes that had achieved a level of socioeconomic advancement comparable to that of non-Indians. The acts also made Indians subject to state laws and jurisdiction in California, Minnesota, Nebraska, Oregon, and Wisconsin. The Indians of terminated tribes would now be regarded as American citizens with the same privileges and responsibilities as any other nontribal American citizens. Termination policy led to the extinguishing of federal recognition of sixty-one tribes, instituted state sovereignty and legal jurisdiction over terminated Indian peoples, ended federal Indian programs, threatened federally guaranteed Indian rights to land and resources, and legislated the loss of both Indian sovereignty and Indian identity (Fixico 1986; Goldberg 1975; Hauptman 1986b; Prucha 1984, 2:1041–59; Wilkinson and Biggs 1977:152–54).

Termination policy, which was yet another form of assimilation, was partly overturned by passage of the Indian Civil Rights Act of 1968, which provided that the institution of Public Law 280 status requires tribal approval and that states that had taken Public Law 280 authority could return this authority to the federal government. This act also imposes the constitutional Bill of Rights upon Indian reservations, and many Indians have regarded it as a further erosion of their sovereignty (*Michigan Law Review* 1976; Burnett 1972; Churchill and Morris 1992:16; Coulter 1971; Jeffrey 1990; Laurence 1990; Winfrey 1986).

In accord with policies outlined by President Nixon in 1970, Congress passed the Indian Self-Determination and Education Assistance Act in 1975. This act repealed termination policy and in effect reinstituted the Indian Reorganization Act by strengthening tribal self-government and providing tribes with the authority and financial assistance necessary to manage their own affairs in the areas of welfare, education, and housing (Barsh and Trosper 1975; Canby 1988:30). The Indian Child Welfare Act of 1978 officially outlawed non-Indian adoption of Indian children, because the practice constitutes an act of genocide in international law (J. Adams 1994; Barsh 1980).

Since 1968 Congress has attempted to promote Indian self-government and aspects of traditional culture, including freedom of religion and the right to use indigenous languages in education. The Supreme Court, on the other hand, in *Delaware Tribal Business Committee v. Weeks* (1977), dismissed the political question doctrine and enforced Fifth Amendment rights in Indian cases arising out of the Constitution, and the Court has tended to interpret Indian treaties in ways favorable to the Indians during cases of financial settlements of treaty violations. Still, Congress's plenary power remains a constant threat to Indian nations. The Supreme Court has recently held that Congress possesses paramount power over Indian land (*United States v. Sioux Nation* [1980]) and may take aboriginal Indian property without compensation (*Tee-Hit-Ton Indians v. United States* [1955]) and that Congress may unilaterally act to extinguish the sovereign existence of the Indian tribes (*United States v. Wheeler*), to limit or eliminate the powers of Indian self-government (*Santa Clara Pueblo v. Martinez* [1978]), to abrogate treaties (*United States v. Sioux Nation; Rosebud Sioux Tribe v. Kneip* [1977]), to reduce the boundaries of Indian reservations without Indian tribal consent or compensation (*Rosebud Sioux Tribe*), and to divest a tribe of criminal jurisdiction (*Oliphant*). Congress also may be able, through the Ancient Indian Claims Settlement Act of 1982, to "extinguish legal land claims of Indian tribes by retroactively extinguishing both title to the land and any claims based on that title" (Newton 1984:233–35). Meanwhile, native Alaskans (Anders 1990; Berger 1995; Bowen 1991; Harring 1989) and native Hawaiians (Anaya 1994; Blaisdell 1997; Hasager and Friedman 1994; Stannard 1992; Trask 1991, 1994), excluded from the Indian Reorganization Act provisions, have waged separate struggles to maintain their cultural heritage and claims to traditional land.

In contrast to the position set forth by Charles F. Wilkinson in *American Indians, Time and the Law* (1987), legal scholar Milner S. Ball argues in "Constitution, Court, Indian Tribe" (1987) that the Supreme Court, historically one of the protectors of the tribes, has now become their chief antagonist. The Constitution empowers Congress to regulate commerce with the Indian tribes, rather than regulating the tribes themselves. For Indians, the "tribe" is the "dominant political-religious-social-aesthetic reality." Most Indian court cases concern Indian land, "tribal identity and religion are tied to the land, and land is, more than anything else, the immediate reason for conflict between Indians and non-Indians." Pointing out that the Indians never relinquished their tribal sovereignty, Ball briefly summarizes the position of the Supreme Court on U.S. Indian law as follows:

> Congress has power over Indian nations and . . . the Court supplies various jurisprudential grounds for its exercise. The Court has either refused to scrutinize the action of Congress in Indian affairs, invoking the political question doctrine, or summoned up constitutional bases for it, or devised what it deemed acceptable extraconstitutional support when none could be found in the Constitution. The Court has never held a congressional exercise of power over Indian tribes to be illegal, and there is no reason to think it ever will. (Ball 1987:11–12)

The origin of the assumption of total congressional authority over Indian tribes is never explained in the Supreme Court's rulings; rather, it is obfuscated. For example, in *National Farmers Union Insurance Companies v. Crow Tribe* (1985), a case dealing with the civil jurisdiction of tribal courts, Justice John Paul Stevens proposes that "at one time [Indian tribes] exercised virtually unlimited power over their own members as well as those who are permitted to join their communities. Today, however, the power of the Federal Government over the Indian tribes is plenary" (Stevens, quoted in Ball 1987:20). Ball questions when and how this loss of power occurred. The Court does not explain, but relies on *United States v. Wheeler*, which proposes that the transfer of Indian sovereignty occurred through treaties and statutes and "by implication as a necessary result of [the tribes'] dependent status."

Ball contends that the historical and documentary record suggests that Indians generally did not relinquish sovereignty through treaties. As for statutes, Ball states that "the inherent sovereignty of another nation cannot be reduced nonconsensually by means of United States legislation. One sovereign may not establish for itself jurisdiction over another by enacting statutes that purport to govern the foreign sovereign" (Ball 1987:22). The proposition concerning "implicit divestiture" requires that the Indian tribes were incorporated into the territory of the United States at some point in time. However, Chief Justice Marshall expressly rejected incorporation of the Indian tribes. Despite small victories such as *County of Oneida v. Oneida Indian Nation* (1985), Indian tribes today are beset with expanding intrusions onto their sovereignty by Congress, through its legally unlimited plenary power; by those states encapsulating Indian country; and by the Supreme Court's expanding independent intervention in Indian affairs.

As for the future of U.S. Indian law, in *The Nations Within: The Past and Future of American Indian Sovereignty* (1984) and *American Indians, American Justice* (1983), Vine Deloria Jr. and Clifford Lytle argue that although the Indian Reorganization Act was superior policy to assimilation and termination, Collier's original proposals were far more insightful than the legislation eventually passed by Congress. They contend that federal Indian law should continue to evolve toward the principles expounded by the Indians in the Twenty Points, a document proposing reinstitution of the treaty relationship, which was presented to the U.S. government following the Trail of Broken Treaties march on Washington, D.C., in 1973.

Deloria and Lytle argue that the current system governing Indian reservations, which creates tribal dependency on the U.S. government and then reduces and threatens to end financial support, is more devastating than colonialism; it is the "final and systematic and perhaps even ruthlessly efficient destruction of Indian society" (Deloria and Lytle 1984:258). In *The Road: Indian Tribes and Political Liberty* (1980), Russel Lawrence Barsh and James Youngblood Henderson call for the establishment of a treaty-federalism consistent with the noble principles of liberty articulated in the original arguments for American independence. Barsh contends that the recent history of U.S. Indian law demonstrates that while international law expands upon the notions of self-determination and the political liberation of peoples, the legal policy in the United States is one of retraction. Barsh cites this as evidence of undeterred, persistent U.S. colonialism, despite statutory claims of support for Indian self-determination and self-governance (Barsh 1983).

Once one acknowledges that Native Americans have been and continue to be systematically precluded from achieving justice—that is, justice in their own terms—in U.S. courts of law or by any other domestic means, then one may recognize the Native American pursuit of justice in international law and international courts as a logical and necessary, rather than radical, alternative. One may also discover American Indian bands, tribes, and nations and their representatives engaged in this pursuit to represent traditional Indian peoples and their aspirations. Consequently, this engagement constitutes another aspect of indigenous political and legal culture that is of profound anthropological interest. As these indigenous peoples have encountered the international law of the twentieth century, they have often found that it resembles the Social Darwinism of the domestic law from which they seek remedy far more than it resembles the enlightened ruminations of Vitoria.

Chapter Three

THE IROQUOIS STRUGGLE

FOR INDEPENDENCE

◆ The political history of the Haudenosaunee, or Six Nations Iroquois Confederacy, provides one of the more manifest examples of the legal and historical foundations of contemporary indigenous demands for self-determination and claims to dispossessed land. At one time a powerful and influential political and military force, the Iroquois Confederacy and the independent nations of which it was composed (originally the Mohawk, Oneida, Onondaga, Cayuga, and Seneca nations, which were later joined by the Tuscarora) entered into numerous treaties, economic arrangements, and political-military alliances with European colonial powers and other Indian tribes or nations. The traditional government of the Iroquois Confederacy continues to operate today, although without federal recognition, and contemporary internal and external conflicts have often involved a struggle between the traditional Iroquois on the one hand and reservation governments and laws imposed by the United States and Canada on the other (Fenton 1965, 1975; *Right to Be Mohawk* 1989; Tooker 1978a, 1978b).

In the 1990s the Mohawk struggle for land rights and sovereignty in Canada created the risk of a violent massacre at the hands of the Canadian military, the Quebec provincial police, and angry Quebecois mobs (Alfred 1991, 1995; Grabowski 1991; Pertusati 1997; York and Pindera 1991; Zannis 1992). In the United States, conflict over Indian-owned casinos threatened to erupt into a Mohawk civil war when reservation governments allied with traditional Iroquois, who find casinos repugnant and inconsistent with Iroquois culture, appealed to the Governor of New York and the New York State Police in an attempt to close the casinos even though their operation was supported by militant defenders of Iroquois sovereignty (Johansen 1993; Starna 1994). Iroquois political struggles extend beyond the reservations. In the 1970s, for example, following attempts to reclaim ancestral lands in New York, militant Mohawks known as the Warriors issued the Ganienkeh Manifesto, which called for the unification of all North American Indian tribes in the formation of an independent Indian state (Landsman 1988; Snow 1994:210).

The People of the Longhouse, or Haudenosaunee, possess an identifiable form of constitutional democratic government in their Confederacy Council, and as a sovereign political power they have established relations with European and Indian nations through the Silver Covenant Chain and other political arrangements (Aquila 1983; Jennings 1984, 1988; Jennings et al. 1985; Jones 1982, 1988; Richter 1992; Richter and Merrell 1987; Tooker 1985). Their form of government emerged from the tradition known as Gayaneshakgwa, or the Iroquois Great Law of Peace, from which was created the League of the Iroquois, a cultural or spiritual system that Onondaga Chief Oren Lyons favorably compares with the United Nations (Lyons 1992). The Iroquois Confederacy, which appeared in the late seventeenth century, is a distinct political and military arrangement like other Indian confederacies, nations, tribes, bands, and villages. It occupied, utilized, and governed recognizable traditional land areas, and it retains claims to traditional territories no longer in its possession, primarily in what is now the state of New York (Richter 1992:6–7; Starna 1988).

The Iroquois Confederacy signed three major treaties with the United States following the Revolutionary War—the treaties of Fort Stanwix (1784), Jay (1794), and Canandaigua (1794)—which guarantee national and collective sovereign status and free trade and individual passage across the "arbitrary" border between the United States and Canada, which divides Iroquois nations (Campisi 1984, 1988; Campisi and Starna 1995; Hauptman 1981, 1988a:67–68). It has continued to claim its independence and its national and international identity by rejecting the unilaterally imposed 1924 Indian Citizenship Act; by making national declarations of war in World Wars I and II; by issuing an Iroquois passport; by sustaining an unrelenting commitment to treaty recognition, treaty rights, and treaty relations (Hauptman 1981, 1986a); and by making determined and ongoing attempts to achieve the preservation and legal recovery of traditional lands (Churchill 1992, 1993; Vecsey and Starna 1988). Like numerous other indigenous nations, the Iroquois have pressed these claims in international arenas, including the League of Nations, its successor the United Nations, and the Russell Tribunal (Emery 1981), and they have been actively involved in the deliberations of the United Nations Working Group on Indigenous Populations.

ORIGINS OF THE HAUDENOSAUNEE

The name *Iroquois* is a Europeanized term of uncertain definition or origin; it is possibly Algonquian for "the killer people." But the Iroquois refer to themselves collectively as the People of the Longhouse, the Haudenosaunee in the Seneca language. The Iroquois Confederacy, which at one time expanded across what is now northern New York, is composed of six independent nations: the Mohawk (the People of the Flint), the Oneida (the People of the Standing Stone), the Onondaga (the People on the Mountain), the Cayuga (the People at the Landing, also known by the Iroquois as the People of the Great Pipe), the Seneca (the People of the Great Hill), and the Tuscarora (possibly the People of the Indian Hemp). The Iroquois also incorporate remnant tribes and Indian refugees within their territories (Richter 1992:1).

Anthropologists first thought that the Iroquois peoples had entered the region of present-day New York and southeastern Canada by migrating sometime after European arrival in the New World, probably during the sixteenth century (Morgan 1851, 1869, 1870a). MacNeish later argued that the Iroquois evolved *in situ* and that they have occupied the same region for several thousand years (MacNeish 1952, 1976). Dean Snow's archaeological analyses suggest to him that the pre-Iroquois cultures in the region, the Point Peninsula people followed by the Owasco, do not represent an unbroken cultural continuity, as MacNeish theorizes. According to Snow, the presence of the Owasco people, a horticultural, matrilineal people whose warfaring society was founded on matrilocal residence, dates back to A.D. 1000 in the region. These people of proto-Iroquoian culture apparently arrived from the south and displaced the hunting, foraging, fishing, and probably Algonquian-speaking Point Peninsula peoples (Snow 1984, 1994:14–33).

During the period from 1150 to 1350 the Owasco people lived in villages that were populated by up to four hundred persons residing in nonstandardized multifamily longhouses. The villages were later palisaded. They principally grew maize, and they supplemented their horticulture with hunting and gathering. The Owasco culture was distinguished by its settlements, which were based on matrilocal residence, and by increasing warfare, including raids on enemy villages, feuds between politically related lineages and villages, and war between tribes involving anywhere from two hundred to two thousand warriors on each side. Matrilocal societies characteristically inhibit raids and feuding within the tribal society but facilitate external warfare, so most Owasco warfare was probably directed toward non-Owasco societies (Tuck 1978:328). According to Snow, a colder climate at the end of the Owasco culture period may have led directly to changes, such as increased village size, from which the Iroquoian culture emerged, (Snow 1994:31–32). Others argue that increased warfare led to clan consolidation and the development of complex, isolated communities (Richter 1992:15). Separate Iroquoian cultural and political identities probably began to take more distinct forms as clustered and fortified villages became more common. During the period from 1350 to 1525, the longhouse developed fully and attained its classic form: the longhouse has five compartments, each housing two cubicles and a hearth supporting two families, with storage chambers at each end (Fenton 1978:303; Snow 1994:40–46).

IROQUOIS POLITICAL ORGANIZATION

Between 1525 and 1600, Iroquois villages began to fuse into larger, more densely populated communities, often located on hilltops and away from principal travel routes and waterways, apparently for better defense. These villages were more massively fortified than before, utilizing ravines, earthworks, and palisades for defense. Iroquois oral history depicts this as a time of intense warfare and brutal violence, and archaeological evidence offers support for suggestions of torture and cannibalism (Snow 1994:54–55).

Within Iroquois villages and between intermarrying villages the people and their lineages were divided into clans, each composed of two or more maternal families. The Iroquois tended to marry outside their own clan, and clan identification signified kinship relations for persons visiting other villages for purposes of commerce. The clans were divided between two moieties, and members of each moiety possessed rights and duties toward the members of the other moiety (Fenton 1978:309–13; Tooker 1971). Elaborate funeral rites, for example, involved the grieving moiety, on the one hand, and the condolence moiety, which performed the rituals for the moiety in mourning, on the other. This process tended to keep the village or villages united, and it directed village rage and the aspersions of evil outside the society (Richter 1992:33; Snow 1994:55–57). Each clan maintained a council, but village decisions were made by an "ad hoc village council of ranking clan chiefs, elders, and wise men" on the basis of consensus; a similar political construction governed each independent nation (Fenton 1978:314).

In contrast with the commitment to peace between trading partners and the political and spiritual alliances based on reciprocal exchange, united or friendly villages engaged in a continuous cycle of raids or warfare against other Iroquoian and non-Iroquoian peoples, although the warfare typically involved ceremonial confrontations and resulted in few actual casualties. Raids known as mourning wars avenged deaths for which an enemy was presumed responsible. Raiders brought back captives who, if they were not ritually executed and eaten, took part in a "requickening" ceremony, through which they replaced and even took the names of persons within the village or cluster who had died. This was done to restore collective spiritual power (Richter 1992:32–36). According to Iroquois legend, when a cycle of particularly violent warfare swept through the region and "everywhere there was peril and everywhere mourning," a few Iroquoian leaders began to pursue the alternative that has since become known as the League of the Iroquois (Richter 1992:31; Snow 1994:58).

THE GREAT LEAGUE OF PEACE AND POWER

The precise date for the genesis of the League of the Iroquois, or the Great League of Peace and Power, remains elusive, but Iroquois oral tradition, historical records, and scholarly research place the origin of the league somewhere between A.D. 1400 and 1600. According to Iroquois oral tradition, the League was created through the efforts of Deganawida (the Peacemaker) and Ayonhwathah (Hiawatha) and the difficult conversion of Thadodaho (Adodarhonh), as recorded in P. A. W. Wallace's *The White Roots of Peace* (1945). The oral tradition of the Seneca suggests that the time they joined the league coincided with a solar eclipse, which might place the date at either 1451 or 1536 (Tooker 1978a:420; Snow 1994:60). The emergence of the league may, in fact, have been the cumulative result of a series of alliances developed over a long period of time (Richter 1987). There is no evidence linking the formation of the League of the Iroquois to any form of European contact or influence.

As the oral legend relates, the league was divided into moiety-like older brothers and younger brothers. The metaphorical symbol of the league came to be a longhouse stretching across Iroquoia. In that longhouse dwelled the five nations—the Haudenosaunee, the People of the Longhouse. The Mohawks guarded the eastern door of the longhouse, the Senecas the western door. The Onondaga, in the center, were both the Keepers of the Fire, the central hearth of the Iroquois longhouse, and the Keepers of the Wampum, the gift that accompanied all important statements. The Tree of Peace towered over the longhouse with an eagle perched in its branches and keeping an eye on the peace between the members of the league. Each league chief, known as a sachem, represented a separate pole of the longhouse, and by linking arms together the chiefs became one (Druke 1987; Richter 1987; Snow 1994:61; Tooker 1978a; R. Williams 1997).

The fifty sachems, who were divided into two moieties that together formed the Grand Council, were chosen by senior women of the dominant clans in each nation. Certain clans traditionally provided the league chiefs; the members of other clans were ineligible. While the positions of chiefs Deganawida and Ayonhwathah were never filled following their deaths, the Mohawk and Oneida each contributed, through the requickening ceremony, nine league chiefs; the Onondaga contributed fourteen, including Thadodaho; the Cayuga ten; and the Seneca eight, for a total of fifty league chiefs. The pine tree chief was chosen from one of the clans that did not provide league chiefs. The war chief could not simultaneously

be a league chief. The purpose of the league was first to establish and preserve peace among the five nations of the Iroquois, and later also to enter
into treaties of peace and friendship with other nations (Richter
1992:39–43; Snow 1994:65; Tooker 1978a:425–29): "the Condolence rituals, words of peace, and exchange of gifts mandated by the Good News of
Peace and Power provided the basic paradigm for diplomatic relations
with outsiders" (Richter 1992:41).

League decisions required consensus, unanimity achieved through debate
among the sachems, occasionally with the assistance of orators. Because the
League of the Iroquois was not a coercive political state but a spiritual or religious union, if agreement could not be reached, individual nations could act
on their own as long as the action did no harm to the league or to any other
member of the league (Tooker 1978a:430). Snow writes:

> Thus the basis of the League was more of a mutual nonaggression pact than a
> political union. It allowed persuasion but not coercion within the longhouse,
> and this in turn allowed nations or even factions of nations to follow their
> own policies. The League was put at risk when those policies conflicted, for
> its consensual/segmented form of government tended to dither when cir-
> cumstances called for quick authoritarian decisions. This weakness some-
> times later allowed brothers within the League to come to blows, and it
> proved fatal when the Iroquois later became caught up in the upheaval of
> the American revolution. (Snow 1994:62)

Formal meetings of the league were usually opened by recitation of the
Deganawida epic and a performance of the Condolence Council, a long
ceremony that mourned the loss of old chiefs and welcomed new chiefs in
their place, reuniting the members and revitalizing the league in classic
Iroquois tradition. The speeches delivered in the council meetings were
accompanied by spiritually empowered wampum shells, a practice deriv-
ing from Iroquois reciprocity and the legend of Deganawida. This rendered the speakers' words truthful and promises sincere (Richter
1992:41–49; Tooker 1978a:437–40).

IROQUOIS INTERNATIONAL RELATIONS IN THE SIXTEENTH AND SEVENTEENTH CENTURIES

European goods began to reach the Iroquois during the sixteenth century. The Mohawk had access to French goods via the St. Lawrence River,
and the Onondaga and Seneca had access to English goods via Chesapeake
Bay and the Susquehanna River. The St. Lawrence Iroquoians and the Algonquians separated the Mohawk from direct contact with the French. By
the end of the sixteenth century, following decimation from European-
introduced diseases and famine, the Huron, the Mohawk, and other In-

dian nations most likely destroyed as nations the formerly powerful St. Lawrence Iroquoians and the Jefferson County Iroquoians. The Huron, the Montagnais, and the Algonquians quickly filled the vacated power niche and blocked Mohawk access to European goods, but the Mohawk's adoption of remnant St. Lawrence Iroquoians and Jefferson County Iroquoians substantially increased their population by the beginning of the seventeenth century (Richter 1992:53; Snow 1994:75–76; Trigger and Pendergast 1978).

In 1609 Mohawk warriors clashed with allied forces of the French under Champlain and Algonquian Indians with whom the Mohawk had been at war for several years. It was in this battle that the Mohawk apparently first encountered the deadly force of European guns (Richter 1992:51, 53; Trigger 1978:348). The confrontation transformed warfare and trade relations in the region. The arrival of the Dutch as trading partners gave the Mohawk—the eastern door of the Confederacy—direct access to European goods for the first time and despite Mahican opposition, and launched the Five Nations of the Iroquois—with its western door (the Seneca) engaged in trade with Europeans (primarily the French) in the Ohio River valley—into the world of global commerce. Dutch trade enriched the Iroquois and transformed the Great League of Peace and Power into a powerful military force.

Before the Dutch trade emerged, the Oneida and the Mohawk had regularly challenged Algonquians for trade supremacy with the French in the St. Lawrence River valley, but by 1624 they had entered into a treaty of peace with the Algonquians as trade with the French declined. Snow argues that the Mohawk now occupied a position of "middleman" between the Dutch and Canadian Indians, particularly in the trade of wampum, which was manufactured by eastern Indians and the Dutch and had become scarce in Iroquoia. Wampum, shell beads that were charged with symbolic significance and were often woven into belts, was required for exchange at treaty conferences and for announcing intentions of war. The Dutch also supplied cloth, which replaced deer hide for clothing. Later they supplied glass beads and silver jewelry, which replaced shells, and guns, which replaced the bow and arrow (Snow 1994:92–93). In exchange, the Dutch primarily sought beaver pelts, which, historian Daniel Richter argues, the Iroquois stole from other Indians who were transporting them via the St. Lawrence River; Iroquoia possessed few beavers. According to Richter, and contra Snow, there is no evidence that any of the Five Nations acted as intermediaries between Europeans and other Indians before 1670 (Richter 1992:57).

During the early 1630s, European-introduced measles and smallpox viruses infested Iroquoia. The Mohawk population is estimated to have fallen from 7,700 to 2,839 in 1634 alone and by as much as 75 percent or more over a decade as a result of these contagions (Snow and Lanphear

1988; Snow and Starna 1989:145; Snow 1994:96), and the Mohawk abandoned their four castled villages for new, smaller ones. The Oneida, Cayuga, and Onondaga populations were reduced by about half, and the Seneca appear to have escaped such severe decimation (Snow 1994:100). The Iroquois tended to blame witches for the afflictions suffered by the nations, and they targeted suspect individuals for excommunication, torture, and execution, or other Indian tribes or nations for revenge through mourning wars. Shamanic medicine societies that utilized medicinal herbs, medicine bundles, ritual masks, songs, chants, rattles, and drums for curing ceremonies flourished at first then were undermined by their ineffectiveness. The population continued to decline as successive waves of epidemics spread throughout Iroquoia during the seventeenth and eighteenth centuries, striking especially the very young and the elders who possessed the cultural knowledge and wisdom of the Iroquois (Richter 1992:60; Tooker 1978a:421; Trigger 1978:352).

Both population decline and the desire for beaver pelts resulted in intense intertribal, or international, warfare among Indian nations in the seventeenth and early eighteenth centuries. These conflicts are known as the Beaver Wars. Population decline is perhaps the most significant cause of these wars; one of the warriors' principal objectives was to capture Indians from other tribes for adoption, essentially to replace those lost to disease (Richter 1992:58–60; Snow 1994:110). But the ferocity and scale of these campaigns went far beyond those of traditional mourning wars. In 1640 Mohawk engaged in the second Mohawk-Mahican War, after which, in 1642, they signed their first separate formal treaty with the Dutch. In 1646 they entered a third Mohawk-Mahican War, which ended in 1653. During the 1640s, in response to a French-inspired Huron military assault in violation of a peace agreement, the Iroquois Confederacy launched a major war against the Huron Confederacy. By 1648, this conflict had engulfed the entire traditional territory of the Huron in turmoil (Churchill 1997:192–93; Richter 1992:60–62; Trigger 1976, 2:546–71, 1978:355).

The Iroquois, by now well armed and skilled in the use of European firearms, attacked Huronia again in 1649. They destroyed the Petun and the few remaining Huron, and the survivors either were absorbed into the Iroquois or moved west and formed the Wyandot Nation. From 1647 to 1643 the Iroquois repeatedly attacked and eventually demolished the Neutral Confederacy, along with the Wenro, and by 1656 the Iroquois had dispersed the Erie Nation. At the urging of the Dutch, the Iroquois attacked their ancient enemies, the Susquehannock, as well. Having destroyed all of the Indian allies of the French in the region, the Iroquois entered into a peace with the French. They then assaulted Indian nations and tribes in the Great Lakes region, first attacking the Illinois and Ojibwa in the mid-

1650s and suffering some defeats, then moving against and defeating the Huron and Ottawa in present-day Wisconsin. The Mohawk entered into the fourth Mohawk-Mahican War in 1658 (Richter 1992:61–74; Snow 1994:114–18; Tooker 1978a:430; Trigger 1978:356).

By 1667 the English had defeated the Dutch in the Second Anglo-Dutch War and had seized New Netherland, which became New York. The Mohawk quickly signed a treaty with the English even though they continued to wage war against English-allied Indian nations. The western Iroquois nations, on the other hand, signed several treaties of peace with the French. The English assisted in a treaty of peace between the Mohawk and the Mahican, which ended the Fourth Mohawk-Mahican War in 1665, but they were unable, in spite of their efforts, to broker a larger peace agreement that would have included several other northeastern Algonquian nations; this failure exposed English limitations.

The Mohawk and the other Iroquois nations were facing French military threats. In 1667 the Mohawk entered into a treaty of peace with the French. The other Iroquois nations, confronted by an overwhelming French military presence that replaced the Company of the Hundred Associates as the governing authority in New France, had entered into a treaty with the French in 1665. These treaties allowed Jesuit missionaries, and consequently French culture, into Iroquoia (Richter 1992:102–32).

During the 1670s the Iroquois engaged in wars against the Shawnee, the Susquehannock, the Mahican and the New England Algonquian, although the Mohawk maintained their sometimes stormy relations with the Mohegans, who were despised by the other Algonquian Indians. The Susquehannock left the Susquehanna Valley region by 1672, and the Shawnee left the Ohio Valley in order to escape incessant Iroquois attacks. By 1673, the Mahican had been rendered powerless, and the Mohawk nation dominated New York. From 1665 to 1687, the Seneca, Cayuga, and Oneida suffered defeats first by a coalition of Ottawa, Mississauga, and Huron, and later by the Mississauga alone, who pushed the expansionist Iroquois settlements out of present-day Ontario and back into present-day New York (Snow 1994:119–22). Although the Dutch temporarily recaptured New York during the Third Anglo-Dutch War (1672–1678), the English regained control in 1674 and established their center of power in present-day Albany. In 1675, the southern New England Algonquians, led by Metacom, or King Philip, attempted to push out the English in what is known as King Philip's War, a conflict in which the Iroquois at first remained neutral. While attempting to solicit the aid of other Indian nations, King Philip's forces were decimated by another epidemic, then from 1675 to 1677 they were attacked by Mohawks acting upon the urging of New York Governor Edmund Andros. Control of New England passed from the Algonquian Indians to the English (Richter 1992:135–36; Snow 1994:122–23).

The Mohawk capitalized on their proximity to the English and their role in the English victory over Metacom, and they gained English support. Many New England Algonquians migrated to the Mohawk territory and converted culturally to become Mohawks. Many Susquehannock, defeated and destroyed as a nation during Bacon's Rebellion, joined the Onondaga and the Cayuga, adopting their culture. Among the western Iroquois, the impact of the French Jesuits and the absorption of the already Catholicized Huron led to many Iroquois conversions to Catholicism. Catholic Mohawks were scorned by Mohawk traditionalists, who commanded authority among the Iroquois as English influence grew. The Catholic Mohawks, Onondagas, and Hurons left for French Canada and created Kahnawake, named after one of their former villages; by 1700, approximately two-thirds of the entire Mohawk population lived at Kahnawake (Richter 1992:135–36; Snow 1994:122, 131).

THE COVENANT CHAIN IN THE EIGHTEENTH CENTURY

The Mohawk continued to attack other non-Iroquois Indian nations in the New York territory, especially the Mohegan and other Algonquian nations that had fled New England and were attempting to establish a new base of power north of Albany. Governor Andros sought to control all of New York and New England by attempting to establish the Mohawk and other Iroquois nations as essentially a police force over all non-Iroquois Indian nations in the region. He then subordinated the Iroquois Confederacy to the authority of New York. In an agreement of 1677, Andros persuaded the Mohawk and the Mahican nations to abstain from conflict with other English-allied Indian nations, agreed to treat with the Iroquois as a whole rather than separately with each nation, and pronounced all non-Iroquois Indian nations to be "children" of the Iroquois. This agreement was the beginning of the creation of the Covenant Chain between England and the Iroquois, through which England claimed hegemony over all Indian nations. The Iroquois, on the other hand, viewed the Covenant Chain as a "linking of arms," and thus an alliance between friendly nations, rather than a hierarchical arrangement of English supremacy and Iroquois subordination (Druke 1987; Haan 1987; Jennings 1984; Richter 1992:136–37; Salisbury 1987; Snow 1994:123–25; R. Williams 1997).

After a period of time the Mohawk eventually adopted the position that the Massachusett and Mohegan nations were English clients and thus protected by the Covenant Chain. Treaty negotiations between the Iroquois and the English, preceded by the condolence ceremony and involving gift exchanges, continually renewed the Covenant Chain, just as similar meetings renewed the League of the Iroquois. Although the English participated in these ceremonies with the Iroquois, they were more interested in defining conclusive treaty terms. At the same time the Iroquois, especially the Seneca, were attacking the French and their Indian allies to the west in an effort to halt expanding French influence in the Great Lakes and Mississippi River regions. The conflict between the Iroquois and the French escalated with the commencement of King William's War between the English and the French. After the signing of the Peace of Ryswick in 1697 officially ended King William's War, the war between the Iroquois and the French, a war that divided the Iroquois between the traditionalists and the Catholics, continued into the eighteenth century (Jennings 1984:186–210; Snow 1994:125–27).

The war with the French threatened to destroy the League of the Iroquois, and eventually, because no single Iroquois nation or division among nations could assume the league's power and authority, only a declaration of neutral status and the establishment of alliances with both the French and the English could preserve the league. In 1701 Iroquois entered into the Grand Settlement with the French that allowed Catholic Iroquois to travel to Quebec and pro-English Iroquois to maintain their ties to Albany. Consequently, the Iroquois established friendly relations with the French-allied Indians of the Ohio River valley and the Great Lakes regions. For the Iroquois, this action did little to alter the Covenant Chain, but the English thought otherwise. They quickly obtained, by purchase from the Iroquois, a "deed" to the interior of the continent that allowed the Indians to occupy their territories as "tenants" (Jennings 1984:210–13; Snow 1994:133–34). In 1727 Cadwallader Colden published the first part of his voluminous *The History of the Five Nations Depending on the Province of New-York in America,* essentially a propaganda piece, in which he attributes the status of "empire" to the Iroquois in order to validate the English assumption and acquisition of sovereignty over the Indians of the interior: "Lacking a reasonable alternative until the French could be forced off the continent, the British donated an empire to the Iroquois in order to claim it for themselves" (Colden, quoted in Jennings 1984:11).

Not all Indian nations, nor even the Iroquois factions, maintained the neutrality to which the league had agreed. In 1702 Queen Anne's War, also called the War of Spanish Succession, broke out, and the English sought the alliance of the Iroquois in the conflict. The Mohawk leader and league sachem Theyanoguin, a converted Protestant, led a group of Mohawks into the conflict on the side of the English. He and three others were later invited to England to meet Queen Anne. There they professed their allegiance to the English and their antagonism toward the French. Upon Theyanoguin's request, the queen later sent missionaries to the Mohawk River valley fort and the community known as Lower Mohawk Castle and financed the construction of a chapel and two houses for the missionaries (Fenton and Tooker 1978:474; Snow 1994:135–36).

The Iroquois accepted the Tuscarora's entry into Iroquoia as refugees following their defeat in the Tuscarora Wars (1711–1713) against European settlers in present-day North Carolina. In 1722 or 1723 the Tuscarora were officially adopted into the league and became the sixth nation of the Iroquois Confederacy. The new Tuscarora village was located between the Oneida and Onondaga villages. Although the Tuscarora participated as an Iroquois nation in all conferences and treaty signings, they did not receive voting representation in the league's Grand Council, and their chiefs were not made sachems (Boyce 1987; Jennings 1984:262; Landy 1978; Snow 1994:138–39; Tooker 1978a:433).

The Iroquois Confederacy did remain neutral during King George's War, also known as the War of Austrian Succession, between the English and the French. However, through the Peace of Aix-la-Chapelle that ended that war, the French persuaded the pro-French Indians in Canada to form a religious (Catholic) and political (pro-French) confederation known as the Seven Indian Nations of Canada. This confederation included the Mohawks, Algonquians, and Nippissings of the Lake of Two Mountains, who would later be known as the Oka or Kanesatake; the Kahnawake Mohawks; the Onondagas and Cayugas at Oswegatchie; the Hurons at Lorette; and the St. Francis Abenaki. The Indians at Oswegatchie later dispersed, and they were replaced in the confederation by the Mohawks at Akwesasne, or St. Regis, who had split off from Kahnawake shortly before (Day and Trigger 1978:795; Snow 1994:140; Tooker 1978a:433).

By the mid to late eighteenth century, following decades of contact with Europeans, international war, and devastation by disease, the traditional Iroquois cultural patterns were breaking down. Few Iroquois lived in longhouses anymore, instead preferring cabins holding smaller family units. The longhouses were used for ceremonial purposes and for housing guests. Economic change altered social patterns, and women were no longer as independent. Traditional leaders, the sachems and the clan mother, received less respect and wielded less authority, and positions such as pine tree chief were no longer restricted to those who did not have access to other traditional positions of leadership (Snow 1994:141).

By 1750 the French were trying to persuade the Mingo, or Ohio River Iroquois, to embrace the pro-French position. The English became alarmed at French efforts in the Ohio River region and feared that the entire Six Nations Confederacy would follow the Ohio River Iroquois and abandon the English for the French. Following the 1754 conference during which Benjamin Franklin introduced the Albany Plan of Union, based partly on the governing principles of the League of the Iroquois, several Iroquois chiefs, including Theyanoguin, were induced to drink alcohol, and, once they were drunk, they were tricked into signing the Wyoming Deed, which granted western land for Connecticut. This unscrupulous transaction later resulted in the Wyoming Massacre of 1778 (Jennings 1988:98–108; Snow 1994:140–43).

By 1755 the Seven Years War, also known as the French and Indian War, was breaking out between the French and English and their Indian allies. Kahnawake Mohawks met New York Mohawks led by Theyanoguin in a battle between the French and the English. Iroquois were pitted against Iroquois in violation of league principles. The Seneca remained pro-French throughout the war, and the New York Mohawks continued to fight on the side of the English. The English captured Montreal in 1760, ending the fighting, and the Seven Years War was officially concluded several years later with the signing of the Treaty of Paris of 1763. According to Francis Jennings, however, the war wasn't truly over until the end of the American Revolutionary War (Jennings 1988; Snow 1994:144–45).

Following the 1763 peace settlement, Pontiac's War immediately broke out, as Indians rebelled against the English in an effort to retain their territory and their independence. King George then signed the Proclamation of 1763, which designated the Appalachian Mountains as the division between Indian territory to the west and English territory to the east, but this line did not establish a clear barrier separating Mohawk and Oneida territories from areas occupied by English settlers. In 1766 Pontiac's Indians signed the Treaty of Oswego, officially ending that conflict. The English voluntarily relinquished two prominent patents to Mohawk land in New York, as recommended by Lieutenant Governor Cadwallader Colden, who was carrying out the instruction of the English Lords of Trade that he should secure land for the Mohawks and promote peace. The 1768 Treaty of Fort Stanwix, another agreement intended to protect Indian land from English settlers, stripped the Iroquois of their English-designated authority over the Shawnee, Delaware, and Wyandot in the Ohio Valley (Prucha 1984, 1:24–35; Snow 1994:149).

THE IROQUOIS AND THE UNITED STATES OF AMERICA

The Revolutionary War caused the metaphorical longhouse of the League of the Iroquois to split apart. The Akwesasne Mohawks signed a treaty with the Americans in 1775, while the Onondaga, Cayuga, Seneca, and New York Mohawks remained loyal to the English. The Oneida and the Tuscarora were decidedly pro-American (Locklear 1988:146). When the league met in 1776, it could not arrive at a consensus on how to proceed. Another epidemic killed off several league chiefs and many other Iroquois, and in 1777 the league symbolically suspended its existence by ceremoniously covering the council fire at Onondaga. The Mohawk were scattered from their territories by American military forces, and some of their territories in the Mohawk Valley were captured by the pro-American Oneida (Graymont 1972; Snow 1994:151).

The pro-American western Iroquois nations remained removed from the fighting until, in 1779, the revolutionary Americans, determined to annihilate them and seize their territories, destroyed their settlements in western New York, and Iroquois led by Joseph Brant attacked Oneida and Tuscarora settlements in retaliation for their support of the Americans. By the end of the campaign, the Iroquois population was reduced by half, and refugee Iroquois Loyalists led by Brant, including members of all six nations, fled to Ontario, Canada, where they were granted 675,000 acres on each side of the Grand River as restitution for their loss of land in New York (Weaver 1978:525). From there the Loyalist Iroquois raided American military outposts and settlements in support of the continuing British war effort. In 1783, concerned that the new American federal government would claim sovereignty over the Iroquois territories on the basis of conquest, New York declared state jurisdiction over the territories and sovereignty over the Indian tribes (Snow 1994:152).

The 1783 Treaty of Paris ended the war between the English and the Americans, but it contained no provisions concerning the Indians. The Iroquois suffered the tremendous loss of their New York territory, and several groups moved permanently to Canada. The Oneida were able to hold on to their territory because they had supported the victorious Americans. The League of the Iroquois was revived at Buffalo Creek in western New York, and a second league was formed at Grand River, Ontario, site of the present-day Six Nations Reserve. Each league had its own set of league chiefs. The 1784 Treaty of Fort Stanwix secured the Oneida and Tuscarora nations in the possession of their land (Locklear 1988:146), but rejected Iroquois claims or legal title to territories in Pennsylvania and the Ohio Valley region, deprived the Seneca of most of their territory in New York (Campisi 1988:61), and removed the Iroquois's right to speak for all other Indian nations, a right that even the Iroquois no longer maintained was appropriately theirs.

In the Constitution the United States asserted federal sovereignty over Indian affairs. New York, however, failed to relinquish its quest for control over the western Indian territories that, New York claimed, remained part of its domain. Massachusetts also claimed western New York as part of its territory.

Oneida land possessions were guaranteed again in the Treaty of Fort Harmar in 1789 and the Treaty of Canandaigua in 1794 (Locklear 1988:146–47), and Seneca land losses were mostly restored by the Treaty of Canandaigua (Campisi 1988:63–64). Akwesasne Mohawks claimed territory in the Adirondacks, but through an agreement between New York and the Seven Indian Nations of Canada, which includes the Akwesasne, they relinquished that claim in exchange for annual payments. The Iroquois did not join the Shawnee, Delaware, and Mingo of Ohio, who rebelled against American domination and repudiated the Treaty of Fort

Harmar, then were defeated at the Battle of Fallen Timbers in 1794. By the end of the eighteenth century, the Iroquois were living on reserves, the beaver population had been decimated, and slash-and-burn, or swidden, cultivation was no longer possible. Traditional Iroquois culture, at least as it was known following the formation of the League of the Iroquois, had been virtually extinguished. The Iroquois succumbed to alcoholism and to internal turmoil that included a new explosion of witchcraft accusations (Snow 1994:155–57; Wallace 1978:443–44).

Dreams are imbued with tremendous significance among the Iroquois. They are believed to express deep desires that require action in order to forestall personal or communal sickness and death. The higher the rank of the dreamer, the more significant were his dreams (Wallace 1958). In 1799, an alcoholic Iroquois man named Handsome Lake, the half-brother of a league sachem, Cornplanter, appeared to have died as a result of his affliction, but he was only in a coma. While he was in the coma, he experienced a vision in which the Creator told him to spread the command that the Iroquois must give up alcohol and that all witches must confess and repent. Later Handsome Lake experienced a second vision in which he was transported to both heaven and hell. On the basis of that vision, he devised a moral code, the Gai'wiio, or "Good Message" (Wallace 1958). During winter Handsome Lake experienced a third vision, in which he was instructed that the Iroquois must observe their traditional ceremonies or the world would be consumed by fire. Handsome Lake immediately revived the midwinter ceremony with four additional sacred rituals appended. Handsome Lake recovered his health and began spreading his visions as a prophet among the Iroquois. Another series of visions led to the construction of a complex code of behavior and the establishment of Handsome Lake's teachings as a new religion among the Iroquois (Snow 1994:159–61; Tooker 1978b:452–54; Wallace 1978:445–47).

Handsome Lake regarded traditional Iroquois medicine societies as witchcraft and outlawed them. He demanded that people confess to witchcraft and executed those who refused, and his antagonism toward Iroquois leaders such as Seneca Pine Tree Chief Red Jacket nearly caused an Iroquois civil war. But the code of behavior that Handsome Lake established, which included proscription of both divorce and malicious gossip, to some extent led the Iroquois out of the anomie, torpor, and self-destructiveness that resulted from defeat and life on the reservation. He also opposed any further Iroquois land sales and Iroquois participation in the U.S. military, particularly during the War of 1812. Handsome Lake died in 1815, but his religious vision survives to this day (Snow 1994:162–64; Tooker 1978b:452–54; Wallace 1978:447–48).

Iroquois land sales continued anyway, and in 1831 some Senecas and Cayugas moved to Indian Territory in present-day Oklahoma. Joseph Brant, arguing that the Grand River land grant was an estate in fee simple over which the Iroquois were guaranteed sovereignty, sold large sections of Six Nations land in Canada to non-Indians, hoping that they would teach the Iroquois how to farm. In 1810 David Ogden purchased the right to acquire Seneca land from the Holland Land Company, which had earlier acquired that right through a fraudulent transaction. The State of New York continued to reduce Iroquois landholdings, often without the knowledge of the Iroquois, by means of a series of unconstitutional legislation. The Iroquois had once again become polarized, this time between those who were Christian and those who had converted to the religion of Handsome Lake; however, following a conference in 1818 the two sides agreed that they should not sell more land and that they should not leave Iroquoia and move west (Tooker 1978b:452). Nevertheless, some Iroquois continued to participate in land sales. The Seneca, for example, sold much of their remaining land to David Ogden through the Treaty of Buffalo Creek (1826), retaining only four large reserves at Buffalo Creek, Tonawanda, Cattaraugus, and Allegany and the small reservation at Oil Spring (Snow 1994:164–65; Tooker 1978b:452).

In 1835 the New York legislature approved leases of land on the Allegany Reserve to non-Indians. In 1838 traditional Seneca sachems sold all of their remaining land including land in Wisconsin, again to Ogden through arrangements resulting from the Buffalo Creek Treaty, and agreed to move to Kansas. They received only $202,000 for land worth more than $2 million. Fewer than half of the Seneca chiefs had signed the treaty, and of those who signed, sixteen had been bribed and others had been coerced. Several signatures were outright forgeries. While some members of the Seneca would later move to Kansas, the majority refused to accept the validity of the treaty and sought help from Quakers and other New Yorkers in overturning it. A compromise agreement was later reached, in 1842, but even it forced the Seneca to relinquish both the Buffalo Creek and Tonawanda reservations. A Christian missionary convinced the Oneida to sell their New York land and move to Wisconsin. Some Oneidas purchased land in Ontario and, with the assistance of the Six Nations Reserve, reestablished their league chiefs and their council of hereditary chiefs. A few Oneidas remained in New York, but their land there was ultimately individually allotted, per New York legislation passed in 1845, and it gradually passed out of their hands. In Kansas, land that had been reserved for the Seneca was usurped by squatters when the Seneca who had left New York for Kansas either died or returned to New York (Snow 1994:166–67; Tooker 1978a:436).

By 1841 the Six Nations of the Grand River in Canada sought to reverse Brant's disastrous policy, which had resulted in the alienation of nearly the entire land grant without relinquishing their claim to sovereignty over their land, and exchanged their claim to 220,000 acres with the British Crown for approximately 20,000 contiguous acres placed in a trust as a protected reserve. Consequently, the Crown evicted all non-Indians on the 20,000 acres, and in 1847 the chiefs of the Six Nations successfully argued for an additional 25,000 acres. In 1847 the reserve community was officially established, and the Six Nations Iroquois Confederacy governed it much like a municipality (Weaver 1978:525–28).

In 1848, fearing that traditional chiefs might once again attempt to sell Seneca land, the Seneca on the Allegany and Cattaraugus reservations in New York elected tribal governments of sixteen chiefs each and formed the Seneca Nation of Indians. The Tonawanda Seneca still believed that because they had signed neither the fraudulent Buffalo Creek Treaty nor the compromise agreement of 1842, and because they had not left their land, their reservation would remain intact. They thought that preserving their traditional government was the key to a just settlement. The Onondaga likewise retained their traditional form of government. The Akwesasne Mohawks continued to be governed by their traditional chiefs; however, in 1802 the New York legislature enacted a statute authorizing the election of three Akwesasne trustees. Since then the state has conducted its business with the three trustees while the traditional government has continued to possess internal tribal authority. In 1818 Akwesasne Mohawks on the United States side of the St. Lawrence River were allowed to form an elected government, a tribal council of three chiefs who continue to serve as the three state-sanctioned trustees (Snow 1994:167–68).

By 1860 the Seneca remained at Allegany, Cattaraugus, and Tonawanda and were still maintaining two separate forms of tribal government, and the Onondaga retained their tribal government at the Onondaga Reserve, but the Cayuga and the Oneida were virtually non-existent in New York. The Grand Council of the League of the Iroquois continued to function among the New York Iroquois and adopted the Akwesasne Mohawk into the League in 1888, but the U.S. government recognized only the individual tribes. The league was able to pursue the Seneca's Kansas claim, and in 1898 it achieved a $2 million settlement (Snow 1994:177–78). In Canada the other Iroquois Council also continued to function although there were few Seneca and Oneida. The Canadian government did not recognize the sovereign-nation status of the Six Nations Iroquois Confederacy, but at least until 1924 it allowed the Confederacy Council to govern as the authority for all the Iroquois on the Six Nations reserve, subject to the Indian Act and its amendments (Weaver 1978:528–33).

The New York Iroquois enlisted in the Union army and fought in the Civil War. The Indian Territory Iroquois remained neutral throughout the conflict; nevertheless, following the conclusion of the war the U.S. government considered the Indian Territory Iroquois to have sided with the government of the Confederate states and therefore classified them as traitors. For an offense they did not commit, the Indian Territory Iroquois were forced to apologize and sell their land (Hauptman 1993). Further alienation of Iroquois land was the intended result of the Dawes Act of 1887. In Canada similar measures were taken, such as the Indian Act of 1869, which encouraged the replacement of traditional governments with elected councils.

THE IROQUOIS IN THE TWENTIETH CENTURY

The Canadian government imposed the Indian Act on the Kahnawake Mohawk in 1877, and an elected band council replaced the traditional council of chiefs. In 1888 the Canadian government enacted an order in council that removed the traditional government of twelve hereditary chiefs at Akwesasne on a charge of malfeasance and replaced them with twelve elected councilors who later became a band council. From that point on, although the traditional Akwesasne Mohawk government continued to operate, it was ignored by both the United States and Canada (Barsh 1982a; Snow 1994:180). The government of Canada imposed an elected council to replace the traditional government at Six Nations Reserve in 1924, and in 1934 it imposed a similar council at Oneida (Hauptman 1981:15; Weaver 1978:533). Despite Canada's official expulsion of the traditional government, the Six Nations league chiefs continue to meet each October or November in one of four remaining longhouses on the Six Nations Reserve (at Onondaga, Seneca, Lower Cayuga, and Upper Cayuga, or Sour Springs). At their meetings they hear the Code of Handsome Lake and the ceremonies of the eight medicine societies. The longhouses continue to be the centers of the perpetuation of traditional Iroquois culture (Weaver 1978:534–35).

In 1920 and 1923, Deskaheh, a Cayuga league sachem traveling with only an Iroquois passport, brought a complaint by the Canadian league before the Council of the League of Nations in Geneva and unsuccessfully attempted to bring a case before the British Crown. He argued that the sovereignty of the Iroquois Confederacy, historically evident in the Covenant Chain and in numerous treaties and land patents, had never been relinquished and that therefore Canada's policies and actions were in violation of Iroquois sovereignty. Deskaheh achieved little more than international applause mixed with derisive laughter, and he died in exile among the Iroquois of New York (Hauptman 1981:16; Veatch 1975).

Into the twentieth century New York continued to pursue its policy of assimilating Indian peoples and alienating Indian land. However, in 1922, following the decision in *United States v. Boylan* (1920), which established that New York Indians were wards of the federal government rather than of the state government, and which restored a portion of illegally possessed land to the Iroquois, the Everett Commission, a New York state commission authorized to investigate the "Indian problem," determined that the Iroquois possessed a legitimate claim to six million acres of western New York that had been illegally acquired from them after the 1784 Treaty of Fort Stanwix. State officials buried the report, but it helped revive Iroquois efforts to recover territories through the legal system (Churchill 1993:87–96; Hauptman 1986a:184; Snow 1994:193).

The religion of Handsome Lake finally made its way to Kahnawake in the 1920s and Akwesasne in the 1930s. Subsequently, Akwesasne reinstituted a traditional government that continues to challenge the authority of the elected government, and Kahnawake established two sets of league chiefs, sending one set to the New York league at the Onondaga Reserve and the other set to the Canadian league at the Six Nations Reserve. In 1925 a Canadian Kahnawake named Paul Diabo was arrested in Philadelphia as an illegal alien in violation of the Immigration Act of 1924. Assisted by the newly created Indian Defense League of America, Diabo won his case by arguing that he is protected by article 3 of the Jay Treaty of 1794, which was reaffirmed in the 1814 Treaty of Ghent and guarantees Iroquois unrestricted and unregulated passage and trade across the United States–Canada border (Hauptman 1986a:148; Snow 1994:193–94).

The Indian Citizenship Act of 1924

In 1924 the United States unilaterally passed the Indian Citizenship Act. Historian Laurence Hauptman notes that "making Indians citizens was an assimilationist goal from the early days of the American Republic and was often identified with policies tied to land-in-severalty, taxation of allotment, land frauds, and a shrinking Indian land base" (Hauptman 1981:6). The Iroquois, especially those of New York, viewed the act as an assault on their never-relinquished, treaty-guaranteed sovereignty as citizens of their own nations within the League of the Haudenosaunee (Hauptman 1986a:4–5). Clinton Rickard, a prominent chief of the Tuscarora, presents Iroquois objections to the Indian Citizenship Act in his autobiography:

> To us, it seemed that the United States government was just trying to get rid of its treaty obligations and make us into taxpaying citizens who could sell their homelands and finally end up in city slums. . . . The Citizenship Act did pass in 1924 despite our strong opposition. By its provisions all Indians were automatically made United States citizens whether they wanted to be so or not. This was a violation of our sovereignty. Our citizenship was in our own nations. We had a great attachment to our style of government. We wished to remain treaty Indians and preserve our ancient rights. There was no great rush among my people to go out and vote in white man's elections. Anyone who did so was denied the privilege of becoming a chief or clan mother in our nation. (Rickard 1973:53)

More recently, concerning their objection both then and now to the unilateral imposition of U.S. and Canadian citizenship, the traditional Haudenosaunee of the journal *Akwesasne Notes* proclaim:

> The 1924 Citizenship Act was an attempt to deny the existence of Native nations, and the rights of these Native nations to their lands. The denial of the existence of Native nations is a way of legitimizing the colonists' claims to the lands. This concept is furthered by the imposition of non-Native forms of government. . . . The Haudenosaunee vigorously objected to the Citizenship Act and maintains to this day that the People of the Longhouse are not citizens of Canada or the United States, but are citizens of their own nations of the League. (*Akwesasne Notes* 1981:69)

Now more than seventy years later, in an undeniable expression of their commitment to sovereign independence, the Iroquois continue to travel internationally with Iroquois passports.

The Indian Reorganization Act of 1934

The Indian Reorganization Act of 1934 encouraged the creation of constitutionally based, elected tribal governments with limited sovereignty under U.S. federal jurisdiction. Traditional Iroquois oppose the Indian Reorganization Act governments, viewing them as a form of "colonial occupation":

> In 1924, Canada's new Indian Act established the legal sanction for the imposition of neo-colonial "elective system" governments within the Native Peoples' territories. In the United States, the same goal was accomplished with the passage of the 1934 Indian Reorganization Act (IRA). Both pieces of legislation provided compulsive chartered political colonies among Native people. These "elective systems" owe their existence and fealty to the United States and Canada, and not to Native peoples. They are, by definition, colonies which create classes of political peasants. (*Akwesasne Notes* 1981:58)

Additional federal legislation, the Criminal Jurisdiction Transfer Act of 1948, transferred jurisdiction for criminal offenses from the Iroquois to the state of New York, further reducing the exercise of Iroquois sovereignty. In 1950 a transfer was effected for civil offenses as well. The Iroquois then had to combat the termination legislation fever of the 1950s.

Traditional tribal government based on hereditary chiefs continues to survive at Tuscarora, Onondaga, and Tonawanda. The Tuscarora fought the United States in the courts in the 1950s in an attempt to prevent the loss of one-fifth of their reservation to the New York Power Authority (Churchill 1993:97–98; Hauptman 1986a:151–78). Although they lost and the land is now part of a reservoir, their legal battle inspired other Indian tribes to similarly resist. In the 1960s Seneca Nation of the Allegany and Cattaraugus reservations, operating with an elected government, lost one-third of the Allegany Reservation, through eminent domain, to the Kinzua Dam project, even though evidence was presented demonstrating that the project was unnecessary and that the U.S. Constitution and treaties with the Seneca protected the Seneca from usual eminent domain proceedings. Congress pushed the project through, and the Seneca sued. They received a 15-million-dollar award, but they lost their homeland, including the original site of the Coldspring longhouse—the place of Handsome Lake's visions—and other sacred sites (Campisi 1984; Hauptman 1986a:85–122).

Some of the Seneca's resistance efforts were more successful, however. In the 1950s, New York constructed two highways through the Seneca Nation reservations without consent or compensation, but Seneca threats to close the highways prompted New York's accession to their requests for negotiation. The Senecas also favorably renegotiated their land leases with the city of Salamanca when the leases expired in 1991, despite protestations and nonpayment by the residents of Salamanca (Churchill 1993:103; Hauptman 1988b; Snow 1994:199–201).

The Oneida have maintained a long-term legal struggle against the state of New York and its counties in order to reclaim ancestral lands lost through treaties and other transactions made in violation of the Nonintercourse Act of the Indian Trade and Intercourse Act of 1790, which prohibits the acquisition of Indian land without federal consent (Churchill 1993:99–101; Hauptman 1986a:179–203; Locklear 1988). The virtually landless Cayuga have also filed suit against counties in New York in order to recover 64,015 acres (Churchill 1993:101–3; Hauptman 1988a:74).

The International Indian Treaty Council

The contemporary worldwide indigenous movement for liberation and self-determination was created largely through the efforts of American Indians, both traditional and urban, in Canada and the United States during the late 1960s and the 1970s. In 1969 Mohawks from Akwesasne, which comprises territory in New York, Ontario, and Quebec, engaged in a blockade of a bridge across the St. Lawrence River in order to force the Canadian government to recognize the Jay Treaty. Two years later Akwesasne Mohawks occupied two islands in the river in order to attain Canadian recognition that those islands belong to the Akwesasne, or St. Regis, Reserve (Hauptman 1986a:148–50; Snow 1994:202).

Following the Trail of Broken Treaties march on Washington, D.C., in 1972, which emphasized the obligation of the United States to honor treaties with Indian nations, including treaties recognizing Sioux rights to the sacred Black Hills of South Dakota, traditional Indians, including the Iroquois, presented a document known as the Twenty Points to the executive branch of the federal government, which had promised to give the document serious consideration (Deloria 1985:61). The Indians were demanding recognition of ratified Indian treaties, legal ratification of unratified treaties, the return of land guaranteed them in those treaties, reinstitution of the treaty relationship, and the formation of a special court to deal with Indian affairs and treaty interpretation and resolution. The U.S. government refused or ignored the demands (Deloria 1985:48–53). Frustration and political divisions then led to the infamous "second war" at Wounded Knee in 1973.

On the Lakota's Pine Ridge Indian Reservation in South Dakota, the reservation government led by Richard Wilson opposed the activity of members of the American Indian Movement (AIM) both on the reservation and off. The original members and leaders of AIM were from urban areas, particularly Minneapolis and San Francisco, but they sought to reclaim their identity as Indians by emphasizing traditional religion and political independence. Federal officials wrongly dismissed the Trail of Broken Treaties march and the Twenty Points as results entirely of AIM activism, but traditional Indians from several nations and reservations formed the largest segment of the marchers and were responsible for the Twenty Points document. Doubtless, AIM activists touched a deep chord among the traditionals, and Wilson's police force, aided by the FBI, attempted a brutal crackdown on members and supporters of AIM that led to a virtual civil war on the reservation. The village of Wounded Knee, site of the last, and perhaps most senseless, massacre of Sioux Indians in the late 1800s, lies within the boundaries of the reservation, but occupation of the village by AIM members and traditional Indians in protest of Wilson and the actions of the U.S. government quickly led to an unwarranted armed confrontation between federal officials and the Indians (Matthiessen 1991; Weyler 1992).

These events led directly to the formation of the International Indian Treaty Council in 1974. Through this organization North American Indians would address the international community as members of the world's community of nations, believing it to be their fundamental right to do so. In 1977 the council helped to organize and participated in the United Nations Non-Governmental Organization Conference on Discrimination against Indians in the Americas, held in Geneva and sponsored by the United Nations Sub-Committee on Racism, Racial Discrimination, Apartheid, and Decolonization, a branch of the United Nations Economic and Social Council Special Committee on Human Rights. The conference attracted Indians from throughout the Americas who presented their grievances and demands before the international body. Indians claimed to be victims of genocide, colonialism, racism, and assimilationist policies that violate their individual and collective human rights. In their Declaration of Principles the Indians demanded both protection under international law and their rights to self-determination as peoples or nations (International Indian Treaty Council 1977:25–26). Indians from Guatemala and Bolivia, two countries where Indians are the majority of the population, described the actions and policies of their countries' governments in terms of extreme human rights violations, if not apartheid. Mapuche Indians from Chile claimed to be victims of government-sponsored genocide (International Indian Treaty Council 1977:7–10, 14–17).

In 1985 the International Indian Treaty Council joined the Indian Law Resource Center, the Four Directions Council, the National Aboriginal and Islander Legal Service, the National Indian Youth Council, and the Inuit Circumpolar Conference to produce a more complete Declaration of Principles of indigenous nations:

1. Indigenous nations and peoples have, in common with all humanity, the right to life, and to freedom from oppression, discrimination, and aggression.

2. All indigenous nations and peoples have the right to self-determination, by virtue of which they have the right to whatever degree of autonomy or self-government they choose. This includes the right to freely determine their political status, freely pursue their own economic, social, religious and cultural development, and determine their own membership and/or citizenship, without external interference.

3. No State shall assert any jurisdiction over an indigenous nation or people, or its territory, except in accordance with the freely expressed wishes of the nation or people concerned.

4. Indigenous nations and peoples are entitled to the permanent control and enjoyment of their aboriginal ancestral-historical territories. This includes surface and subsurface rights, inland and coastal waters, renewable and non-renewable resources, and the economies based on these resources.

5. Rights to share and use land, subject to the underlying and inalienable title of the indigenous nation or people, may be granted by their free and informed consent, as evidenced in a valid treaty or agreement.

6. Discovery, conquest, and settlement on a theory of *terra nullius* and unilateral legislation are never legitimate bases for States to claim or retain the territories of indigenous nations or peoples.

7. In cases where lands taken in violation of these principles have already been settled, the indigenous nation or people concerned is entitled to immediate

restitution, including compensation for the loss of use, without extinction of original title. Indigenous peoples' desire to regain possession and control of sacred sites must always be respected.

8. No State shall participate financially or militarily in the involuntary displacement of indigenous populations, or in the subsequent economic exploitation or military use of their territory.

9. The laws and customs of indigenous nations and peoples must be recognized by States' legislative, administrative and judicial institutions and, in case of conflicts with State laws, shall take precedence.

10. No State shall deny an indigenous nation, community, or people residing within its borders the right to participate in the life of the State in whatever manner and to whatever degree they may choose. This includes the right to participate in other forms of collective action and expression.

11. Indigenous nations and peoples continue to own and control their material culture, including archaeological, historical and sacred sites, artifacts, designs, knowledge, and works of art. They have the right to regain items of major cultural significance and, in all cases, to the return of the human remains of their ancestors for burial in accordance with their traditions.

12. Indigenous nations and peoples have the right to be educated and conduct business with States in their own languages, and to establish their own educational institutions.

13. No technical, scientific or social investigations, including archaeological excavations, shall take place in relation to indigenous nations or peoples, or their lands, without their prior authorization, and their continuing ownership and control.

14. The religious practices of the indigenous nations and peoples shall be fully respected and protected by the laws of States and by international law. Indigenous nations and peoples shall always enjoy unrestricted access to, and enjoyment of, sacred sites in accordance with their own laws and customs, including the right of privacy.

15. Indigenous nations and peoples are subjects of international law.

16. Treaties and other agreements freely made with indigenous nations or peoples shall be recognized and applied in the same manner and according to the same international laws and principles as treaties and agreements entered into with other States.

17. Disputes regarding the jurisdiction, territories and institutions of an indigenous nation or people are a proper concern of international law, and must be resolved by mutual agreement or valid treaty.

18. Indigenous nations and peoples may engage in self-defence against State actions in conflict with their right to self-determination.

19. Indigenous nations and peoples have the right freely to travel, and to maintain economic, social, cultural and religious relations with each other across State borders.

20. In addition to these rights, indigenous nations and peoples are entitled to the enjoyment of all the human rights and fundamental freedoms enumerated in the International Bill of Human Rights and other United Nations instruments. In no circumstances shall they be subjected to adverse discrimination. (reprinted in Burger 1987:271–73)

The International Indian Treaty Council and its allied indigenous organizations presented these international twenty points to the United Nations Working Group on Indigenous Populations for consideration in its effort toward developing the Declaration of the Rights of Indigenous Peoples.

The Mohawk Nation and the Fourth Russell Tribunal

The Mohawk Nation presented a claim before the Fourth Russell Tribunal in 1980 that the United States denied the Mohawk Nation their right to their homeland on the basis of a fraudulent treaty and that the State of New York imposes an alien government on the Mohawk peoples. The Mohawk Nation argued that treaties between the Haudenosaunee and the English guaranteed Haudenosaunee territories and that these guarantees were repeated in the 1784 Treaty of Fort Stanwix between the Haudenosaunee and the United States.

The Mohawk Nation claimed that no treaty-guaranteed territories were ever ceded. The State of New York, however, claimed title to and sovereignty over most of Mohawk land based on a 1797 treaty signed by representatives of the State of New York and two individuals claiming to represent the Mohawk Nation. The Mohawk claim put forth that neither individual was a Mohawk chief or a member of the Grand Council of the League of the Iroquois. Since Mohawk land is possessed communally, it cannot be sold by individuals. Consequently, neither individual possessed the authority to act on behalf of the Mohawk Nation or the individual right to sell Mohawk land.

Furthermore, the State of New York, with the support of the U.S. government, created through legislation the St. Regis Tribal Council that governed

Mohawk people and land. The Mohawk Nation argued that neither the traditional Mohawk government nor the Mohawk people were consulted about or consented to this arrangement. The nation contended that there is no basis in Mohawk law for the authority of a such a tribal council or for the police force that the St. Regis Tribal Council created and that both interfered with the traditional government and the rights and property of the Mohawk people. Mohawk people were under indictment in New York courts for refusing to submit to the illegally imposed authority of the Tribal Council, and the State of New York used and threatened to use armed force to arrest Mohawk people and remove them from their own territory if they refused to submit to the authority of the Tribal Council.

The Fourth Russell Tribunal found in favor of the Mohawk Nation, citing violations of the United Nations Charter, the Declaration of Human Rights, the right of peoples to self-determination, treaties entered into by the U.S. with the Mohawk Nation, and the American Convention of Human Rights. Further Mohawk Nation negotiations with New York state courts that same year resulted in the lifting of indictments and the dismissal of all charges against traditional Mohawks. Later, a traditional Mohawk was elected as a trustee, and the tribal police were disbanded (Ismaellilo and Wright 1982:119).

Chapter Four

INDIGENOUS RIGHTS IN

INTERNATIONAL LAW

✦ In 1969 journalist Norman Lewis focused the world's attention for one significant moment on the destruction of the indigenous peoples of the Brazilian Amazon in his renowned *Sunday Times Magazine* article "Genocide: From Fire and Sword to Arsenic and Bullets—Civilisation Has Sent Six Million Indians to Extinction." The Indian Protection Service, the Brazilian government's special agency charged with the protection of indigenous peoples, had recently been exposed by the ruling military regime for its direct participation in the Indians' extermination. In Lewis's words, the Brazilian minister of the interior announced that the Indian Protection Service, "had been converted into an instrument for the Indians' oppression, and had therefore been dissolved" (Lewis 1969:41). The United Nations Commission on Human Rights accused the Brazilian government of complicity in the massacres. In response to the United Nations, Brazil launched a judicial inquiry into the conduct of 134 functionaries of the service, and the Brazilian attorney general stated informally that perhaps not even ten of the service's one thousand employees would be fully cleared of guilt (Lewis 1969:34–41).

The government's official report describes the atrocities in a matter-of-fact manner. Lewis summarizes: "Pioneers leagued with corrupt politicians had continually usurped Indian lands, destroyed whole tribes in a cruel struggle in which bacteriological warfare had been employed, by issuing clothing impregnated with the virus of smallpox, and by poisoned food supplies. Children had been abducted and mass murder gone unpunished" (Lewis 1969:41). The Brazilian attorney general estimated that property valued at $62 million or more had been stolen from the Indians in the previous ten years, and said that the Indian Protection Service had been "for years a den of corruption and indiscriminate killings."

In his article Lewis explores the odious history of Portuguese and Brazilian contact and relations with the indigenous people. Drawing on the works of Las Casas and Lévi-Strauss, he briefly chronicles the scandalous and murderous acts of the Peruvian Amazon Company, other rubber companies, and diamond miners. He interviews employees of the government and of the *fazendeiros,* the great landowners who are anachronistic despots of virtual fiefdoms. Lewis sketches the histories and near-extinction of several Brazilian Indian tribes, including Lévi-Strauss's Bororo, and introduces the unprecedented efforts of the Vilas Boas brothers, Brazilian anthropologists who were instrumental in the creation of the great Xingú National Park for the preservation of indigenous cultures, a park that by 1969 had already been invaded by roads and miners. The Indian Protection Service was for the most part merely a tool of the *fazendeiros,* Protestant missionaries, land-hungry settlers, all of whom engage in pointless cruelty toward the Indians. "Officially it is the Indian Protection Service and 134 of its agents that are on trial, but from all these reports the features of a more sinister personality soon emerge, the fazendeiro, . . . and in his shadow the IPS agent shrinks to a subservient figure, too often corrupted by bribes" (Lewis 1969:45). Lewis describes vast societal machinations aimed toward the destruction of the indigenous inhabitants and the confiscation of their land; the government agency charged with the protection of indigenous peoples was an instrument furthering that result. The Brazilian government's exposé, Lewis's article, and the international outcry and protest spurred United Nations–sponsored investigations into the conditions of indigenous peoples worldwide.

INDIGENOUS PEOPLES AND THE UNITED NATIONS

In 1969 Special Rapporteur Hernán Santa Cruz submitted the preliminary report of the Special Study on Racial Discrimination in the Political, Economic, Social, and Cultural Spheres to the Sub-Commission on the Prevention of Discrimination and Protection of Minorities. The final report was complete in 1971. Santa Cruz devoted a chapter to "measures taken in connection with the protection of indigenous peoples." He concluded that because information on specific policies was generally not available to him, an appropriate agency of the United Nations should conduct a comprehensive study that would identify the forms of discrimination faced by indigenous peoples and propose the national and international measures needed to resolve this discrimination (Alfredsson 1986:22; United Nations 1987:3).

Acting on the special rapporteur's proposal, the subcommission recommended in Resolution 4B(XXIII) of August 26, 1970, that the Commission on Human Rights authorize a comprehensive study. The Economic and Social Council, in Resolution 1589(L) of May 21, 1971, empowered the Sub-Commission on the Prevention of Discrimination and Protection of Minorities "to make a complete and comprehensive study of the problem of discrimination against indigenous populations and to suggest the necessary national and international measures for eliminating such discrimination, in co-operation with the other organs and bodies of the United Nations and with the competent international organizations. The subcommission, in Resolution 8(XXIV) of August 18, 1971, appointed José R. Martínez Cobo as special rapporteur to engage in the study. Canadian law professor and indigenous rights advocate Douglas Sanders notes that the subcommission's emphasis on its discrimination mandate was inadequate for the range of areas under investigation, but that this was preferable to emphasizing the protection-of-minorities mandate; "indigenous populations" would now be distinguished as a category separate from that of "minorities" (Sanders 1989a:407).

The Study of the Problem of Discrimination against Indigenous Populations took more than a decade to complete; it was finished in 1987 (Martínez Cobo 1986–1987). It covers international and national actions taken to protect indigenous populations; social issues, including indigenous health, education, employment, and housing; cultural issues, including the preservation of indigenous languages, religions, and cultures; and political issues, such as political rights, land rights, equality in the administration of justice and the availability of legal assistance, and the status of indigenous political and legal institutions. Sanders contends that Special Rapporteur Martínez Cobo's study is inaccessible, lengthy, and incomplete, and that because it was seriously outdated by the time of its completion, it generated less of an impact than was anticipated (Sanders 1989a:408), but the study does propose a constructive definition for the term *indigenous populations,* identifies various widespread forms of persistent discrimination against indigenous populations, and exposes the incapacity of international law to deal appropriately and successfully with the uniqueness of indigenous cultures and peoples. Martínez Cobo recommends that the study "be regarded as an appeal to the international community to take heed of the painful discrimination practised against indigenous peoples, one of the largest but weakest sectors of the world's population" (United Nations 1987:2).

Martínez Cobo's definition of *indigenous populations* is controversial, but it remains the definition of reference in the United Nations. According to Martínez Cobo, for the purpose of international action taken affecting their interests, indigenous populations may be defined as follows:

Indigenous communities, peoples and nations are those which, having a historical continuity with pre-invasion and pre-colonial societies that developed on their territories, consider themselves distinct from other sectors of the societies now prevailing in those territories, or parts of them. They form at present non-dominant sectors of society and are determined to preserve, develop and transmit to future generations their ancestral territories, and their ethnic identity, as the basis of their continued existence as peoples, in accordance with their own cultural patterns, social institutions and legal systems.

This historical continuity may consist of the continuation, for an extended period reaching into the present, of one or more of the following factors:

(a) Occupation of ancestral lands, or at least part of them;

(b) Common ancestry with the original occupants of these lands;

(c) Culture in general, or in specific manifestations (such as religion, living under a tribal system, membership of an indigenous community, dress, means of livelihood, life-style, etc.);

(d) Language (whether used as the only language, as mother-tongue, as the habitual means of communication at home or in the family, or as the main, preferred, habitual, general or normal language);

(e) residence in certain parts of the country, or in certain regions of the world;

(f) Other relevant factors.

On an individual basis, an indigenous person is one who belongs to these indigenous populations through self-identification as indigenous (group consciousness) and is recognized as one of its members (acceptance by the group).

This preserves for these communities the sovereign right and power to decide who belongs to them, without external interference. (United Nations 1987:29)

This definition of *indigenous populations* is controversial but insightful, and it remains the definition of reference in the United Nations. Martínez Cobo's working definition and his additional recommendations require that census statistics of indigenous populations take into account the subjective criteria for self-identification and membership and that the decision regarding membership belongs, as an exclusive and fundamental right, to the indigenous community. In other words, "No State may take, by legislation, regulations or other means, measures that interfere with the power of indigenous nations or groups to determine who are their members; . . . artificial, arbitrary or manipulatory definitions must . . . be rejected" (United Nations 1987:28–30).

Martínez Cobo gives particular attention to the uniqueness and diverse expressions of indigenous cultures, and his assessment of the relationship between indigenous peoples and the land is no less insightful than his working definition of *indigenous populations.* He concludes that to indigenous peoples land represents far more than a commodity or exploitable resource; in order to understand indigenous peoples, it is "essential to understand the special and profound spiritual relationship of indigenous peoples with Mother Earth as basic to their existence and to all their beliefs, customs, traditions and culture" (United Nations 1987:39). When their territories, which they have sometimes occupied for thousands of years, have been illegally taken from them, they experience an overwhelming sense of deprivation, and, in the words of the special rapporteur, "no one should be permitted to destroy that bond" (United Nations 1987:39).

Martínez Cobo calls for an immediate end to the systematic violation of indigenous peoples' rights to the land and its natural resources. He declares their natural and inalienable right to their territories; their right to freely use the land in their possession, including exclusive right to all natural resources therein; and a right to demand the return of land of which they have been unjustly deprived. "Millenary and immemorial possession" is appropriate to constitute legal indigenous title to land. National and international guarantees specifically providing for these rights should be enacted and implemented. States should immediately recognize inviolable indigenous ownership of land, assign to indigenous peoples all public land of sacred and religious significance, and permit and protect indigenous access to such historical sites that are on private land. All illegal acquisitions of indigenous land should be immediately pronounced null and void *ab initio,* and no rights should be vested in subsequent purchasers of such land. Indigenous peoples should be compensated for all indigenous lands and designated reserves that have been taken from them. Furthermore, the state should not unilaterally terminate or extinguish the right of indigenous possession of land or natural resources (United Nations 1987:39–40).

Special Rapporteur Martínez Cobo goes farther by declaring the necessity of recognizing indigenous communal or collective rights:

> There should be international and national recognition and full protection by law of the right of indigenous populations to own their land communally and to manage it in accordance with their own traditions and culture. The natural resources of indigenous land are entirely the property of the indigenous communities.
>
> In the case of communities whose ecological equilibrium has not been destroyed, the territory they occupy should be recognized as their property.

> Where ecological equilibrium has been destroyed, the communities should be offered new opportunities for activities compatible with the respect due to their cultural identity. Plans should be made to rescue communities in such a situation, without ignoring their right to their ancestral land; existing reserves should be maintained, protected and extended and new territories should be given to indigenous communities which lack, or have insufficient, land. (United Nations 1987:40–41)

International law of human rights, including law that pertains to minority rights, provides for individual rights and freedoms. It does not promote or protect the collective rights that the special rapporteur finds so fundamental to the rights and freedoms of indigenous peoples.

Martínez Cobo suggests that the subcommission recommend the ratification and strict enforcement of a number of international conventions for the protection of human rights, such as the Slavery Convention (1926), the Convention on the Prevention and Punishment of the Crime of Genocide (1948), the Convention against Discrimination in Education (1960), the International Convention on the Elimination of All Forms of Racial Discrimination (1965), the International Covenant on Civil and Political Rights (1966), the International Covenant on Economic, Social, and Cultural Rights (1966), and the American Convention on Human Rights (1969). He finds that the existing international law of human rights and fundamental freedoms has clearly not been fully implemented and respected in all countries.

Greater adherence to the rights and duties provided for in these and other United Nations conventions and declarations would substantially improve the indigenous situation, but Martínez Cobo also concludes:

> It is . . . clear that the provisions contained in the instruments in question are not wholly adequate for the recognition and protection of specific rights of indigenous populations as such within the overall societies in which they now live.
>
> It is essential, therefore, that all the consequences of existing provisions should be made clear, together with the measures entailed in ensuring effective observance of the rights recognized in them, as well as the additional provisions which would have to be formulated and observed. In the view of the Special Rapporteur, specific principles should be formulated for use as guidelines by Governments of all States in their activities concerning indigenous populations, on the basis of ethnic identity of such populations and for the rights and freedoms to which they are entitled. (United Nations 1987:45)

The special rapporteur explains that his own study offers numerous observations and recommendations that form the basis of implicit principles, and in some cases explicit principles, from which a declaration and a convention on the rights of indigenous peoples could proceed.

THE STATUS OF INDIGENOUS PEOPLES UNDER POSITIVE INTERNATIONAL LAW

Federal Indian law in the United States developed out of the Law of Nations and the international protocol established by the British, French, and Spanish colonial powers. The origins of modern international law on indigenous peoples, on the other hand, are to be found largely in the domestic law of the former European colonies. International legal reasoning and three early-twentieth-century international arbitration cases addressing the rights and status of indigenous peoples exhibit the prevailing Social Darwinist and statist ideological convictions that were the cornerstones of the pacification, dispossession, domestication, and extermination of indigenous nations in the Americas, Oceania, Africa, the Middle East, and Asia.

The declaration of the Berlin Africa Conference of 1884–1885, during which European colonial powers effectively divided up Africa among themselves, defined the "aboriginal tribes" as "wards of the State," toward whom, in recognition of the sovereignty of those colonial powers, the states held legal and financial obligations (Sanders 1983:17). These paternalistic themes of protection of aboriginal populations, just treatment, and trusteeship were further developed by the Institute of International Law in 1888, in Alpheus Snow's *The Question of Aborigines in the Law and Practice of Nations* (1921), and in Articles 22 and 23(b) of the Covenant of the League of Nations (Sanders 1983:18).

The late 1800s and early 1900s witnessed the near-complete transformation of international law from the natural law of the Law of Nations to the positive law of the family of nations, which "ensured that international law would become a legitimizing force for colonization and empire rather than a liberating one for indigenous peoples" (Anaya 1990:204). According to Native American law professor and indigenous rights advocate S. James Anaya, in contradistinction to natural law, positive law concerns the rights and duties of states exclusively; it upholds the extreme sovereignty of states and the equality of those states; and it is a law between states as specifically revealed in treaties and agreements, rather than a law that transcends states and written documents. Those states that create international legal rights and duties constitute a limited domain that excludes indigenous peoples and other political entities that are based on non-European political and legal principles (Anaya 1990:204–5). These characteristics of positive law receive perhaps their most thorough early rationalization in British publicist John Westlake's *Chapters on the Principles of International Law* (1894). Emphasizing the superiority of civilization over savagery, Westlake contends that the white races will inevitably expand in their utilization of natural resources, that civilized government must preside over the territories of expansion, and that people indigenous to those territories should be treated as uncivilized: "It does not mean that all rights are denied to such natives, but that the appreciation of their rights is left to the conscience of the state within whose recognized territorial sovereignty they are comprised, the rules of the international society existing only for the purposes of regulating the mutual conduct of its members" (Westlake, quoted in Anaya 1990:206). The governing of indigenous peoples, by this formulation, is the sole responsibility of the state in which they are found.

Later legal theorists dropped the necessity of rationalizing the exclusion of indigenous peoples from international law. William Edward Hall, in *A Treatise on International Law* (1924), for example, contends that the exclusion of indigenous peoples from international law is necessary because international law developed from and applies only to European states, other cultures being unable to understand or appreciate that law. The European jurist Lassa Oppenheim, in *International Law* (1920), argues essentially that indigenous peoples were excluded as subjects of international law because the subjects of international law did not include them; the Law of Nations, reasons Oppenheim, could not apply to "organized wandering tribes." The American jurist Charles Hyde, in *International Law Chiefly as Interpreted and Applied by the United States* (1922), simply asserts that "at the time of European explorations in the Western Hemisphere in the fifteenth and sixteenth centuries . . . States were agreed that the native inhabitants possessed no rights of territorial control which the European explorer or his monarch was bound to respect," and in the United States, "the American Indians have never been regarded as constituting persons or States of international law." Moreover, Hyde continues, "if inhabitants of the territory concerned are an uncivilised people, deemed incapable of possessing a right of property and control, the conqueror may, in fact, choose to ignore their title, and proceed to occupy the land as though it were vacant" (Hyde, quoted in Anaya 1990:208–9). As to the universal impact of international legal positivism on the rights of indigenous peoples, Anaya concludes that

> The revisionism of the positivists was necessary . . . in order to maintain a semblance of coherence in their vision of international law as law made *by* states and *for* states, exclusive of indigenous peoples and their rights.
>
> . . . For international law purposes, indigenous lands prior to any colonial presence were considered legally unoccupied and accordingly cloaked in the legal jargon of *terra nullius* (vacant lands). Under this fiction, discovery could be employed as a means of upholding colonial claims to indigenous lands and bypassing any claim to possession by the natives in the "discovered" lands. In order to acquire indigenous lands, there was no longer any need to pretend conquest where war had not been waged, or to rely on the rules of war where it had. Likewise, the treaties with American tribes and other indigenous peoples could simply be ignored. (Anaya 1990:209–10)

These principles were then codified in international case law concerning indigenous peoples. In 1928 the *Cayuga Indians* case was brought before the Anglo–United States Arbitral Tribunal to determine the obligations of the United States to the Cayuga Indians living in Canada. The Cayuga had entered into treaties with the State of New York in 1789, 1795, and 1807, but then the Cayuga nation had split into three parts. One part remained in New York, another moved to Canada under the jurisdiction of Great Britain, and a third moved to Oklahoma. The British sought to enforce New York's treaty obligations to the Canadian Cayuga nation. The court ruled that Great Britain could not assert a claim for the "Cayuga Nation" which, the court stated, is an Indian tribe and therefore not a legal unit of international law because the American Indian tribes were never regarded as such. The Indian tribes have been regarded from the time of discovery "as under the exclusive protection of the power which by discovery or conquest or cession held the land which they occupied," and consequently the Cayuga in New York exist as a legal unit under New York law, while the Cayuga in Canada exist only as individuals under British law (Green 1989:84–85). Anaya notes that the court relied on Hyde, among other thinkers, for their position that American Indians never possessed international status; Hyde would later use the *Cayuga Indians* case to support the same position in the second edition of his own work (Anaya 1990:210).

In 1928 the Permanent Court of Arbitration decided the *Islands of Palmas* case, a dispute between the United States and the Netherlands over jurisdiction of an island in the former Dutch East Indies. The United States claimed sovereignty over the island through Spanish discovery and subsequent succession via U.S. conquest of Spain in the Philippines through the Treaty of Paris (1898). The Netherlands based their claim to sovereignty on possession and exercise of the rights of sovereignty beginning with the arrival of the East India Company in 1677, and even earlier in 1648, and continuously demonstrated by the Netherlands through the present. The Netherlands also introduced as part of their central argument the existence of treaties or conventions entered into between the East India Company and two native chiefs representing the indigenous inhabitants. According to the court the treaties and conventions were irrelevant to the case: "Contracts between a State . . . and native princes or chiefs not recognized as members of the community of nations . . . are not, in the international law sense, treaties or conventions capable of creating rights and obligations." Still the court ruled in favor of the Netherlands; that country's effective occupation and demonstration of sovereignty prevailed over the U.S. claim of sovereignty by discovery.

In 1933 the Permanent Court of International Justice decided the *Legal Status of Eastern Greenland* case, in which both Norway and Denmark claimed sovereignty over an uncolonized portion of Greenland. Norway argued that the portion of Greenland in question was *terra nullius,* and that through occupation and a 1931 proclamation Norway had established its sovereignty. Denmark argued that it had maintained and peacefully displayed state sovereignty over all of Greenland for a considerable time prior to and up to the time of Norwegian occupation. The court considered neither the presence of indigenous Inuit people in the area, nor the fact that the Inuit had militarily driven the Norwegian settlers out of the region, which might have given the Inuit sovereignty by conquest. The court held that a territory occupied by "backwards" people was considered *terra nullius,* but that in this case Denmark's demonstration of sovereignty prevailed.

Through these three cases international law endorsed the sovereignty of the colonizer over the colonized and the domestication, or de-internationalization, of indigenous peoples. There were apparent exceptions to doctrine of absolute state sovereignty during this period of European colonialism. One is the League of Nations' 1926 adoption of the Slavery Convention, which entered into force in 1927. The Slavery Convention allows one state party to the convention to lodge a complaint for arbitration with the Permanent Court of International Justice against another state party believed to be in violation of the prohibition against slavery. In spite of these apparent limitations on absolute sovereignty, because indigenous peoples have no status in international law, and because they are entirely encapsulated in aggressively expansionist states, they have no recourse but to the laws and courts of the colonizer. It is no wonder that until quite recently the destructive forces confronted by indigenous peoples worldwide have been accepted, at least until recently, as the status quo.

HUMAN RIGHTS IN CONTEMPORARY INTERNATIONAL LAW

Not until northern Europeans themselves were colonized and twentieth-century weapons of mass destruction fully exposed the true face of colonialism did the family of nations begin to amend the European state-centered, noninterventionist, positive international law regime. With the establishment of the United Nations, new concepts and ideals achieved prominent status in international legal discourse: self-determination, decolonization, the protection of human dignity, and the preservation of world peace. These came to the fore beginning with the completion of the Charter of the United Nations (1945), the Declaration Regarding Non-Self-Governing Territories (1945), and the Universal Declaration of Human Rights (1948).

The United Nations as an Assembly of States

The Charter of the United Nations (1945), which requires the signature of all United Nations member states, opens with the following words in its preamble "WE THE PEOPLES OF THE UNITED NATIONS DETERMINED to save succeeding generations from the scourge of war, . . . and to reaffirm faith in fundamental human rights, in the dignity and worth of the person, in the equal rights of men and women and of nations large and small . . . HAVE RESOLVED TO COMBINE OUR EFFORTS TO ACCOMPLISH THESE AIMS." The central purposes of the United Nations are, in addition to the preservation of international peace and security (Chapter 1, Article 1.1), "to develop friendly relations among nations based on respect for the principle of equal rights and self-determination of peoples, and to take other appropriate measures to strengthen universal peace" (Chapter 1, Article 1.3), and "to achieve international co-operation in solving international problems of an economic, social, cultural, or humanitarian character, and in promoting and encouraging respect for human rights and for fundamental freedoms for all without distinction according as to race, sex, language, or religion" (Chapter 1, Article 1.3). In Chapter 9, Article 55, the member states are once again called upon to respect the principles of equal rights, self-determination of peoples, and universal respect for and observance of human rights and fundamental freedoms for all.

Membership in the United Nations, however, is expressly limited to states, and Chapter 1, Article 2(7) states: "Nothing in the present Charter shall authorize the United Nations to intervene in matters which are essentially within the domestic jurisdiction of any state or shall require the Members to submit such matters to settlement under the present Charter." The exceptions to this principle of territorial integrity and noninterference, found in Chapter 7, include international acts of aggression and threats to international peace. The charter does, however, recognize the importance of decolonization in Chapter 11, the Declaration Regarding Non-Self-Governing Territories. Member states that administer non-self-governing territories—territories whose peoples have not attained self-government—must regard as paramount both the interests of those inhabitants and their own obligation as administering states to promote the well-being of the non-self-governing peoples. This includes respect for the peoples' culture and sociopolitical systems and the development of self-government, taking into account the aspirations of the peoples.

The United Nations system operates through six branches: the General Assembly, the Security Council, the Secretariat, the Economic and Social Council, the Trusteeship Council, and the International Court of Justice. The General Assembly is the assemblage of representatives of all member states. Among its duties are encouraging the progressive development and the codification of international law and assisting in the realization of human rights and fundamental freedoms. The General Assembly fulfills these mandates in part through its resolutions and declarations on principles of international law. These resolutions and declarations are technically nonbinding, but they often carry the moral force of law.

The decisions of the Security Council do carry the force of law. The council is a committee of fifteen members, five of which have permanent veto power: France, Russia, China, Great Britain, and the United States. Under Chapter 7 of the charter, the Security Council possesses the authority to impose sanctions and, when necessary, to use military force.

The Secretariat (office of the secretary general) (Chapter 15) attempts to influence member states to abide by the principles of the United Nations. The Trusteeship Council (Chapter 13) presided over the administration of non-self-governing territories following the fall of the Ottoman Empire in World War I and of the Axis powers in World War II; the last territory under its jurisdiction, Palau, gained independence in 1994.

The International Court of Justice is a world court. It is the principal judicial organization of the United Nations, and it authors advisory opinions upon the request of the Security Council or the General Assembly (Chapter 14). However, it is small, understaffed, under-utilized, and available only to member states. The court has no enforcement procedures for its decisions, but the decisions do have moral authority, and the Security Council may decide upon measures to enforce the court's decisions (Article 94[2]).

The Economic and Social Council (Chapter 10) focuses on international economic, social, cultural, educational, health, and related issues and may make recommendations to the General Assembly or other members or organs of the United Nations, including recommendations for the purpose of promoting respect for and observance of human rights and fundamental freedoms (Article 62). In addition, the Economic and Social Council may prepare draft conventions for submission to the General Assembly (Article 62[3]) and call for United Nations–sponsored international conferences (Article 62[4]) on issues falling under its mandate.

The Commission on Human Rights

In one of its earliest endeavors, the Economic and Social Council authorized its subsidiary organization, the Commission on Human Rights, to draft a convention on human rights. In 1948, without a dissenting vote, but with eight abstentions, the General Assembly adopted the Universal Declaration of Human Rights, which asserts in its preamble that "*Whereas* it is essential, if man is not to be compelled to have recourse, as a last resort, to rebellion against tyranny and oppression, that human rights should be protected by the rule of law," and its first article that "All human beings are born free and equal in dignity and rights." The rights in this declaration apply to every human being regardless of whether that person belongs to a state, a trust territory, or a non-self-governing territory. These rights include the right to life and liberty (Article 3); to recognition everywhere as a person before the law (Article 6); to effective remedy by a competent tribunal for violations of the rights granted by constitution or law (Article 8); to be free from slavery (Article 4), torture, cruel and inhuman punishment (Article 5), and arbitrary arrest and detention (Article 9); to own property alone or in association with others, and to not be arbitrarily deprived of that property (Article 17); to freedom of thought, conscience, and religion (Article 18); to freedom of opinion and expression (Article 19); to equal access to the state's public services (Article 21); to an adequate standard of living (Article 25); to an education directed to the full development of the human personality and to the strengthening of respect for human rights and fundamental freedoms, an education that promotes understanding, tolerance, and friendship among nations and among racial and religious groups (Article 26); and "to a social and international order in which the rights and freedoms set forth in this Declaration can be fully realized" (Article 28).

The legal status of the charter is not without controversy, but the charter does create legal obligations on member states to respect the human rights of their citizens and inhabitants. The legal status of covenants, protocols, and conventions make them legally binding on those states that agree to them through ratification or accession. The legal status of declarations, principles, guidelines, standard rules, and recommendations have no legally binding effect; however, depending on their recognition and acceptance, these instruments carry significant moral force, and because they are declaratory of accepted international legal principles, they are intended to guide the behavior of states.

The unanimously adopted Universal Declaration of Human Rights states in its preamble that it is "a common standard of achievement" to be attained through education, rather than a statement of existing law. However, it may be argued that resolutions interpreting the charter, expressing customary international law, and stating rules of law carry the legal weight of international treaties. An unofficial Assembly for Human Rights meeting in Montreal in 1968, the International Year of Human Rights, proclaimed that the "*Universal Declaration on Human Rights* constitutes an authoritative interpretation of the *Charter* of the highest order, and has over the years become a part of customary international law" (Henkin, Pugh, Schechter, and Smit 1987:987). Similarly, in the Proclamation of Teheran (1968), the official International Conference on Human Rights announced that the "Universal Declaration of Human Rights states a common understanding of the peoples of the world concerning inalienable and inviolable rights of all members of the human family and constitutes an obligation for the members of the international community."

The unanimously adopted 1963 Declaration on the Elimination of All Forms of Racial Discrimination recognizes that every state shall "fully and faithfully observe the provisions of . . . the Universal Declaration of Human Rights." The 1965 International Convention on the Elimination of All Forms of Racial Discrimination, which entered into force in 1969, declares that all forms of racial discrimination are illegal and that "racial discrimination shall mean any distinction, exclusion, restriction or preference based on race, colour, descent or national or ethnic origin which has the purpose or effect of nullifying or impairing the recognition, enjoyment or exercise, on an equal footing, of human rights and fundamental freedoms in the political, economic, social, cultural or any other field of public life" (Article 1[1]). All state parties are compelled to engage in efforts to eliminate all forms of discrimination and to promote understanding among all races (Article 1[1]). Apartheid and racial segregation are condemned as particularly reprehensible, and eradication of these practices is required (Article 3). Moreover, in Article 4, the states party to the declaration condemn "all propaganda and all organizations which are based on ideas or theories of superiority of one race or group of persons of one colour or ethnic origin, or which attempt to justify or promote racial hatred and discrimination in any form." They will "undertake to adopt immediate and positive measures designed to eradicate all incitement to, or acts of, such discrimination and, to this end, with due regard to the principles embodied in the Universal Declaration of Human Rights and the rights expressly set forth in Article 5 of this Convention." The rights set forth in Article 5 include equal treatment before tribunals; protection against bodily harm; political rights; civil rights; and economic, social, and cultural rights.

Part II of this convention establishes a Committee on the Elimination of Racial Discrimination, which examines alleged crimes of racial discrimination. Cases may be brought before the committee by a state party that believes that another state party has not implemented the provisions and protections required by the convention (Article 11). A state party may also authorize the committee to receive and consider communications from "individuals or groups of individuals" within the state party's jurisdiction who claim violations by that state party, but the committee cannot receive and consider communications from "individuals or groups of individuals" within state parties that have not so authorized (Article 14). The committee brings communications of violations to the attention of the state party without revealing the identity of the petitioners, although no anonymous complaints are considered (Article 14[6][a]), and complaints are considered only after all available domestic remedies have been exhausted (Article 14[7][a]). The committee presents its suggestions and recommendations, if any, to the state party and the petitioner (Article 14[7][b]).

The fundamental human rights presented in the declaration were clarified in subsequent legally binding international treaties and covenants. These treaties include most notably the International Convention on the Elimination of All Forms of Racial Discrimination (1965) and the three United Nations instruments that form the International Bill of Rights: the International Covenant on Civil and Political Rights (1966), the Optional

Protocol to the International Covenant on Civil and Political Rights (1967), and the International Covenant on Economic, Social, and Cultural Rights (1967). Each of these entered into force in 1976. Both covenants emphasize equality before the law and nondiscrimination on the basis of race, language, religion, or national or social origin. They declare the right of all peoples to self-determination, including the right to freely determine their political and cultural status, the obligation of states party to the covenants to promote the realization of the right to self-determination, and the right of peoples to their natural resources.

The Covenant on Civil and Political Rights emphasizes the right and opportunity of all peoples to take part in the conduct of public affairs (Article 23). Although indigenous peoples consistently insist that "minorities" is an inappropriate classification, Article 27 provides that "in those States in which ethnic, religious or linguistic minorities exist, persons belonging to such minorities shall not be denied the right, in community with other members of their groups, to enjoy their own culture, to profess and practice their own religion, or to use their own language." This and all but a handful of the human rights provided for in this covenant may be voided in times of a "public emergency which threatens the life of the nation and the existence of which it is officially proclaimed," provided that measures taken are not inconsistent with other obligations in international law and do not discriminate solely on the basis of race, color, sex, language, or religion (Article 4). Although the Covenant on Civil and Political Rights declares the right to life, it allows the death penalty for serious crimes, but prohibits this penalty if the enactment of it violates the Genocide Convention (Article 6). Also prohibited are torture and cruel and inhuman punishment (Article 7), slavery and servitude (Article 8[1] and [2]), imprisonment for unfulfilled contractual obligations (Article 11), and imprisonment for an act that was not illegal at the time it was committed (Article 15). The covenant also endorses the right to recognition as a person before the law (Article 17) and the right to freedom of thought, conscience, and religion (Article 18). Although the Covenant on Civil and Political Rights protects some rights of individuals belonging to minority groups, and the Covenant on Economic, Social, and Cultural Rights provides some protection for trade unions, the principal object of international human rights law from the declaration through the covenants remains the individual.

Part IV of the Covenant on Civil and Political Rights establishes a process for the redress of grievances through the Committee of Human Rights. The committee maintains three basic functions. The first two are outlined in Article 41 of the covenant: to examine state reports on compliance with the covenant, and to examine state complaints about another state's treaty violations. The third function is set forth in the Optional Protocol to the International Covenant on Civil and Political Rights: to examine an individual's complaints of a state's treaty violations if the state has signed both the convention and the protocol, but only after the exhaustion of available domestic remedies. The committee forwards its opinions to the state party concerned and to the individual (Higgins 1992).

Limits of International Human Rights Law for Indigenous Peoples

Since 1981 there have been several attempts by indigenous peoples, primarily from Canada, to utilize the Committee on Human Rights for the redress of alleged human rights violations covered by the Covenant on Civil and Political Rights. Leonard Peltier's communication alleging violation of Article 7 was dismissed on the grounds that the allegations were not established (Sanders 1989a:421). In *Lovelace v. Canada* (1981), Sandra Lovelace, a Canadian Indian, claimed that the Canadian Indian Act (1869) discriminated against her on the basis of her gender by depriving her of legal access to her Indian community. The committee found that the Canadian Indian Act violated Article 27 of the covenant, and consequently Canada amended the act in 1985 (Turpel 1992:583). In *Kitok v. Sweden* (1988), Ivan Kitok, an indigenous Sami, challenged his deprivation under Swedish law of participating in traditional reindeer breeding because he had taken a second job. Sweden took its position due to environmental concerns. The Sami village, which under the law could have restored Kitok's rights, endorsed the Swedish position; Kitok unsuccessfully appealed. The Committee on Human Rights examined an alleged violation of Article 27, but found the exclusion under Swedish law to be legitimate and nondiscriminatory because it has "a reasonable and objective justification" and is "necessary for the continued viability and welfare of the minority as a whole" (quoted in Sanders 1989a:422).

The committee is obviously prepared to act on behalf of individual rights, but it has ruled elsewhere that it does not possess the authority to determine collective claims of a people's right to self-determination, despite the fact that in Article 1 the covenant expressly provides for those rights (Barsh 1993b:217). In *Bernard Ominayak, Chief of the Lubicon Lake Band v. Canada* (1990), Ominayak brought an unresolved land claim before the committee. Canada was found to be in violation of the covenant, but it had already taken action to improve the situation (Churchill 1993:217–58; Turpel 1992:583). The committee denied Chief Ominayak's attempt to bring an individual claim as a victim of an alleged violation of a people's right to self-determination, even though it is a right that the covenant does "recognize and respect in most resolute terms" (quoted in Turpel 1992:586; Barsh 1994:80). Self-determination, argued the committee, is a right conferred upon peoples, not individuals, and the committee lacks the authority to determine cases involving collective rights (Barsh 1993b:217).

In *Mikmaq Tribal Society v. Canada* (1991), three members of the traditional Mikmaq tribal council submitted a communication to the committee alleging that they were individual victims and the Mikmaq tribe was a victim of violations of the right of peoples to self-determination (in Article 1 of the covenant). The Mikmaq, an indigenous people occupying territories in eastern Canada, are governed by a grand council that constitutes a political alliance of seven Mikmaq territorial districts. The Mikmaq offered historical support for their claim to the right to be recognized as "peoples" under international law:

1. Mikmakik (the Mikmaq homelands) had long been recognized as an independent, federal state through the negotiation of Crown treaties and alliances with its national council, the Sante'Mawi'omi or Grand Council.

2. In addition to commercial and defensive arrangements with France and the United Kingdom extending over two centuries, Mikmakik received Catholicism under concordat with the Holy See.

3. Mikmakik was the first state to recognize the independence of the United States of America under a military-assistance treaty of 1776.

4. A Halifax Treaty of Peace and Friendship of 1752, while acknowledging the Mikmaq as British subjects for certain purposes, confirmed the separate national identity and rights of hunting, fishing and trading of the Mikmaq throughout what was then Nova Scotia. (*Mikmaq Communication*, in Turpel 1992:587)

The Mikmaq claim centered on Article 37(1) of the Canadian Constitution Act of 1982, which involves the participation of aboriginal peoples of Canada in discussions on the future constitutional relations between Canada and the aboriginal peoples. Canada refused to invite Mikmaq representatives, despite specific written requests, on the grounds that the four aboriginal organizations invited, the Assembly of First Nations representing "status Indians," the Native Council of Canada representing nonstatus people, the Metis National Council, and the Inuit Committee on National Issues, effectively represented all of Canada's aboriginal populations. The Mikmaq Tribal Society regarded this position as racist and contended that the premise of the government was that "any members of the 'Indian' race can exercise the Mikmaq people's right to self-determination" (*Mikmaq Communication*, in Turpel 1992:585).

In response to Canada's submission to the committee that the Mikmaq do not constitute a people under current international law, the Mikmaq submitted a complaint alleging violation of Article 25(a) of the Covenant on Civil and Political Rights, which affirms the right of citizens "to take part in public affairs, either directly or through freely chosen representatives." The Mikmaq discussed the critical differences between the two legal positions:

> It is likewise important to distinguish self-determination from the right of popular participation found in Article 25 of the Covenant. Self-determination is a people's choice of a state and a framework of government, and for this reason has been described as an essential condition or prerequisite, although not necessarily excluding other conditions, for the genuine existence of the other human rights and freedoms enumerated in the Covenant. Popular participation is the right of individuals, subsequent to the exercise of self-determination, to participate freely and effectively in the state and form of government chosen. (*Mikmaq Communication,* in Turpel 1992:591–92)

The contrast is crucial for indigenous peoples, whose existence as distinct cultural and political entities can not always be adequately represented or safeguarded within the individualistic European tradition of "one person, one vote."

In its admissibility hearing the Committee on Human Rights refused to consider the Mikmaq complaint on violations of Article 1, noting that although the Optional Protocol does resolutely guarantee a people's right to self-determination, neither individuals nor peoples can invoke this article under the Optional Protocol procedure (Turpel 1992:589). The committee did agree to consider the alleged violation of Article 25(a), but decided that Canada did not violate this article. The committee explained that "article 25(a) of the Covenant cannot be understood as meaning that any directly affected group, large or small, has the unconditional right to choose the modalities of participation in the conduct of public affairs. That, in fact, would be an extrapolation of the right to direct participation by the citizens, far beyond the scope of article 25(a)" (*Mikmaq Tribal Society v. Canada,* in Turpel 1992:596). The committee essentially defined Article 25 and the Covenant as culturally exclusive rather than universal (Turpel 1992:594–95) and ignored International Labor Convention No. 169, which identifies indigenous peoples as possessing a legal identity superior to that of an "interest group," such as a minority group or a trade union (Barsh 1994:80). Native American professor of law and indigenous rights advocate Mary Ellen Turpel contends that the decision in the *Mikmaq* case indicates "that the Human Rights Committee and the United Nations is now out of touch with the struggles of indigenous peoples in Canada, and illustrates the insensitivity of these bodies to the political context of indigenous peoples' situations" (Turpel 1992:601). The door to indigenous peoples' official legal appeals for decolonization and complaints of violations of the right to self-determination appears with this decision to be effectively closed, both domestically and internationally.

Additional international instruments have clarified or expanded various aspects of human rights that have some relevance to indigenous peoples. At the request of the Sub-Commission on the Prevention of Discrimination and Protection of Minorities, the United Nations Educational, Scientific and Cultural Organization (UNESCO) drafted and adopted the Convention Against Discrimination in Education (1960), which entered into force in 1962. This convention prohibits the establishment of separate educational systems based on race or religion, but provides that members of national minorities possess the right to carry on their own educational activities and that education in general shall promote understanding, tolerance, and friendship among nations and respect for human rights and fundamental freedoms. UNESCO's Declaration on Race and Racial Prejudice (1978) proclaims in Article 2 that "any theory which involves the claim that racial or ethnic groups are inherently superior or inferior, thus implying that some would be entitled to dominate or eliminate others, presumed to be inferior, or which bases value judgements on racial differentiation, has no scientific foundation and is contrary to the moral and ethical principles of humanity." The United Nations Convention Against Torture and Other Cruel, Inhuman or Degrading Treatment or Punishment (1984), which entered into force in 1987, provides in Part II for the establishment of a Committee Against Torture that functions similarly to the Committee on Human Rights. The Convention Relating to the Status of Refugees (1954), which entered into force in 1960; the Declaration on Territorial Asylum (1967); the Declaration on the Elimination of All Forms of Intolerance and Discrimination Based on Religion and Belief (1981); the Convention on the Elimination of All Forms of Discrimination Against Women (1979), which entered into force in 1981; the Convention of the Rights of the Child (1989), which entered into force in 1990; and the Declaration on the Protection of All Persons from Enforced Disappearance (1992) promote protection against numerous social and political acts and conditions commonly faced by indigenous peoples.

The United Nations Declaration on the Rights of Persons Belonging to National or Ethnic, Religious and Linguistic Minorities (1992) promotes, in its preamble, the realization of principles professed in all previous human rights instruments, and it specifically urges states to protect the existence and identity of minorities within their territorial jurisdiction (Article 1) in addition to all other human rights and fundamental freedoms of individuals and individuals in association with others. States must take measures to create conditions favorable for minorities to express and develop their cultural, linguistic, and religious identities, except where those expressions are in violation of national law or contrary to international standards (Article 4). Barsh explains that "proposals to include the rights of geographically distinct groups to local autonomy, self-development, and demographic integrity were lost in the negotiations" and that the declaration's guarantee of effective participation in the political process (Article 2[3]), like the Covenant on Civil and Political Rights, disregards minorities' status as "legal entities with collective political rights" (Barsh 1994:79). Barsh contends that this Declaration indicates an expanding resistance to the appeals of indigenous peoples in the General Assembly.

THE INTERNATIONAL CRIMES OF GENOCIDE AND APARTHEID

Hurst Hannum, a leading American scholar of international law, contends that genocide is the context in which the existential situation of indigenous peoples, in every part of the world, must first be understood (Hannum 1988:649). States and state populations, in attempting to resolve the "indigenous problem," have consistently resorted to political, legal, military, and paramilitary strategies constituting genocide. In Article 1 of the Convention on the Prevention and Punishment of the Crime of Genocide (1948), contracting parties define genocide, whether committed in times of war or peace, as an international crime that they agree to prevent and punish. In Article 2, genocide is defined as follows:

> In the present Convention, genocide means any of the following acts committed with *intent* to destroy, in whole or in part, a national, ethnical, racial or religious group as such:
>
> (a) Killing members of the group;
>
> (b) Causing serious bodily or mental harm to members of the group;
>
> (c) Deliberately inflicting on the group conditions of life *calculated* to bring about its physical destruction in whole or in part;
>
> (d) Imposing measures to prevent births within the group;
>
> (e) Forcibly transferring children of the group to another group.

Article 3 specifies the acts that shall be punishable under this convention: genocide, conspiracy to commit genocide, direct and public incitement to commit genocide, attempt to commit genocide, and complicity in genocide.

All persons committing acts of genocide, whether public officials or private individuals, shall be punished (Article 4). Persons charged with genocide will be brought before a competent national tribunal of the state in which the act was committed or before an international penal tribunal that has jurisdiction (Article 6). Competent organs of the United Nations, upon request by a contracting party, may take appropriate action under the terms of the charter to prevent and suppress acts of genocide (Article 8), and the International Court of Justice shall resolve disputes between contracting parties concerning the interpretation, fulfillment, or application of the convention (Article 9).

Professor of law Rennard Strickland (1986) and Professor of Native American Studies and indigenous rights advocate Ward Churchill (1994), among others, poignantly characterize the systematic destruction of indigenous populations in the United States through legal, extra-legal, and illegal means as a classic case of genocide. Moreover, Strickland proposes that often those who considered themselves undeniable friends of the Indians were, in the end, unwittingly the Indians' worst enemies, imposing upon them inappropriate and alien laws and other vehicles of social engineering and social control, such as the Dawes Act, the Curtis Act, and the Indian Civil Rights Act of 1968.

Some American Indians claim that genocide has occurred recently or is now occurring in Paraguay (the Aché people), Brazil, the United States, Guatemala, and other countries (ICIHI 1987:84). Concerning Indian claims that assimilation policy constitutes genocide, and with particular reference to genocide in Guatemala, members of the Independent Commission on International Humanitarian Issues (ICIHI) pointedly ask:

> Are governments actively pursuing policies aimed at the eventual destruction of their indigenous populations? In some countries it is difficult to believe otherwise. In Guatemala both presidents Garcia Lucas and Ríos Montt characterized Indians as subversive and instructed the army to treat all indigenous communities as potential or active guerilla bases. . . . The Guatemalan Conference of Bishops estimated that more than one million people have been displaced by the violence, and a further 200,000 have fled across the borders into neighboring countries. The Inter-Church Committee on Latin America in January 1984 called these acts in Guatemala "the clearest example in Central America of genocide of indigenous peoples. Men, women, children and the elderly are tortured and murdered. Whole communities have been massacred." (ICIHI 1987:87)

Such acts committed against indigenous peoples are not limited to Guatemala, yet the international community has failed to forcefully apply its laws to these indigenous peoples and to their oppressors. Prior to the election of a civilian government in the 1990s that has attempted to curb human rights abuses, recruits into the Guatemalan army were taught that Indians are a subhuman species and were encouraged to abuse them (ICIHI 1987:89; Americas Watch 1983, 1984). Similar accounts come from Indonesia, Bangladesh, Australia, and elsewhere (ICIHI 1987:89–90). Until its recent application to the Bosnian conflict, the Genocide Convention had not been effectively utilized to prevent and suppress the deliberate destruction of indigenous or minority cultures. The General Assembly made attempts to declare genocide in Guatemala throughout the 1980s, only to have its resolutions defeated by the veto power of permanent members of the Security Council and their allies.

Apartheid is declared a second crime against humanity and a dangerous threat to international peace and security in the International Convention on the Suppression and Punishment of the Crime of Apartheid (1973), which entered into force in 1976. In it organizations, institutions, and individuals practicing apartheid are declared criminals (Article 1). According to Article 2, apartheid comprises all acts "committed for the purpose of establishing and maintaining domination by one racial group of persons over any other racial group of persons and systematically oppressing them." Entities that practice apartheid may follow policies of racial segregation and discrimination; deny members of a racial group the right to life and liberty; murder, inflict serious bodily or mental harm on, or arbitrarily arrest and illegally imprison members of a racial group; deliberately impose living conditions calculated to cause the physical destruction of the group in whole or in part; pursue legislative measures calculated to prevent a racial group from participating in the political, social, economic, and cultural life of the nation; deny members of the racial group the right to earn a living; create reserves or ghettos designed to separate populations; prohibit interracial marriage; and expropriate the property of, exploit the labor of, and otherwise persecute those who oppose apartheid (Article 2). International criminal responsibility applies to everyone who commits, participates in, directly incites, or conspires in the commission of the acts mentioned in Article 2 (Article 3). Persons charged with these acts will be tried by a competent tribunal of any state party to the convention or by an international penal tribunal that has jurisdiction (Article 4).

DECOLONIZATION AND THE PRINCIPLES OF INTERNATIONAL LAW

Algeria's war of national liberation against France in the late 1950s and early 1960s and other national liberation struggles waged against colonial powers throughout the twentieth century led directly to the General Assembly's Declaration on the Granting of Independence to Colonial Countries and Peoples (1960), which was adopted unanimously. In the preamble the General Assembly recognizes "the passionate yearning for freedom in all dependent peoples and the decisive role of such peoples in the attainment of their independence" and asserts that "the peoples of the world ardently desire the end of colonialism in all its manifestations." The General Assembly proclaims the beliefs that "the process of liberation is irresistible and irreversible" and that "all peoples have an inalienable right to complete freedom, the exercise of their sovereignty and the integrity of their national territory." It thus declares that states have the duty to "faithfully and strictly" observe the provisions of the United Nations charter and the Universal Declaration of Human Rights and that the "subjection of peoples to alien subjugation, domination and exploitation constitutes a denial of fundamental human rights and is contrary to the Charter of the United Nations and is an impediment to the promotion of world peace and cooperation" (Article 1).

The Declaration on the Granting of Independence affirms that all peoples have the right to self-determination and may freely determine their political status (Article 2), and it demands that all armed actions or other repressive measures taken against dependent peoples shall cease immediately in order that those peoples may establish their independence (Article 3). However, the declaration maintains the sanctity of the principle of territorial integrity (Article 6). Although declarations are not normally regarded as binding international law, the liberation and independence of formerly dependent and colonized peoples following the adoption of the declaration (United Nations 1980) and the General Assembly's 1961 creation of a special committee on decolonization indicate that the Declaration on the Granting of Independence has been generally accepted as binding international law, at least in customary practice.

Expressions of the international principles of nonintervention and territorial integrity include Article 2(7) of the Charter of the United Nations, which prohibits the United Nations from intervening in matters that are essentially within the domestic jurisdiction of a state, except as provided by Article 7 concerning situations regarded as acts of aggression or threats to international peace and security. The Declaration on the Inadmissibility of Intervention into the Domestic Affairs of States (1965) prohibits one state from intervening in the internal or external affairs of another state for any reason. A state may not organize, foment, finance, incite, or tolerate "subversive, terrorist or armed activities directed towards the violent overthrow of the régime of another State, or interfere within civil strife in another State." These prohibitions are understood in association with respect for the right to self-determination of peoples, for human rights and fundamental freedoms, and for the right of peoples to be free of foreign pressure (Article 6). This declaration recognizes that *every state* possesses an inalienable right to choose its political, economic, social, and cultural systems—rather than *all peoples,* as expressly recognized by the Declaration on the Granting of Independence to Colonial Countries and Peoples. This is a notable distinction.

The Declaration of Principles of International Law Concerning Friendly Relations among States in Accordance with the Charter of the United Nations (1970) was adopted by consensus as an accurate interpretation of the principles of the charter, and it was considered at that time to be the major legal achievement of the United Nations (Henkin, Pugh, Schechter, and Smit 1987:114). It develops and codifies seven major principles regulating international relations among states. These principles focus primarily on the prohibition of armed aggression and threats of force, the nonintervention of states into the internal or external affairs of other states, recognition of the sovereignty and equality of states, agreement among states to settle international disputes through peaceful means, and the duty of cooperation in accordance with the charter. The declaration also affirms the principle of equal rights and self-determination of peoples; the right of peoples to freely determine their political status without external interference; and the duty of every state to promote the realization of the self-determination of peoples, including the speedy end of colonialism. It reaffirms principles that the subjection of peoples to alien subjugation, domination, and exploitation is a violation of the right to self-determination and contrary to the charter and that peoples engaging in resistance to such subjugation are entitled to receive support in accordance with the purposes and principles of the charter. Furthermore, "the establishment of a sovereign and independent State, the free association or integration with an independent State or the emergence into any other political status freely determined by a people constitute modes of implementing the right of self-determination by that people."

Finally, this declaration states that nothing in the foregoing shall authorize the violation of

> the territorial integrity or political unity of sovereign and independent States conducting themselves in compliance with the principle of equal rights and self-determination of peoples as described above and thus possessed of a government representing the whole people belonging to the territory without distinction as to race, creed or color.

The declaration is vague, although ardent, in its endorsement of the end of colonialism and alien subjugation, domination, and exploitation, and its promotion of the equality and self-determination of peoples. What it offers in substance toward the protection of indigenous peoples and the resolution of their claims remains in question.

In Resolution 5(30) of February 20, 1974, the Commission on Human Rights appointed Héctor Gros Espiell special rapporteur with a mandate to clarify the right of self-determination in relation to the rights of peoples under colonial and alien domination and to study the implementation of United Nations resolutions in this regard. Gros Espiell first defined the subject under study:

> "Colonial and alien domination" means any kind of domination, whatever form it may take, which the people concerned freely regards as such. It entails denial of the right to self-determination to a people possessing that right, by an external, alien source. Conversely, colonial and alien domination

does not exist where a people lives freely and voluntarily under the legal order of a State, whose territorial integrity must be respected, provided it is real and not merely a legal fiction, and in this case there is no right of secession. (United Nations 1980:6)

The implementation of the right of self-determination involves both independence and the recognition of people's political and cultural sovereignty. Self-determination is a lasting force that does not lapse having once been exercised, and it is relevant to situations of neocolonialism and other forms of imperialism (United Nations 1980:8). The right to self-determination is enshrined in the charter and in numerous additional instruments, including most notably the declaration on decolonization, and it is recognized as a collective right of peoples, not nations or states, although under contemporary international law minorities do not possess this right (United Nations 1980:8–9). The right to self-determination is simultaneously an individual right and a collective right. The collective right of peoples to self-determination not only requires states to not violate this right but to promote it and secure its realization. The right of peoples under colonial and alien domination is not subject to any other condition, such as the pretext that a people is not prepared for independence. Furthermore, peoples under colonial and alien domination possess an international personality, as do their national liberation movements (United Nations 1980:10).

It is Gros Espiell's position that the principle of the self-determination of peoples is so important in the contemporary world that it constitutes *jus cogens*, a "peremptory norm of general international law." It is an element of natural law, and thus is increasingly, though not without opposition, recognized to occupy a position at the summit of the international legal hierarchy (United Nations 1980:11–13). When peoples under colonial and alien domination have exhausted all opportunity of exercising their right to self-determination by peaceful means, they possess the right to engage in struggle by every means available against colonial powers that suppress their aspirations for freedom and independence. These armed struggles are recognized as international conflicts, not civil wars, and therefore states are allowed to provide support to national liberation movements (United Nations 1980:14–15). The special rapporteur concludes that the "self-determination of peoples and their right to be rid of colonial and alien domination is today a fundamental principle which all States are bound to accept under international law" (United Nations 1980:65).

Gros Espiell does not discuss the special status of indigenous peoples, for his report precedes the formation of the Working Group on Indigenous Populations and the completion of the Study of the Problem of Discrimination against Indigenous Populations. Therefore, he does not provide clarification of their status as peoples under colonial or alien subjugation, domination, or exploitation. Nor does he directly discuss the issue of "internal colonialism." However, Gros Espiell does not endorse the Blue Water Thesis, an extralegal concept that has been used to conceptually limit decolonization to territories separated from the governing political entity by an expanse of water, generally an ocean. The Blue Water Thesis has been promoted to protect the territorial integrity of Russia (for example, in the case of Chechnya) and of the states of the Americas. Barsh argues that, consistent with Gros Espiell's position, the Declaration on Friendly Relations requires that before a state's territorial integrity becomes inviolable, it must first demonstrate that its territories in question were legally acquired. This places the states of America and elsewhere in question (Barsh 1983:88). Eminent international law scholars Ian Brownlie, Richard Falk, and Rosalyn Higgins extend the application of the principle of decolonization to the Indians of the Americas in opinions they have prepared for Canada's indigenous peoples concerning their right to self-determination in contradistinction to the original Canadian Indian Act (Opekokew 1987:3–4); the writings and opinions of leading legal scholars provide one of the bases of international law.

OPINIONS OF THE INTERNATIONAL COURT OF JUSTICE

The Charter of the United Nations provides that the International Court of Justice, formerly the Permanent Court of International Justice under the League of Nations and popularly known as the World Court, shall be the principal judicial organ of the United Nations (Article 92). All members of the United Nations are ipso facto parties to the Statute of the International Court of Justice (Article 93) and agree to comply with the decisions of the court; otherwise, the other party or parties in a dispute may have recourse to the Security Council, which may make recommendations or decide upon measures necessary to render a judgment (Article 94).

The Statute of the International Court of Justice (1945) provides that the court will be composed of fifteen independent judges (Article 3) elected by the General Assembly and the Security Council for nine-year periods and eligible for reelection (Article 4). The seat of the court is The Hague, and the court remains in permanent session. It is open only to states party to the statute (Article 35), and states alone may be parties in cases before the court (Article 34). The jurisdiction of the court covers all cases referred to it according to the provisions of the United Nations charter and through treaties and conventions (Article 36). States may request the jurisdiction of the court in treaty interpretation, questions of international law, questions of fact that may constitute treaty violation or abrogation, and issues of reparations.

In arriving at decisions in accordance with international law, the court shall apply international conventions, international custom, general principles of law, and "judicial decisions and the teachings of the most highly qualified publicists of the various nations, as subsidiary means for the determination of rules of law" (Article 38). Judicial decisions, the writings of scholars, pronouncements of states on rules of international law, and the declaratory resolutions of international organizations are regarded as evidence of whether a rule has become international law (Henkin, Pugh, Schechter, and Smit 1987:37). Decisions of the court are binding only on the states that are parties to that particular case (Article 59).

In accordance with the Charter of the United Nations the court may also render advisory opinions on issues of international law at the request of an authorized body (Article 65). Four organs and fifteen specialized agencies of the United Nations have been authorized to request advisory opinions, but states are not eligible to make such requests. Advisory opinions are not legally binding (Henkin, Pugh, Schechter, and Smit 1987:650–51). The court has rendered at least two advisory opinions with relevance to the liberation of indigenous peoples: *Namibia* (1971) and *Western Sahara* (1975).

In *Namibia,* an advisory opinion requested by the Security Council, the International Court of Justice was asked to determine "What are the legal consequences for States of the continued presence of South Africa in Namibia, notwithstanding Security Council resolution 276 (1970)?" The Security Council's resolution had affirmed a previous termination by the General Assembly of South Africa's trusteeship mandate for South West Africa (Namibia) and declared that South Africa's continued presence in Namibia was illegal. The court concluded that South Africa had deliberately and persistently violated the terms of the mandate, which had stipulated that South Africa possessed an obligation in the form of a "sacred trust" to ensure the moral and material well-being and the security of the indigenous inhabitants, thereby compelling the termination of the mandate in Namibia and rendering the occupation illegal. The court declared that "elementary considerations of humanity" may be based upon the human rights provisions of the United Nations charter, the Universal Declaration of Human Rights, and the human rights covenants, even though those instruments were established long after the mandate was issued.

In *Western Sahara,* an advisory opinion requested by the General Assembly, the court was asked: "(1) Was Western Sahara at the time of colonization by Spain a territory belonging to no one *(terra nullius)?* If the answer to this question is in negative, (2) What were the legal ties between this territory and the Kingdom of Morocco and the Mauritanian entity?" Following the withdrawal of Spain from the Western Sahara territory as part of the ongoing process of decolonization, Morocco, Mauritania, and the indigenous nomadic Sahrawi people each advanced claims to the territory otherwise known as Rio de Oro and Sakiet El Hamra. The court answered the first question in the negative, thereby effectively eliminating the concept of *terra nullius* as a means of territorial acquisition; in answering the second question, the court determined that there had been legal ties but no tie of territorial sovereignty with either Morocco or Mauritania and that the principles of decolonization, including the principle of the self-determination of peoples, fully apply to non-self-governing territories.

The court used anthropological research extensively in arriving at its decisions in the case. It first acknowledged that at the time of Spanish colonization Western Sahara was populated with nomadic tribal peoples, pastoral nomads who had social and political organization, political leaders who were competent to represent them, legal regimes, and territorial control, and who entered into ties of alliance or dependence with other tribes. Furthermore, and in answer to the second question, Saharan tribes such as the Regheibat were essentially autonomous and independent, even though nomadic routes may have passed through Algeria, Morocco, and Bilad Shinguitti, or present-day Mauritania. Although nonbinding and limited only to this case, the *Western Sahara* advisory opinion single-handedly pronounces as moribund the early arbitration decisions and the general practice of states denying indigenous peoples international legal status and the right to self-determination.

The Canadian Mohawks attempted to bring their territorial claims before the International Court of Justice in 1967 (Barsh 1983:98), but the court will not hear complaints from indigenous peoples, and so far there have been no "friendly" states willing to sponsor indigenous peoples' complaints before the court (Indian Law Resource Center 1984:22–23). The reason may partially lie in the fact that third-world and newly independent states have been reluctant to utilize the World Court, fearing that its European-centered legal reasoning will not render favorable results. They have turned rather to the development of General Assembly resolutions, declarations, and covenants (Opekokew 1987:8).

OTHER COMPLAINT PROCEDURES WITHIN THE UNITED NATIONS

The United Nations has established at least two complaint procedures for exposing human rights violations in addition to those established by the Optional Protocol, the Apartheid Convention, the Convention on the Elimination of Racial Discrimination, the Convention Against Torture, and the Statute of the International Court of Justice. These two procedures are known as the "1235 Procedure" and the "1503 Procedure." UNESCO and the International Labour Organization (ILO), two United Nations special agencies, also provide complaint procedures for human rights violations related to their particular fields of expertise.

Through Resolution 1235 (1967), the Economic and Social Council established a procedure whereby international nongovernmental organizations (NGOs) with consultative status may forward complaints about situations that "appear to reveal a consistent pattern of gross and reliably attested violations of human rights and fundamental freedoms, including policies of racial discrimination and segregation and of apartheid." Oral and written complaints are received in Geneva by either the Commission on Human Rights or the Sub-Commission on the Prevention of Discrimination and Protection of Minorities. Individuals and groups seeking to present complaints of human rights abuses must seek out a sympathetic NGO that is "willing to lend its support and its NGO credentials" to the particular human rights issue (Indian Law Resource Center 1984:27). More than 600 NGOs are capable of assisting indigenous peoples in presenting their complaints. This is open to the public, and the international news media report the procedures, creating public knowledge of human rights violations and embarrassment for the violating state (Indian Law Resource Center 1984:27–28).

United Nations Economic and Social Council Resolution 1503 (1970) authorizes the Sub-Commission on the Prevention of Discrimination and Protection of Minorities to appoint a five-member working group to hear communications that, again, "appear to reveal a consistent pattern of gross and reliably attested violations of human rights and fundamental freedoms," but only in "situations affecting a large number of people over a protracted period of time" (United Nations 1989a:5). Complaints may involve violations by nonmember and nonparty states. The Indian Law Resource Center, an indigenous NGO and advocate of human rights, describes the 1503 Procedure as limited to "massive violations" only, and explains that "complaints under the 1503 procedure will not be considered if they are about individual or isolated violations of rights, or if the alleged human rights violations are not well-documented and credible" (Indian Law Resource Center 1984:32). The subcommission is authorized to investigate the complaints and request additional information from states. The information gathered remains confidential, and the accuser has no opportunity to challenge the state's response. Review of complaints is done in secret, and extremely few complaints result in decisions that directly benefit the victims of human rights violations. The final decisions also remain confidential, and for many this secrecy renders the 1503 Procedure almost useless for correcting human rights abuses (Indian Law Resource Center 1984:33). The subcommission does forward the most serious cases to the Commission on Human Rights, which will conduct a further inquiry and exert additional pressure on the violating state. In the rarest of cases the commission will forward a complaint to the Economic and Social Council or the General Assembly, where violations may be made public.

UNESCO has established a procedure for receiving communications regarding massive human rights violations related to the field of education, including the violation of individual rights such as the right to education;

the right to participate freely in cultural life; the right to freedom of thought, conscience, and religion; and the right to freedom of assembly and association for the purposes of activities connected with education, science, culture, and information. UNESCO also protects two special group rights as a result of its commitment to cultural rights: the right to cultural development in the exercise of the right to self-determination; and the right of minorities to enjoy their own culture, religion, and language. Complaints may be made in writing to the Executive Board's Committee on Conventions and Recommendations by an individual, group, or NGO. Complaints that are considered admissible will generally result in an attempt by the board to achieve a mutually agreeable resolution of the situation. The Indian Law Resource Center suggests that UNESCO's complaint procedure may eventually prove more valuable to indigenous peoples than the 1503 Procedure as a result of UNESCO's commitments and specialized area of expertise (Indian Law Resource Center 1984:34–36).

BINDING INTERNATIONAL LAW: CONVENTION NO. 169

The only current form of binding international law specifically addressing the rights and needs of indigenous peoples is the International Labour Organization's Convention No. 169 (1989), which entered into force in 1991. It revises the ethnocentric, paternalistic, and assimilation-oriented Convention No. 107 (1957), which, in fairness, was for thirty-two years the only international convention protecting indigenous people's customary laws and rights to land (Swepston and Plant 1985). Convention No. 169 was drafted in cooperation with the United Nations, the Food and Agriculture Organization (FAO), UNESCO, the World Health Organization (WHO), and the Inter-American Indian Institute of the Organization of American States, but no indigenous organizations.

Convention No. 169 promotes respect for all human rights and fundamental freedoms and recognition of indigenous peoples' collective ownership of land. In Article 1(1), it offers its own working definitions for *tribal peoples* and *indigenous peoples,* affirming that the convention applies to:

(a) tribal peoples in independent countries whose social, cultural and economic conditions distinguish them from other sections of the national community, and whose status is regulated wholly or partially by their own customs or traditions or by special laws or regulations;

(b) peoples in independent countries who are regarded as indigenous on account of their descent from the populations which inhabited the country, or a geographical region to which the country belongs, at the time of conquest or colonisation or the establishment of present state boundaries and who, irrespective of their legal status, retain some or all of their own social, economic, cultural and political institutions.

The convention emphasizes "self-identification" as the "fundamental criterion for determining the groups to which the provisions of this convention apply" (Article 1[2]), but qualifies its use of the term *peoples* as having no implications "as regards the rights which may attach to the term under international law."

Convention No. 169 asserts that governments shall respect the integrity of indigenous peoples, who possess the right to participate in the development of policies and actions for their own protection; that indigenous peoples shall share all rights of citizenship while their religious traditions, cultural institutions, and languages shall be retained, respected, and protected when they do not violate internationally recognized human rights; that indigenous peoples have the right to decide their own priorities for development including development of the land they occupy; that governments have a responsibility to protect and preserve the land and environment that indigenous peoples inhabit (Articles 2–8); that land not exclusively occupied by indigenous peoples but traditionally utilized for subsistence activities or cultural traditions shall be safeguarded, with particular attention paid to nomadic peoples and swidden cultivators; that "adequate procedures shall be established within the national legal system to resolve land claims by the peoples concerned" (Article 14[3]); that indigenous rights to natural resources shall be safeguarded, and that indigenous peoples shall retain the right to participate in the management and conservation of these resources; that relocation from traditional land may occur only with the free and informed consent of indigenous peoples, who then may return when the conditions necessitating relocation no longer exist, and who shall receive compensation for any loss or injuries due to relocation; that traditional transmission of land rights shall be respected; that agrarian programs making additional land available for sectors of the population shall also make land available to indigenous peoples when their land base is too small to permit normal existence; that unauthorized intrusion upon or use of land of indigenous peoples shall be prevented by governments and that adequate penalties shall be assessed (Articles 14–19); that governments shall develop and maintain special programs for the welfare and well-being of indigenous peoples (Parts 3, 4, 5, and 6); and that governments shall facilitate contacts between indigenous and tribal peoples across borders (Part 7, Article 32).

Under international law, Convention No. 169 legally binds those states that formally ratify the document (Part 10, Article 38). The ILO maintains supervision of its own conventions and recommendations, and specific complaints of violations of the convention's provisions may be communicated to the ILO, but the complaint procedure is open only to governments, trade unions, employers' associations, and delegates to the ILO (Swepston 1992).

While many state governments thought that Convention No. 169 went too far, several indigenous representatives and scholars and the first state to sign the convention have expressed dissatisfaction, describing it as paternalistic and asserting that it endows states with ultimate authority (United Nations 1989c:10–11, 1990b:12). Indigenous peoples are especially concerned about the convention's qualification that the use of the term *peoples* does not imply rights associated with the legal definition of *peoples* in international law. When ILO spokesperson Lee Swepston appeared before the Working Group on Indigenous Populations to explain that the convention constitutes the minimum standards for the protection of indigenous peoples, standards to which a maximum number of states would be willing to bind themselves, and that in no way inhibit the principles and aspirations that should be presented in the forthcoming Universal Declaration on the Rights of Indigenous Peoples (United Nations 1989c:10; Swepston 1990), over three hundred indigenous people in attendance "left their seats and walked out of the conference room in protest" (Venne 1989:65).

Native American attorney and indigenous rights activist Sharon Venne criticizes Convention No. 169, saying that it is Eurocentric, assimilationist, and, because of its more cautious language, "far more destructive than its predecessor," Convention No. 107 (Venne 1989:53). Venne argues that Convention No. 169 totally ignores the indigenous worldview and is therefore irreconcilably written from a nonindigenous point of view. She rejects ILO's peculiar use of the term *peoples* and opposes the preference for inclusion of indigenous representation in the framework of the nonindigenous political system and the "lip service" given to indigenous legal systems. She condemns the use of the word *customary* in describing the indigenous legal system, considers protection of internationally recognized human rights to be meaningless if the fundamental right to self-determination is denied, and condemns the authority vested in governments to determine and control the development and destruction of indigenous land and to appropriate compensation (Venne 1989). Venne argues:

> Whose rights are being protected; those of the indigenous peoples or of the non-indigenous peoples? We did not invade the non-indigenous territories. We did not impose our values, laws, cultures, languages and educational systems upon the non-indigenous peoples. It appears to me, as an indigenous person, that the ILO revision is meant to protect the non-indigenous peoples from the indigenous peoples. Perhaps the revised convention should be called the Convention Concerning Non-indigenous Peoples in Indigenous Peoples' Territories and Their Right to Exist in Those Territories. (Venne 1989:56)

Professor of law Howard Berman essentially agrees with Venne's position. He describes Convention No. 169 as "an instant anachronism that may well prove a drag on the future substantive development of indigenous rights" (Berman 1988:56).

Anaya, on the other hand, asserts that despite its shortcomings the convention successfully affirms the value of indigenous communities and cultures; advances the general theme of "the right of indigenous communities to live and develop by their own designs as distinct communities"; and attempts to preserve the integrity of indigenous cultures, land, and resource rights and to promote nondiscrimination in the areas of labor, education, and health. Perhaps most importantly, the convention creates treaty obligations for states to observe these provisions (Anaya 1991:7–8). Barsh argues that indigenous people and their advocates can utilize the convention, which represents the "bottom floor" of indigenous rights, to enhance the promotion and protection of those rights. In the process they can expand the understanding of the rights provided for in the convention: "Unlike national legislation, international standards begin weak but may grow stronger over time" (Barsh 1990). Indigenous organizations are increasingly supporting adoption of Convention No. 169, including the Nordic Sami Conference, the Inuit Circumpolar Conference, the World Council of Indigenous Peoples, and the National Indian Youth Council (Anaya 1991:8).

THE RIGHT OF PEOPLES TO SELF-DETERMINATION

Numerous United Nations conventions and declarations recognize two fundamental principles from which all other inalienable rights and freedoms flow: the principle of the dignity of the individual and that of the right of peoples to self-determination. Indigenous organizations such as the International Indian Treaty Council, the Inuit Circumpolar Conference, and the World Council of Indigenous Peoples consistently assert indigenous peoples' right to unqualified self-determination, including secession and self-defense against state actions conflicting with that right. The 1985 Indigenous NGO Draft Declaration of Principles on indigenous rights states:

> All indigenous nations and peoples have the right to self-determination, by virtue of which they have the right to whatever degree of autonomy or self-government they choose. This includes the right to freely determine their political status, freely pursue their own economic, social, religious and cultural development, and determine their own membership and/or citizenship, without external interference.

Robert A. Williams Jr. considers this indigenous theme of self-determination to be the most significant challenge to contemporary and established notions of international law:

> Under the European doctrine of discovery, Western settler states unilaterally denied indigenous peoples' rights to complete sovereignty over their territories. Since Justice Marshall's elaboration of this principle in *Johnson,* Western legal systems have extended the denial of indigenous self-determination far beyond the doctrine's original limitation to indigenous peoples' "power to dispose of the soil at their own will to whomsoever they pleased." Settler states in the Americas, New Zealand and Australia have denied indigenous peoples the right to practice their own religions, speak their own languages, teach their own children, engage in their traditional means of subsistence, and govern their lives according to their own traditions and institutions. (R. Williams 1990b:691–92)

In the United States, the denial of indigenous peoples' right to self-determination on the basis of the Doctrine of Discovery reached its ultimate expression in the doctrine of Congressional plenary power over the Indian tribes. Clinebell and Thomson (1978) and Morris (1987) advance scholarly arguments for the recognition that indigenous peoples, in the present and in the past, possess the characteristics necessary for international legal status, that they are essentially political entities equivalent to states and consequently possess the right to self-determination.

In its Resolution 1865 (LVI) of May 17, 1974, the Economic and Social Council authorized the Sub-Commission on the Prevention of Discrimination and Protection of Minorities to appoint a special rapporteur for a study of the historical and current development of the right of peoples to self-determination on the basis of the Charter of the United Nations and other instruments adopted by United Nations organs. The subcommission appointed Aureliu Cristescu to complete the study *The Right to Self-Determination* (1981). Cristescu concludes his thorough study of relevant United Nations instruments and their legal interpretations by stating that "the right to self-determination has become one of the most important and dynamic concepts in contemporary international life" and that this right "exercises a profound influence on the political, legal, economic, social and cultural planes, in the matter of fundamental human rights and on the life and fate of peoples and individuals" (United Nations 1981:117). The embodiment of the principle of self-determination in the charter marks its recognition as a legal principle in contemporary international law

The principle of self-determination is the most important principle of international law concerning friendly relations and cooperation between nations. It is reaffirmed in several United Nations declarations, and it represents the driving force of decolonization, including the elimination of apartheid and neocolonialism. The right to self-determination is both a collective right, the beneficiaries of which are peoples, and an individual right exercised by minorities through Article 27 of the International

Covenant on Civil and Political Rights. The violation of a people's right to self-determination constitutes an "offence against international legality and a threat to world peace" (United Nations 1981:118–19). Furthermore, the right to self-determination constitutes the general framework and foundation for the implementation of all other human rights and fundamental freedoms. Special Rapporteur Cristescu recommends that the right to self-determination must be the basis of any action taken by the United Nations and member states, and in order to ensure the complete expression of this right,

> the elimination of colonialism, neo-colonialism, racism, apartheid, and other forms of the violation of the right to self-determination, and the adoption of strong measures to establish truly democratic relations between States and peoples are urgent at this time. The United Nations and the Member States must take effective measures to ensure the immediate and complete liberation of all peoples from any form of foreign subjugation, to eliminate all forms of exploitation and discrimination, racism and apartheid, and to repress any action intended to revive such practices. (United Nations 1981:123)

The special rapporteur was unable to develop a precise definition of who constitutes "peoples" entitled to the collective right of self-determination, but he provides the following guidelines: "(a) the term 'people' denotes a social entity possessing a clear identity and its own characteristics; (b) it implies a relationship with a territory, even if the people in question has been wrongfully expelled from it and artificially replaced by another population" (United Nations 1981:41). Indigenous peoples are not excluded from these guidelines.

The instruments of international law have not yet unequivocally distinguished "peoples" possessing a right to self-determination from "minorities," who possess no such right. The Mikmaq nation, in a 1982 submission to the Commission on Human Rights, offer their perspective:

> If a people exercise their right to self-determination by incorporating themselves freely into another people—by immigration or voluntary cession—they surrender their separate status and become one, politically, with the host State.
>
> . . . The situation is different where no voluntary incorporation of peoples has occurred, and there has been no free consolidation of two peoples' political rights. A people lawlessly annexed or taken from their country by force do not thereby lose their separate voice or choice of destiny, but retain it until given an unrestrained opportunity for its exercise. They do not become, by force of seizure, colonization or enslavement, a minority, but remain a people still.

The distinction therefore between a minority and a people, in our conception flows from the quality of consent. A people can become a minority, if it
chooses. Minorities cannot be made by violence or oppression, however.

We think all nations can agree that map-makers are powerless to destroy a
people's right to determine its own future. (Mikmaq Nation, quoted in Barsh
1983:94)

The Mikmaq position, as Barsh explains, requires states to "show how and
when they lawfully annexed or assumed control over an aggrieved group,"
and then "if no lawful incorporation, such as by treaty or immigration,
can be shown, it is to be presumed that the group is a separate people that
has yet to exercise its right of self-determination" (Barsh 1983:94–95).

In their 1992 submission to the Commission on Human Rights, the
Grand Council of the Cree, caught in the crossfire of Quebecois declarations of independence from Canada and Quebecois refusal to recognize
similar rights of independence or secession for the indigenous peoples
whose territories make up the largest part of Quebec, offer their own perspective on indigenous peoples' right to self-determination:

In the context of Quebec, the Quebec people and indigenous peoples constitute "peoples" under international law. The reality is that there are poten-
tially conflicting claims to self-determination and territory that must be im-
partially and equitably addressed.

The right to self-determination is not absolute. It does not automatically
include the right to secede from the Canadian federation. In each specific
case, there may be various other international principles that must be taken
into account.

. . . The ongoing colonized treatment of indigenous peoples by Canada
and Quebec serves to significantly strengthen the claim of indigenous peoples to external self-determination under international law. Colonialism in
all of its manifestations has been unanimously condemned by the United
Nations and all its Member States. The internationally recognized remedy to
achieve decolonization is self-determination. (Grand Council of the Cree,
quoted in Stamatopoulou 1994:78–79)

The Grand Council of the Cree thus endorses the recognition of indigenous peoples as peoples under international law who are subjugated by
the alien domination of a colonizing state.

Among his proposals and recommendations in the published results of
the Study of the Problem of Discrimination against Indigenous Populations, Special Rapporteur Martínez Cobo offers a progressive and enlightening approach to question of the relevance to indigenous populations of
peoples' right to self-determination. No doubt his approach emerged in
large part from his commitment to reflecting in the study the views and

aspirations of indigenous peoples (Stamatopoulou 1994:67). It should also be recalled that colonialism and decolonization represent the general context from which the special rapporteur's definition of "indigenous populations" was constructed. According to Martínez Cobo:

> Self-determination, in its many forms, must be recognized as the basic precondition for the enjoyment by indigenous peoples of their fundamental rights and determination of their own future.
>
> It must also be recognized that the right to self-determination exists at various levels and includes economic, social, cultural and political factors. In essence, it constitutes the exercise of free choice by indigenous peoples, who must, to a large extent, create the specific content of this principle, in both its internal and external expressions, which do not necessarily include the right to secede from the State in which they live and to set themselves up as sovereign entities. (United Nations 1987:42–43)

Self-determination is not available, collectively, to minorities, so the special rapporteur's use of the term *indigenous peoples* in the context of the right of peoples to self-determination is instructive. Martínez Cobo recommends, in agreement with special rapporteurs Gros Espiell and Cristescu, that the United Nations appoint a special rapporteur to prepare a study on self-determination with particular attention to the right of indigenous peoples to self-determination. In a statement that perhaps also illumines his carefully studied position on indigenous peoples' right to self-determination, Special Rapporteur Martínez Cobo recommends a separate United Nations study on the current situations of the indigenous populations of Africa, about which little information was made available by African governments.

TREATIES BETWEEN STATES AND INDIGENOUS PEOPLES

According to legal scholars, the first truly contentious case of the Permanent Court of International Justice was one in which the court decided that the conclusion of a treaty by a state that entails obligations on that state does not indicate an abandonment of its sovereign rights in international law, but demonstrates an exercise of its sovereignty (Henkin, Pugh, Schechter, and Smit 1987:6). This early holding discussed treaties between states only; the early arbitration cases applicable to indigenous peoples, however wrongly decided, simply dismissed the international standing of treaties with indigenous peoples.

The Vienna Convention on the Law of Treaties (1969), which entered into force in 1980, represents the principal authoritative source of the law of treaties. It is invoked by tribunals and states in the interpretation of treaty agreements and the resolution of treaty disputes. The Vienna Convention is limited to treaties between states, however, and it is not retroactive. A draft Convention on Treaties between States and International Organizations or between Two or More International Organizations, submitted to the General Assembly in 1986, has provisions that largely resemble those of the Vienna Convention. It also appears to hold no relevance at this time for treaties between states and indigenous peoples.

REGIONAL HUMAN RIGHTS REGIMES

Several regional legal instruments provide for and protect human rights. These include the European Convention for the Protection of Human Rights and Fundamental Freedoms (1950) and its five protocols, the American Declaration of the Rights and Duties of Man (1948), the American Convention on Human Rights (1969), and the African Charter on Human and Peoples' Rights (1981). These regional conventions, declarations, and charters, representing regional organizations that resemble the United Nations but on a smaller scale, generally reaffirm the fundamental human and individual rights promoted and protected in United Nations international legal instruments, especially the Universal Declaration of Human Rights. None of these instruments directly addresses indigenous peoples or situations that are clearly unique to indigenous peoples.

The European Convention, an instrument of the Council of Europe that entered into force in 1953, established as an organ of the European Commission a European Court of Human Rights that is empowered to ensure that member states observe the standards of the convention and its protocols but provides that only the "High Contracting Parties" and the commission itself may bring cases before the court (Article 44). Twenty-two member states, however, have recognized both the compulsory jurisdiction of the court and the right of individuals to petition the commission (Brownlie, ed., 1992:326). The jurisdiction of the European Court of Human Rights extends to all cases concerning the interpretation and application of the convention (Article 45).

The American Convention on Human Rights, an instrument of the Organization of American States that entered into force in 1978, organized the autonomous Inter-American Commission on Human Rights, which is empowered to promote respect for human rights and to make recommendations to states for the progressive adoption of measures to enhance human rights (Chapter 7), and established an Inter-American Court of Human Rights, which is available only to states party and the commission (Chapter 8). The jurisdiction of the court includes all cases concerning the interpretation and application of the convention. The court was inaugurated in 1979 and is located in San José, Costa Rica.

The African Charter on Human and Peoples' Rights, an instrument of the Organization of African Unity that entered into force in 1986, established an African Commission on Human and Peoples' Rights for the purpose of promoting human rights and peoples' rights and ensuring their protection in Africa, including the formulation of principles and rules aimed at resolving legal problems concerning those rights and fundamental freedoms (Part 2, Chapter 2). The commission may receive communications concerning violations from anyone and "may resort to any appropriate method of investigation" (Chapter 3). The African charter addresses certain collective rights such as the equality of peoples, and the right of all peoples to be free of domination by another people (Article 19). It states that all peoples possess the inalienable right to self-determination (Article 20); that "colonized or oppressed peoples shall have the right to free themselves from the bonds of domination by resorting to any means recognized by the international community" (Article 20[2]); and that "all peoples shall have the right to the assistance of the States party to the present Charter in their liberation struggle against foreign domination, be it political, economic or cultural" (Article 20[3]). The Organization of African Unity has been particularly restrictive, however, in identifying cases of foreign domination, oppression, and colonization and has been opposed to special rights for and recognition of indigenous peoples.

INDIGENOUS PEOPLES AND INTERNATIONAL POPULIST TRIBUNALS

While indigenous peoples, indigenous NGOs, and advocates of indigenous rights have struggled, usually unsuccessfully, to bring their grievances before competent United Nations and regional organs, they have received the attention of nonbinding, grassroots tribunals. The Fourth Russell Tribunal during the 1980 session on the Rights of the Indians of the Americas held in The Netherlands, heard indigenous testimony and reviewed documentation concerning massive human rights and treaty violations. Founded in honor of the philosopher Bertrand Russell, the Russell Tribunal's moral authority depends upon the independence and integrity of the tribunal members, all of whom are nongovernmental personnel, to rely upon objectivity and conscientiousness in their determinations. The philosopher Jean-Paul Sartre served as the executive president of the First Russell Tribunal, which investigated American intervention in Vietnam. In his opening statement he expressed the uniqueness and importance of the tribunal:

> It is certainly true that our Tribunal is not a body clothed with power. . . . We are not being given help by anyone, except for some relief committees, which are, like we, groups of people without power. We do not have any power and that is the very guarantee for our independence. Since we do not

represent a government or a party, we cannot receive orders: "in honour and decency" as it is called, or, if one prefers: in total freedom, we examine the facts. (Sartre, quoted in van Vree, ed., 1980:18)

Tribunal members composing the jury are chosen from among intellectuals who by virtue of their scholarly achievements and human rights activism command international respect (van Vree, ed., 1980:6; Emery 1981).

The aim of the Fourth Russell Tribunal was first to serve as a platform for the Indians to speak for themselves as victims of discrimination, dispossession, ethnocide, and genocide. The Indians were also allowed to have expert witnesses provide further testimony based on their expertise. Charges in the tribunals may be directed against states, institutions, multinational corporations, and so on. Cases must meet certain criteria to be selected for deliberation; for example, they must be solidly based on factual evidence, and the persons bringing forth the case must have a direct relationship to the victims involved. The Fourth Russell Tribunal heard fourteen cases, after which the tribunal jury endeavored to recognize legitimate claims of the Indian peoples of the Americas, including the right to self-determination, and to bring these claims to international public attention through the tribunal's written resolution (van Vree, ed., 1980:16). The jury, in this case composed of five anthropologists, two philosophers, a professor of criminal law, a jurist, a labor activist, an editor and author, and an indigenous leader, utilizes the appropriate legal instruments of the international community and of the states involved in order to render its determinations. The jury may also request information and assistance from an international advisory council in this respect.

The Fourth Russell Tribunal returned verdicts of guilty in all fourteen cases. The government of Guatemala, for example, was found to have violated the Genocide Convention, the International Covenant on Civil and Political Rights, the International Convention on the Elimination of All Forms of Racial Discrimination, the Universal Declaration of Human Rights, and the American Convention on Human Rights. The government of Panama was found guilty of similar violations in relation to the Guaymí, as was the government of Colombia in relation to the Regional Council of the Indians of Cauca. In relation to its treatment of the Shoshone and its violation of the Treaty of Ruby Valley (1863), the U.S. government was found guilty of violating the Universal Declaration of Human Rights; the American Convention on Human Rights; the International Convention on the Elimination of All Forms of Racial Discrimination; the International Covenant on Civil and Political Rights; the International Covenant on Economic, Social, and Cultural Rights; and the Declaration on the Granting of Independence to Colonial Countries and People. Unable to impose sanctions, the Fourth Russell Tribunal appeals to human conscience and human reason.

The Permanent People's Tribunal is a permanent judicial body that promotes popular sovereignty and has procedures comparable to those of the Russell Tribunal. In 1983 in Madrid the Permanent People's Tribunal heard testimony of witnesses and reviewed documents presented by human rights groups concerning human rights violations committed against Indians and non-Indians in Guatemala. In its final statement the tribunal estimated that between fifty thousand and one hundred thousand—or more—persons may have been murdered by the military and by civil patrols and death squads (Permanent People's Tribunal, in Jonas, Mc-Caughan, and Martínez, eds., 1984:237). The tribunal asserts that the treatment of the indigenous peoples by successive Guatemalan governments constitutes ethnocide and genocide:

> The reduction of the Indian to the category of subhuman is referred to, for example, in frequent expressions by officers of middle and high rank who proclaim they will exterminate whole populations that, according to them, support the guerrillas, until "we do not leave a single seed." . . . To eliminate an ethnic microgroup [villages] with the intention of totally destroying it, including the very small children, is an action that has not only political motives but also racist motives. It is believed that crime is biologically transmittable. We are talking about genocide in the strict sense of the word. (Permanent People's Tribunal, in Jonas, McCaughan, and Martínez, eds., 1984:241–42)

The tribunal declared the Guatemalan government, at least through the administration of General Ríos Montt, guilty of crimes against humanity and of genocide against indigenous peoples (Permanent People's Tribunal, in Jonas, McCaughan, and Martínez, eds., 1984:265–66).

INTERNATIONAL CONFERENCES ADDRESSING INDIGENOUS RIGHTS

The writings of leading legal scholars, the pronouncements of states on the rules of international law, and declaratory resolutions of international organizations such as those of the United Nations General Assembly are regarded as means of establishing and clarifying the substance of international law. The declaratory resolutions and recommendations of United Nations–sponsored conferences, on the other hand, carry no legal weight, but like the populist tribunals, they may serve to promote public and institutional awareness of issues and opinions relevant to international law and its interpretation and development. Several conferences sponsored by the United Nations and other international organizations in the last two decades have touched on, if not directly addressed, issues concerning indigenous peoples. Until the 1980s, however, direct indigenous participation in these conferences had tended to be minimal, with the exception of those conferences sponsored by indigenous organizations such as the International Indian Treaty Council, the World Council of Indigenous Peoples, and the Inuit Circumpolar Conference.

For example, the 1978 World Conference to Combat Racism and Racial Discrimination, held in Geneva and attended by representatives of 125 states, engaged in a legally nonbinding attempt to clarify racism specifically in relation to indigenous peoples. It stated in its declaration that the conference "endorses the right of indigenous peoples to maintain their traditional structure of economy and culture, including their language, and also recognizes the special relationship of indigenous peoples to their land and stresses that land, land rights and natural resources should not be taken away from them" (in United Nations 1986, 1:31). The conference called on states to facilitate the creation of indigenous organizations through which indigenous peoples can promote their interests and to allow indigenous peoples to develop cultural and social links with their "kith and kin" across state borders. However, the conference opposed the application of the international principle of self-determination to indigenous situations and explicitly reaffirmed the necessity of the territorial integrity of existing states (United Nations 1986, 1:31).

In 1981 UNESCO held a conference in San José, Costa Rica, on ethnocide and ethnodevelopment in Latin America. With the participation of indigenous people, the conference stated in the San José Declaration "that ethnocide, i.e. cultural genocide, is a crime against international law, as is genocide. . . . We affirm that ethnodevelopment is an inalienable right of Indian groups" (San José Declaration, in United Nations 1986, 1:123). Ethnocide thus represents a massive human rights violation of the highest order. It includes the denial of members of an ethnic group, either individually or collectively, to enjoy, develop, and transmit their culture, their language, and their cultural identity. *Ethnodevelopment* means the "strengthening and consolidating" of a culturally distinct people's culture, increasing its self-government and its exercise of self-determination. The San José Declaration furthermore rejects the deliberate falsification of the history of indigenous peoples, which has amounted to the negation of their existence. And recognizing the indigenous relationship with the natural world, the declaration pronounces an inalienable right of indigenous peoples to keep the territories they possess and to claim lands taken from them (San José Declaration, in United Nations 1986, 1:124).

The 1992 United Nations Conference on Environment and Development, or Earth Summit, held in Rio de Janeiro, was not originally intended to address the issues of indigenous peoples. Instead, the Earth Summit was planned as a conference for industrialized countries to arrive at agreements on issues of global warming and deforestation. Indigenous organizations, however, placed a high priority on having their positions heard in this forum. At issue here were not human rights and self-determination, but less controversial concepts, such as "indigenous land management." The Rio Declaration, "a summary of basic principles intended as a new charter of international environmental law" (Barsh 1993b:208), states in Principle 22 that "indigenous peoples and their communities, and other local communities, have a vital role in environmental management and development because of their knowledge and traditional practices. States should recognize and duly support their identity, culture and interests and enable their effective participation in the achievement of sustainable development." Agenda 21, the United Nations global program of action on the environment that was adopted at the conference, calls for the empowerment of indigenous peoples, stating that they should have greater control over their lands, self-management of their resources, and participation in development decisions affecting them. Barsh argues that the "agreements adopted at Rio acknowledge a unique status for indigenous peoples that is justified by their traditional reliance on and sustainable management of renewable resources." Those agreements "involve collective property rights as well as political rights necessary to maintain distinct institutions and participate effectively in decisionmaking" (Barsh 1994:48). The total impact of the Earth Summit on state policy and on the practices of transnational businesses with regard to indigenous peoples and the environment remains in question.

The United Nations World Conference on Human Rights, held in Vienna in 1993, was the site of another international intellectual and legal battleground for indigenous peoples. Differences on self-determination erupted into a public confrontation. During the drafting of the Vienna Declaration a provision that would obligate states to treat indigenous and nonindigenous peoples equally became the focus of debate between indigenous peoples and states. The indigenous peoples demanded that the *s* be included in *peoples* and that collective rights be recognized, while states were determined to undercut indigenous peoples' claims to self-determination and to reject the possibility of secession. During a ceremony commemorating the International Year of the World's Indigenous People, indigenous participants wore shirts bearing the emblem *s* and the word *peoples*. The outburst over the *s* eventually made it impossible to include an otherwise noncontroversial paragraph on decolonization in the declaration (Barsh 1994:51–52).

THE GENERAL ASSEMBLY AND INDIGENOUS PEOPLES

Special Rapporteur Martínez Cobo recommended that the appropriate United Nations organs should authorize the appointment of special rapporteurs to study the situations of indigenous peoples in Africa and the principle of peoples' right to self-determination with emphasis on indigenous peoples. They should also establish a Working Group on Indigenous Populations with a mandate to prepare a draft declaration followed by a draft convention on the rights of indigenous peoples; appoint a special rapporteur for the study of treaties and other agreements entered into with indigenous peoples; and declare 1992, otherwise recognized as the five hundredth anniversary of Columbus's arrival in the Americas, as the International Year of the World's Indigenous Populations (United Nations 1987). By the time Martínez Cobo's study was finally completed, the working group had been established and was already pursuing its mandate, and a special rapporteur for the study of treaties and other agreements was soon appointed. His recommendations for special studies of Africa's indigenous peoples and of self-determination and indigenous peoples have not yet been observed.

The United Nations General Assembly, through Resolution 45/164 of December 18, 1990, proclaimed 1993 as "the Year for the World's Indigenous People, with a view to strengthening international cooperation for the solution of problems faced by indigenous communities in such areas as human rights, the environment, development, education, health." This decision allowed Spain to enjoy the five hundredth anniversary of Columbus's voyage in 1992, celebrated by UNESCO and the Organization of American States as the year of the Encounter of Two Worlds. Spain's attempt to overturn all plans for the Indigenous Year was supported by European countries, but the defection of Canada from the European position as a result of the Mohawk crisis in Oka, Quebec, and growing support among the states of Central and South America turned the tide in the year's favor (Barsh 1993:211). Leaders in Latin American countries believed that their support for the Indigenous Year and for the expanding United Nations interest in the rights of indigenous peoples would be attractive to possible providers of monetary funds for Indian development programs (Barsh 1993:211–12).

The theme of the Indigenous Year, "Indigenous People—A New Partnership," implied a forward-looking approach rather than one that contemplated the genocidal destruction of the previous five hundred years, but over the objections of the subcommission, the organizational planning was placed in the hands of the Commission on Human Rights rather than shared equally with indigenous organizations. Two technical meetings designed to incorporate indigenous input in the planning stage were unsuccessful both because the initial meeting was held in Geneva and was poorly advertised so that indigenous attendance was low, and because no agreements could be reached during the next meeting, which was dominated by indigenous organizations insisting that they should control the activities for the Indigenous Year. One indigenous organization proclaimed that the relationship between indigenous peoples and states at the latter technical meeting represented not a new partnership, but a new paternalism (Barsh 1994:64).

The Indigenous Year opened with a special ceremony in New York City in December 1992, with thirteen leaders from indigenous nations addressing the United Nations General Assembly for the first time. Unfortunately, although numerous enthusiastic indigenous delegates participated, few representatives to the General Assembly were present (The Native American Council of New York City, in Ewen, ed., 1994:25–26). A large number of conferences, seminars, lectures, cultural and artistic performances, and publications commemorated, supported, and celebrated the International Year of the World's Indigenous People, but overall the Indigenous Year was inadequately financed. It was also poorly publicized, with perhaps the exceptions of the near riot at the World Conference of Human Rights in Vienna and the efforts of Nobel laureate Rigoberta Menchú Tum, who traveled extensively throughout the world in 1993 spreading the message of the urgency of promoting and protecting the rights of indigenous peoples (United Nations 1994b:20).

Menchú, a Quiché Mayan human rights activist and victim of Guatemalan genocide (Menchú 1984), addressed the assemblage at the World Conference on Human Rights in Vienna in 1993 on behalf of indigenous peoples and as goodwill ambassador for the International Year of the World's Indigenous People (United Nations 1994b:19). There, Menchú proposed both a Permanent Forum for Indigenous Peoples in the United Nations, which would promote indigenous rights, and the declaration of a Decade of the World's Indigenous Peoples, which would continue to pursue the objectives of the Indigenous Year (United Nations 1994b:19–20). Menchú recalled the recommendations that indigenous peoples had made in the resolutions of the First Summit of Indigenous Peoples, a satellite conference held at B'oko'Chimaltenango, Guatemala, from May 24 to May 28, 1993, as part of the World Conference on Human Rights; she requested that governments ratify all instruments that protect the rights of indigenous peoples, recognize treaties made with indigenous peoples, support the Draft Declaration on the Rights of Indigenous Peoples, and create a post of high commissioner for indigenous peoples (United Nations 1994b:20). The delegates to the world conference endorsed by consensus two of Menchú's proposals and included them in the Vienna Declaration, which recommends that the General Assembly enact these provisions of the declaration on the condition that the term *people* prevail over *peoples* (Barsh 1994:69). The World Conference on Human Rights also requested the swift conclusion of the Working Group on Indigenous Population's drafting of the Declaration on the Rights of Indigenous Peoples.

The General Assembly, in Resolution 48/163 of December 21, 1993, proclaimed the International Decade of the World's Indigenous People, which commenced on December 10, 1994. Because December 10 was a Saturday, the United Nations was not in session, and therefore the day passed without official notice or celebration. The main objective of the decade is "the strengthening of international cooperation for the solution of problems faced by indigenous people in such areas as human rights, the environment, development, health, culture and education" (United Nations 1995h:3). Other major objectives of the decade include "the education of indigenous and nonindigenous societies concerning the situation, cultures, languages, rights and aspirations of indigenous people"; the promotion and protection of the rights of indigenous people; the empowerment of indigenous people to retain their cultural identity while participating in national economic and social life; the implementation of the recommendations of high level conferences concerning indigenous people, such as the Rio Declaration and the Vienna Declaration; the adoption of the draft Declaration on the Rights of Indigenous Peoples; further development of international standards and national legislation promoting and protecting the human rights of indigenous people; and the implementation of effective methods of monitoring and guaranteeing these rights (United Nations 1995h:3).

General Assembly Resolution 48/163 also provides for the institution of a Voluntary Fund for the Indigenous Decade and for the establishment of a permanent forum for indigenous peoples in the United Nations system. During a technical meeting to discuss the Indigenous Decade, an indigenous African representative argued for the establishment of a committee to study cases of internal colonialism, and another indigenous representative suggested that this could be one task of the permanent forum. A North American indigenous representative proposed that the permanent forum could possess the power to settle conflicts arising from states' noncompliance with treaties and agreements signed with indigenous peoples (United Nations 1995d:25). An indigenous speaker from the Pacific region suggested that to meet the objectives of the Indigenous Decade a permanent peoples' court to which indigenous peoples may submit their claims should be established (United Nations 1995d:28). The permanent forum for indigenous peoples remains, at present, without a mandate, without authority, without a location in the United Nations system, without membership, and without guidelines for indigenous participation (United Nations 1994f, 1994g, 1995g).

INDIVIDUAL RIGHTS, THE RIGHTS OF MINORITIES, AND THE COLLECTIVE RIGHTS OF PEOPLES IN INTERNATIONAL LAW

Special Rapporteur Martínez Cobo recognized that contemporary international law, including nascent human rights laws and principles, is inadequate to protect the unique needs and interests of indigenous peoples. "Western thought," Robert N. Clinton explains, "begins with the isolated individual separated from organized society," which is why "it focuses extensively on the relationship of the individual to the state" (Clinton 1990:740). Human rights are regarded as limitations on society, on government, and on the state, in favor of the individual; therefore, "rights are legal constructs that limit state action." The fundamental themes of Western legal thought "pit the individual against the state and presume that individual rights emerge from the limited nature of the social compact and the restraints imposed by the notion of popular consent" (Clinton 1990:741–42). There is little or no space in these theoretical approaches for group or collective rights. For example, "while organized religious groups constitute groups which might presumably seek *group* protection for their religious autonomy, American law recognizes only the right of the individual adherent to the free exercise of his or her religion" (Clinton 1990:741).

The General Assembly's recently adopted Declaration on the Rights of Persons Belonging to National or Ethnic, Religious, and Linguistic Minorities (1992) provides only for individual rights of persons belonging to minorities. States are obliged to protect the existence of minorities, eliminate discrimination, and create favorable conditions for members of minorities to express their cultural identity. Individuals belonging to minorities possess the right to participate effectively in the national and regional political process on decisions that affect them. Minorities have no right to self-determination as do peoples, and they are not recognized as legal entities possessing any collective political rights (United Nations 2000c). As noted earlier, this declaration may indicate a deepening resistance among the member states to the claims and demands of indigenous peoples (Barsh 1994:78–79).

Indigenous peoples derive their notions of law, legal relationships, and human rights from a very different theoretical perspective, a different vision from that of Western legal thought. The indigenous worldview derives from tribal culture, kinship, and relations in natural ecology. Clinton observes that "Native peoples see humans as inherently social beings" born into a close network of relationships rather than in isolation. The idea of group rights based on principles of mutual respect is the natural way of thinking about legal rights for indigenous peoples, and thus "an individual's right to autonomy is not a right *against* organized society, as it is in western thought, but a right one has *because* of one's membership in the family, kinship and associational webs of the society" (Clinton 1990:742).

Indian tribes and other indigenous peoples have legitimate claims to group rights as a result of treaties entered into with states. These treaties recognize the tribal political entity and sovereignty and the involuntary cession of that sovereignty to states. Indigenous peoples have been dispossessed of their territories as a collective group, and they have experienced forced assimilation into the nation state and have suffered ethnocide and genocide as a result of their cultural and political collective identity. According to Clinton:

It is truly ironic that western legal theory now questions the validity or existence of such group rights when indigenous peoples demand vindication of those group rights, the very same rights that western governments promised to the disadvantaged indigenous groups. . . . Because indigenous peoples have no structural political guarantees that the nation in which they find themselves located will respect their group rights to land, culture, religion and political autonomy, special legal protection that limits the power of the state is critically important. . . . Because majorities, however, rarely vote to limit their political autonomy in favor of indigenous, sometimes disenfranchised, minorities, international protection of such group rights is also terribly important. (Clinton 1990:746)

Without protected collective rights, indigenous peoples will not be able to continue to express their unique cultural identities, which include relations with the natural ecology as well as self-determination, and consequently they will not continue to exist as peoples.

Chapter Five

THE UNITED NATIONS

AND INDIGENOUS PEOPLES

◆ As his study on discrimintion against indigenous populations progressed, Special Rapporteur José Martínez Cobo recommended the formation of a United Nations working group that would investigate the evolving legal and political situation of indigenous peoples. His recommendation was reinforced by the conclusions and recommendations of the nongovernmental organization (NGO) conferences on discrimination against indigenous peoples and on indigenous peoples and the land, held in Geneva in 1977 and 1981, respectively. Subsequently, the United Nations Sub-Commission on Prevention of Discrimination and Protection of Minorities proposed, in Resolution 2(34) of September 8, 1981, the creation of the Working Group on Indigenous Populations. This proposal was endorsed by the Commission on Human Rights in Resolution 1982/19 of March 10, 1982.

The Economic and Social Council's Resolution 1982/34 enacted on May 7, 1982, authorized the subcommission to form the Working Group on Indigenous Populations, which would meet annually to review developments pertaining to indigenous rights in light of Martínez Cobo's report on the problems of discrimination against indigenous populations. With this resolution, the working group became the "first permanent United Nations forum devoted to the consideration of the rights, elimination of discrimination and the problems of indigenous populations" (Daes 1986:131). Special Rapporteur Martínez Cobo also suggests that, pursuant to the second part of its mandate, the working group should "formulate a body of basic principles, based on those to be duly formulated in the text of a draft declaration, and propose in due course a draft convention on the subject for the competent bodies of the United Nations" (Martínez Cobo 1986–1987:24).

THE UNITED NATIONS WORKING GROUP ON INDIGENOUS POPULATIONS

The Working Group on Indigenous Populations is composed of five persons, independent experts who are members of the Sub-Commission on Prevention of Discrimination and Protection of Minorities and who represent different geopolitical regions of the world. Asbjørn Eide of Norway was selected as the first chairperson-rapporteur of the working group, and his brief leadership was instrumental in determining the group's direction, particularly as he allowed "any indigenous person or indigenous representative to speak. The working group became the most open body in the UN system. Everywhere else the right to speak is limited to states, intergovernmental agencies, and accredited nongovernmental organizations (NGOs)" (Sanders 1989:408). Eide was particularly sympathetic to and experienced with the application of international law to indigenous situations, having previously defended Sami rights to cultural survival and nomadic reindeer herding in Norway, and he allowed indigenous persons and groups to address the working group during its sessions with complaints of human rights violations. Eide also maintained that the issue of indigenous land rights should be given top priority by the working group (Eide 1985:211–12). Several member states were dissatisfied with Eide's leadership, and in 1984 the representative of India orchestrated a third-world vote that rejected the election of four of the five members, including Eide. The one member who was reelected believed that questions of indigenous rights should remain embedded in international law concerning the rights of minorities (Sanders 1989:409).

From 1985 to the present, Erica-Irene Daes of Greece, a professor of international law, has served as chairperson-rapporteur of the working group. During her tenure Daes has become highly committed to the protection of indigenous peoples and to the evolution of indigenous rights in international law, and has recommended that the fundamental rights of indigenous peoples be recognized and constitutionally protected within states. Daes has noted in particular that indigenous peoples "constitute a vital force which should be properly educated and advanced in order to realize their full potential," and that the United Nations Working Group on Indigenous Populations should oversee international efforts to that end. "Faith in fundamental human rights and the dignity of every human person," Daes concluded, "should be the guiding spirit of our current movement for a better human world" (Daes 1986:132–33).

However, Daes still contends that the liberation or self-determination of indigenous peoples does not include external self-determination, political independence, or secession; rather, it is a form of internal self-determination in cases where indigenous peoples are the majority, or self-governing regional autonomy in those cases where indigenous peoples are an enclave population within the borders of a state (Daes 1986, 1989, 1993). She most recently states that

> in coming to this conclusion, I have taken into account that indigenous peoples themselves have overwhelmingly expressed their preference for constitutional reform within existing States, as opposed to secession. I have also been conscious that most indigenous peoples acknowledge the benefits of a partnership with existing States in view of their small size, limited resources, and vulnerability. It is not realistic to fear indigenous peoples' exercise of the right to self-determination. It is far more realistic to fear that the denial of indigenous peoples' right to self-determination will leave the most marginalized and excluded of all the world's peoples without a legal, peaceful weapon to press for genuine democracy in the states in which they live. (Daes 1993:9–10)

In this passage, Daes eloquently expresses her belief in the capacity of democratic governments to protect and enhance the rights of indigenous peoples; in the process of peaceful and enlightened negotiations they can avert any necessity on the part of indigenous peoples to resort to armed rebellion against an oppressive state. Special Rapporteur Martínez Cobo, on the other hand, suggests that the full right of self-determination for indigenous peoples should apply in at least two situations: when indigenous peoples are the majority population; and where their independence was recognized in a treaty with a colonial power and therefore, in his opinion, established under international law (Sanders 1989:429). The conclusions and recommendations of several conferences on indigenous issues strongly suggest that indigenous peoples and organizations are more in agreement with Martínez Cobo than with Daes on this issue.

The working group has met annually for approximately one week in Geneva since 1982, with the exception of 1986, when Daes chaired a conference on indigenous rights cosponsored by the Anti-Slavery Society and the World Council of Indigenous Peoples (United Nations 1990a) and "general financial problems within the United Nations led to the cancellation of the sub-commission meeting and of the working group session" (Sanders 1989:409). As first implemented by Eide, the annual sessions of the working group have continued to be open to participation by indigenous persons and organizations, indigenous nongovernmental organizations with consultative status, academics, representatives of member states, and representatives of other concerned organizations. This openness to indigenous participation has been essentially endorsed by the General Assembly, which established through Resolution 40/131 of December 13, 1985, the United Nations Voluntary Fund for Indigenous Populations, a monetary fund that is used to help indigenous representatives and organizations to attend and participate in the working group's sessions. Administered by the United Nations secretary-general with the advice of a five-member board of trustees that includes two indigenous persons, the voluntary fund has received contributions from the governments of Australia, Canada, Denmark, Finland, the Netherlands, New Zealand, Norway, and Sweden and from the Baha'i International Community, the Grand Council of the Cree, and the Shimin Gaikou Center of Japan (United Nations 1990a:9–10). In 1995 the voluntary fund helped fifty-two indigenous representatives to attend the sessions of the working group.

Although no official definition of *indigenous populations* or *indigenous peoples* has been adopted by the Working Group on Indigenous Populations or other United Nations agency, the definition accepted by the working group is that proposed by Special Rapporteur Martínez Cobo in his report. Several African and Asian states have consistently argued that there are no indigenous populations or indigenous peoples within their countries because all are indigenous, so these countries have so far rejected the application of the special rapporteur's definition and the efforts of the working group to establish special rights for indigenous peoples or populations (Sanders 1989a:416–17).

INTERNATIONAL CONFERENCES ON THE RIGHTS OF INDIGENOUS PEOPLES

The Working Group on Indigenous Populations owes its existence, at least to some degree, to the 1977 NGO Conference on Discrimination against Indigenous Peoples and the 1981 NGO Conference on Indigenous Peoples and Land. International conferences on indigenous peoples have made significant intellectual contributions to the working group and have highlighted the urgency of the completion of the working group's draft declaration. Indigenous peoples' political positions and aspirations sometimes sound foreign to nonindigenous people, who tend to prematurely dismiss and denounce those positions and aspirations; these conferences serve to highlight the voice of indigenous peoples in international arenas.

The Third Nuclear Free and Independent Pacific Conference

In 1983, 140 indigenous representatives from thirty-three island and oceanic nations met in Vanuatu for the third Nuclear Free and Independent Pacific Conference, an event that "marked a historic point in the struggle to decolonise the Pacific" (Moody, ed., 1993:522–23). In the conference's final document, titled *We, Being the Inhabitants of the Pacific,* the Pacific peoples and nations demanded an end to nuclear testing, nuclear dumping, and the use of nuclear power in the region, and the withdrawal of all colonial powers from the Pacific; an end to U.S.-directed policy against the liberation of indigenous peoples in Central America, especially an end to the genocidal war against the Mayans of Guatemala; recognition of the inalienable right of East Timorese to self-determination and independence, and pressure in the United Nations on this issue from the governments of Pacific islands, New Zealand, and Australia; cessation of the French government's nuclear testing in the Pacific; the French government's recognition of the independence of "French" Polynesia; an end to U.S. neocolonialism, militarization and nuclearization in the Philippines; an end to Indonesian transmigration and cultural genocide in West Papua (Irian Jaya); recognition of the Free Papua Movement as a legitimate liberation movement; an immediate end to French colonialism in Kanaky (New Caledonia); support for the Kanak Independence Front; an end to cruise missile testing on American Indian lands in upper North America; uncompromised independence for Micronesia; an end to U.S. colonialism in Guam; self-determination for the Chamorro people of Guam; an end to U.S. colonialism in Hawaii; and self-determination for *na Kanaka Maoli,* the indigenous people of Hawaii (in Moody, ed., 1993:522–38).

The World Council of Churches Integrity of Creation Conference

In 1989 the World Council of Churches Programme to Combat Racism convened a global consultation called Integrity of Creation: Our Land Is Our Life in Darwin, Australia. It was attended by 125 indigenous people from several parts of the world, including a large number of Australian Aborigines, and by Erica-Irene Daes, Chairperson-Rapporteur of the United Nations Working Group on Indigenous Populations. The objectives of the consultation were to identify obstacles to indigenous self-determination and self-governance and to petition international organizations to actively support indigenous concerns. The consultation produced a document called the Darwin Declaration, which warns of a worldwide "state of emergency" concerning the survival and status of indigenous peoples (United Nations 1989c:36). Regarding treaties and the legal status of indigenous nations and territories, the Darwin Declaration demands that indigenous peoples retain an inalienable right to self-determination, to control of their traditional territories, to establishment of their own governments, and to the maintenance of traditional cultural and religious practices. The declaration also asserts that indigenous peoples never freely consented to the cession of their rights and territories. The indigenous voices in this document further demand full rights of self-determination in international law, including the right to reassert their own nation states, and international rejection of the proposal to abolish Aboriginal Australian land rights and rejection of the suppression of Aboriginal people's sovereign rights. They demand that the World Council of Churches and the United Nations urge New Zealand to honor the Treaty of Waitangi, compel the French Government to move out of the Pacific island of Kanaky (New Caledonia), insist that Indonesia withdraw from occupied East Timor and recognize the sovereignty of the indigenous people there, place Hawaii on the Special Committee of Decolonization list of non-self-governing territories, and pressure Canada to conclude its proposed treaty with the First Nation Indians (United Nations 1989c:36–38).

The World Conference of Indigenous Peoples on Territory, Environment, and Development

Indigenous peoples and organizations met for the World Conference of Indigenous Peoples on Territory, Environment, and Development in Kari Oca, Brazil, from May 25 to May 30, 1992, and adopted a declaration that they titled the Indigenous Peoples' Earth Charter. The recommendations of indigenous peoples embraced in this charter include recognition of collective human rights in international law; revision of the Genocide Convention to include genocide committed against indigenous peoples; recognition of their right as peoples to self-determination; elimination of the concept of *terra nullius* in international law and reversal of state political and legal policies that are founded on this concept; indigenous peoples' consent about their future as opposed to democratic, majoritarian imposition of state projects, and the immediate end to development projects that do not have the consent of indigenous peoples; international recognition of indigenous political and legal systems and rejection of the assertion of nonindigenous states' laws onto indigenous lands; free passage through traditional territories intersected by state-imposed boundaries; freedom from forced population transfers; freedom from the encroachment of transnational corporations on their lives and lands; recognition of treaties signed with indigenous peoples as treaties under international law; United Nations creation of a special procedure for dealing with violations of these treaties; extension of World Court jurisdiction to include complaints made by indigenous peoples; recognition of the inalienable rights of indigenous peoples to their lands and resources and the right of indigenous peoples to demarcate those traditional territories; the removal of nonindigenous peoples from traditional indigenous territories; an end to the concept of "land claims" for indigenous peoples because it is the nonindigenous peoples who are making "claims" to indigenous lands; the cessation of the dumping of toxic wastes and nuclear products on indigenous territories; an end to profit-motivated deforestation; an end to state-created artificial entities known as "district councils," which deceive the international community by suggesting the consent of indigenous peoples to state projects; and recognition of the right of indigenous peoples to their languages and cultures, including cultural knowledge, material artifacts, and sacred places (United Nations 1994g:2–11).

Conference on the Effects of Racism and Racial Discrimination on the Social and Economic Relations between Indigenous Peoples and States

In 1989 the United Nations Centre for Human Rights sponsored its first international seminar devoted solely to indigenous issues, which convened January 16–20 at the Palais des Nations in Geneva. Indigenous peoples and the Working Group on Indigenous Populations aggressively and successfully lobbied the Centre for Human Rights to include experts nominated by indigenous organizations as equals among the seminar participants. For the first time participants included representatives of indigenous NGOs; the selection of Ted Moses of the Grand Council of the Cree as rapporteur for the seminar established another first (Barsh 1994:56).

Following the expert presentations, seminar discussions were held that focused on the impact of racism against indigenous peoples on the application of international human rights standards in indigenous situations. Chairperson-Rapporteur Daes reported in her address that the information received by the Working Group on Indigenous Populations "presented an irrefutable pattern of oppression and discrimination against millions of indigenous peoples." Additionally, participants dealt with issues of defining racism and racial discrimination, collective versus individual rights, the continuing history of colonialism, and existing legislation. They discussed the question of treaties with indigenous peoples and suggested that where treaties exist they should be assessed in terms of their effectiveness and equitability, and that where no treaties exist the practice of treaty relations with indigenous peoples should be instituted (United Nations 1989b:7).

The participants in the seminar adopted several conclusions by consensus, including: that indigenous peoples are victims of racism, and that the imposition of arbitrary regimes inevitably deny the human rights and freedoms of indigenous peoples; that "the concepts of *'terra nullius,'* 'conquest' and 'discovery' as modes of territorial acquisitions are repugnant, have no legal standing, and are entirely without merit or justification to substantiate any claim to jurisdiction or ownership of indigenous peoples' lands and ancestral domains, and the legacies of these concepts should be eradicated from modern legal systems"; that "colonial laws and colonial concepts are used to justify the imposition of 'trusteeship,' and other demeaning, prejudicial and racially founded systems which prevent indigenous peoples from exercising their human rights and fundamental freedoms, and result in their impoverishment, disenfranchisement, debasement, demoralization and disintegration"; that only recognition of collective rights can fully protect the rights of indigenous peoples; that "the principle of self-determination as set forth in the charter of the United Nations and in article 1 of the Covenant on Civil and Political Rights and the Covenant on Economic, Social and Cultural Rights is essential to the enjoyment of all human rights by indigenous peoples" and

that "self-determination includes, *inter alia,* the right and power of indigenous peoples to negotiate with states on an equal basis the standards and
the mechanisms that will govern relationships between them"; that the
destruction of indigenous peoples and cultures is the result of racism and
deprivation; that "treaties and agreements between indigenous peoples
and States, and treaties between States that affect indigenous peoples,
should be subject to international supervision to secure their enforcement"; that development policies that despise and destroy indigenous cultures are racist; that the lack of available information concerning indigenous rights issues allows racism to persist; that the destruction of
indigenous cultures results from prohibitions against indigenous languages and religions; that indigenous peoples are not minorities—that in
some states indigenous peoples are the majority and in other states they
constitute a majority in their traditional territories; and that elimination
of racism against indigenous peoples necessarily includes the reestablish-
ment of indigenous peoples' control over their own lives and future
(United Nations 1989b:7–9).

Seminar participants also recommended that relations between states
and indigenous peoples be founded upon "free and informed consent and
co-operation" rather than "consultation and participation"; that indigenous peoples be recognized as proper subjects of international law; that
collective rights be recognized; that states explicitly recognize indigenous
rights and implement all existing human rights instruments; that the
working group's draft declaration of indigenous rights be adopted by the
United Nations General Assembly and followed by an international
covenant on the rights of indigenous peoples; that more comprehensive
monitoring of human rights abuses be instituted; that a commissioner
be appointed by the Centre for Human Rights to study issues related to
indigenous peoples' rights and report to the Commission on Human
Rights and state governments; that new communications procedures in
the United Nations for receiving and responding to complaints be implemented; that the United Nations participate in the dissemination of
information on indigenous peoples' rights; that the dignity of indigenous peoples be recognized and respected; that "all States and relevant
entities recognize and respect indigenous peoples' rights to lands and
resources, and provide *just restitution* and compensation for *past infringements* of these rights"; and that the fundamental relationship of respect
between indigenous peoples and the environment should be explicitly
recognized in the work of the United Nations Environment Programme
(United Nations, 1989b:8–10).

The seminar "condemns imposition of non-indigenous social, cultural
and economic judgements and values upon indigenous peoples, and calls
for the prohibition of assistance and support by the United Nations agencies and other international, regional and national organizations for pro-

jects and development that threaten the human rights and fundamental freedoms of indigenous peoples, or adversely affect indigenous social, cultural, and economic rights." It "urges full recognition of the indigenous peoples' right to development, and the requirement for the full participation and consent of indigenous peoples in the selection, planning, implementation, and evaluation of development projects, consistent with the indigenous peoples' right to benefit from and control their own lands and resources." The seminar demands that states prevent the removal and alien adoption of indigenous children, which constitutes genocide, and "requests that Governments recognize that the realization of indigenous peoples' rights in the economic, social and cultural fields will result in breaking the cycle of poverty" (United Nations 1989b:9–11).

In her article "On the Relations between Indigenous Peoples and States" (1989), Chairperson-Rapporteur Daes offers her assessment of the seminar, which she regards as a "milestone in the protection of the rights of indigenous peoples." According to Daes the most important features of the conference were the equality of participation of indigenous representatives and representatives of governments, the adoption of the term *indigenous peoples* rather than *indigenous populations,* the establishment of a distinction between "indigenous rights" and "minority rights," the rejection of the concept of *terra nullius,* and the assertion of the right of indigenous peoples to self-determination. Moreover, Daes asserts that seminar participants' adoption of a seminar report without a vote customarily establishes a moral edict for the participants to respect and implement all of the conclusions and recommendations (Daes 1989:42).

Participant Russel Lawrence Barsh writes in his review of the event: "If it accomplished nothing else, the seminar demonstrated the practicality of indigenous participation in UN decision making. Heretofore, indigenous representatives, like other non-governmental organizations, have had a voice in UN policy but no vote. Representation on an equal footing at future meetings of a technical nature, at least, now appears increasingly likely" (Barsh 1989:604). Barsh contends that the report of the seminar reflects the indigenous viewpoint far more than any previous official document does and that the recommendations on indigenous self-determination are particularly notable positions. In a third overview and criticism of the seminar, Douglas Sanders advances that the key provisions are the attacks on *terra nullius,* conquest, discovery, and trusteeship; the recognition of indigenous peoples as proper subjects of international law; and the recognition of the need to protect the collective rights of indigenous peoples (Sanders 1989b). Although the seminar's conclusions and recommendations are not legally binding, they serve collectively as an educational instrument. The recommendations have been distributed to the United Nations General Assembly and other United Nations and international committees and organizations, and they were made available to the general public as a United Nations publication despite opposition from some Western governments.

The Meeting of Experts on the Experience of Countries in the Operation of Schemes of Internal Self-Government for Indigenous Peoples

The Commission on Human Rights sponsored a meeting of experts on September 24–28, 1991, on "the experience of countries in the operation of schemes of internal self-government for indigenous peoples" as an activity of the Second Decade to Combat Racism and Racial Discrimination. This second United Nations–sponsored conference focusing entirely on indigenous peoples' issues was held in Nuuk, Kalaallit Nunaat (Greenland), at the invitation of both the Greenland Home Rule Government and Denmark. It was the first United Nations conference focusing exclusively on self-government and autonomy.

In background papers prepared for the conference, experts examined self-government and autonomy, focusing on forms of self-determination that do not entail secession and that, in their opinion, could strengthen national unity in a pluralist state. Examples investigated were the reservation systems in the United States and the Philippines; regional autonomy in Nicaragua; the Comarca system for the Kuna Indians in Panama; constitutional provisions for the protection of indigenous peoples in Brazil; and home rule in Greenland, which was generally regarded as a constructive example (United Nations 1992e). Several participants argued that indigenous peoples possess a right to self-determination as provided in the international covenants on human rights and that states are therefore obliged to promote this right. An indigenous representative from Australia noted that although Australia was declared decolonized, the Aboriginals were not involved in that process and consider themselves to remain in a colonial situation (United Nations 1992d:5). The representative of New Zealand's government remarked that because 90 percent of Maori people now live in urban areas, self-government there would prove impractical; however, he noted that the Cook Islands and Niue, for which New Zealand remains responsible for foreign policy and defense, are independent in every other way and thus should be considered as notable examples of successful autonomous arrangements (United Nations 1992d:5, 10).

In his opening address to the meeting, the premier of Kalaallit Nunaat, Lars Emil Johansen, praised the United Nations for reestablishing over the previous few years its viability as a protector of the weak against the strong. An Inuit, Johansen eloquently expresses an indigenous perspective of the meeting and of the efforts of the United Nations to restore dignity and justice for the 300 million indigenous peoples:

... it is the merit of the United Nations that many of the former colonies were able to free themselves from the bondage of colonialism in a peaceful and dignified manner, and become independent nations. It is, in fact, the decolonization and the full securing of the right, of States as well as of individuals, to live in freedom and equality, which is the core basis of the United Nations. And it is the United Nations' combat against oppression and racism which has led so many small peoples in the world to place such high hopes in the Organization.

And this is precisely the perspective from which this meeting must be understood. For while a number of former colonies are now free and independent States, there are still peoples who live in conditions where they feel that their claim for lawful self-determination is not given the space and freedom to unfurl. People who still feel oppressed and deprived of their right to equality. People whose land and livelihood, culture and distinctiveness are not yet secured from coercive powers stronger and greater than they. People for whom the colonial structure is not abolished. (United Nations 1992e:6-7)

Unfortunately, Johansen goes on to say, indigenous peoples are still denied human rights, and the decolonization processes of the United Nations, as currently constructed and implemented, are not applied to them. Johansen calls for the immediate end of assimilation policies directed at indigenous peoples. He proposes that indigenous peoples and cultures have much to offer the world and that Greenland represents a potent example of the implementation of indigenous self-government and autonomy (United Nations 1992e:5–9).

In the preamble to the *Nuuk Conclusions and Recommendations on Indigenous Autonomy and Self-Government,* the experts at the meeting recognized indigenous peoples as historically self-governing peoples with unique cultures and as distinct peoples possessing the right to self-determination, which comprises autonomy, self-government, and self-identification. The participants concluded that self-determination of peoples is in fact the precondition for freedom, peace, and justice; that indigenous peoples possess the right to self-determination as declared in international law, to be implemented with respect to other principles of international law; that self-government, self-administration, and self-management constitute elements of indigenous political autonomy, but do not pose a threat to territorial integrity of the state; that indigenous autonomy and self-government are prerequisites to achieving equality, dignity, freedom, and all human rights; that indigenous peoples' territories should be guaranteed to them because they are essential to their physical, spiritual, and cultural existence; that the autonomy and self-government of indigenous peoples preserves the natural environment and the ecological balance necessary for sustainable development; that indigenous peoples themselves must respect human rights in their jurisdictions; that it is necessary for treaties and other agreements entered into between states and indigenous peoples to be honored; that treaty relations and constitutional or statutory provisions should be created affirming indigenous territories, autonomy, and self-government, which are essential for survival, development, and international cooperation; that autonomy and self-government include control over matters concerning land resources and subsistence strategies, development, law, health and social welfare, trade, culture, religion, and the right to impose taxes; and that an independent court or other mechanism for adjudicating conflicts between the indigenous self-government and the state should be established by constitutional or statutory provisions (United Nations 1992d:11–13).

The Nuuk meeting of experts also recommends that states regularly address obstacles to indigenous autonomy and self-government; allow the free movement of indigenous peoples and trade and communications between indigenous peoples across national and international boundaries; ratify relevant international instruments; and assist in the education and training of indigenous peoples to prepare them for the exercise of autonomy and self-government. It recommends that the United Nations permanently address the rights and protection of indigenous peoples; establish international monitoring mechanisms; and distribute the materials resulting from the Nuuk meeting of experts to all agencies, organs, governments, and organizations and publish these materials as a United Nations publication.

The Santiago Technical Conference

The third United Nations conference devoted entirely to indigenous issues, the Technical Conference on Practical Experience in the Realization of Sustainable and Environmentally Sound Self-Development of Indigenous Peoples, was held in Santiago, Chile, May 18–22, 1992. It also was sponsored by the Commission on Human Rights. An indigenous representative, Ingmar Egede of the Inuit Circumpolar Conference, was selected to be the rapporteur. In the preamble to the resulting document, *The Santiago Conclusions and Recommendations on Indigenous Peoples and the Environment*, the participants of the technical conference recognize that:

> Traditionally, indigenous peoples lived in sustainable and harmonious relationships with their lands and environment. They possessed a deep knowledge, understanding and management experience of the ecological systems on which they depended. The ability of indigenous peoples to apply and develop this knowledge to their lands, and to share this knowledge with others, is vital for overcoming environmental degradation throughout the world. It is also an important factor in the achievement of equitable and sustainable living conditions for all the peoples of the world.

The survival of indigenous peoples and their ecosystems depends upon the realization of indigenous peoples' rights and redress of injustices, including restoration of land and resources, which will allow them to pursue their own sustainable and environmentally sound development (United Nations 1992b:16). The conference recommended that indigenous peoples participate directly and effectively in the socio-environmental impact studies, decision-making processes, and implementation processes of national development projects affecting them; that the United Nations take measures to protect the property rights, including intellectual property, of indigenous peoples; that the meetings of all United Nations agencies on indigenous peoples include indigenous representation, and when possible be held on indigenous territories; that the World Bank and other multilateral financial institutions take appropriate steps to assist in indigenous self-development programs; that appropriate funding be provided to indigenous peoples in order to enable them to participate in negotiations directly affecting them; "that mechanisms and resources be developed at the national and international levels to ensure the peaceful resolution of conflicts which may occur between indigenous peoples, States and other sectors of society"; "that appropriate mechanisms and resources be developed to provide legal and technical assistance to indigenous peoples for the promotion of their rights and sustainable management of their environment"; that biosphere reserves and natural parks be established on indigenous lands only with the consent and active participation of the indigenous peoples; that indigenous knowledge be utilized in rehabilitating environments; "that appropriate mechanisms be developed at the international and national levels to identify, prevent and provide sanctions against environmental degradation"; and "that the contribution and effective participation of women be taken into account in all issues and activities related to development and the environment which affect indigenous peoples" (United Nations 1992b:17–18).

The Working Group on Indigenous Populations receives these reports, incorporates them into its analysis of developments on the rights of indigenous peoples, and makes them available to those in attendance at its annual sessions. The Centre for Human Rights has published the final report of the seminar in Geneva, and in response to the meetings in Nuuk and Santiago the working group requested that the Centre for Human Rights, with the assistance of indigenous peoples, prepare a handbook on the experience of indigenous self-government (United Nations 1992c:39).

THE DRAFT DECLARATION ON THE RIGHTS OF INDIGENOUS PEOPLES

The working group has carried out its mandate by receiving information from member states, agencies and organizations of the United Nations, regional organizations, and indigenous peoples and organizations regarding developments in state relations with indigenous peoples. The chairperson-rapporteur is authorized to visit member states in order to observe these developments first hand. The working group does not have a mandate to examine or decide on indigenous complaints concerning alleged human rights violations, but such complaints are often voiced to the group and are recorded in its annual reports. The working group records these complaints "not to apportion guilt, but to identify pressing issue areas, to examine the policies, laws and practices of the governments as well as the reactions and aspirations of the Indigenous populations and thereby to formulate views on future improvements in relations between the Indigenous populations and the governments" (Eide 1985:203). Indigenous peoples are advised to pursue other complaint procedures, but they have not regarded those procedures as satisfactory.

The working group has pursued the second part of its mandate by preparing the document known as the Universal Declaration on the Rights of Indigenous Peoples. Early on in the group's maturation, Chairperson Eide determined that it would be better to draft a declaration than to draft a convention because a declaration is nonbinding; therefore, it would be easier to negotiate and could be far more advanced in its explication of rights and protections, while still influencing national politics and legislation (Eide 1985; Alfredsson 1986).

In 1986 the draft declaration consisted of eleven articles. With the assistance of indigenous peoples and organizations and an obviously deepening appreciation for the uniqueness of indigenous cultures and the seriousness of indigenous peoples' grievances and aspirations, evident in the substitution in 1988 of *indigenous peoples* for *indigenous populations* in its documents and discussion, the working group completed a final draft version of the declaration, numbering forty-five articles, during its eleventh session, in 1993 (reprinted in United Nations 1993a). The Four Directions Council, a North American Indian NGO with consultative status at the United Nations, comments perceptively on this evolution:

> A breakthrough occurred at the Working Group's eleventh session, which was attended by the representatives of more than 125 indigenous nations, organizations, and peoples. The Working Group abandoned its effort to negotiate some kind of consensus, which it realized now would have to be achieved at higher, political levels of the United Nations. Instead, its members accepted the fact that the indigenous peoples' position was legally correct—even if it thus far lacked political consensus. On this basis, the Working Group agreed that indigenous peoples are peoples, and have the right to self-determination, the same as other peoples.
>
> In our view, the Working Group has already accepted nearly all of the indigenous peoples' proposals substantively, if not always in the same words or

style. Further redrafting of the text may result at best in some stylistic improvements, but nothing more. Meanwhile, indigenous peoples face destruction, displacement and ethnocide in many parts of the world. We feel the time has come to move ahead from legal debates to political actions. (United Nations 1993d:1–2)

Despite the length of the process to date, the rights presented in this document must be approved by the United Nations Sub-Commission on Prevention of Discrimination and Protection of Minorities and by the United Nations Commission on Human Rights.

According to Part 9, Article 42 of the draft, the rights declared in this document constitute "the minimum standards for the survival, dignity and well-being of the indigenous peoples of the world." The preamble of the draft declaration affirms the equality of indigenous peoples with all other peoples and demands respect for their differences from other peoples. It expresses concern for the colonization and dispossession of indigenous peoples and recognizes that treaties and agreements made with indigenous peoples are "matters of international concern and responsibility." Article 3 declares the right of indigenous peoples to self-determination, and Article 4 asserts the right of indigenous peoples to strengthen their unique political, legal, economic, and cultural systems without relinquishing their rights as citizens of the state in which they are located unless they choose to.

Article 1 affirms the application to indigenous peoples of all fundamental rights guaranteed by existing international conventions, and Article 6 declares the right to protection from genocide. Article 7 posits a right previously nonexplicit in international law by outlawing ethnocide and cultural genocide and requiring redress for injustices, such as any action violating indigenous peoples' "integrity as distinct peoples," any form of forced assimilation, dispossession of land and resources, enforced population transfers that violate their rights, and propaganda directed against them. Similarly, Article 10 forbids forcible relocation and allows relocation only when the affected peoples consent, when fair compensation is provided, and when the option is left open for return when such return becomes possible. Article 8 also creates a new right when it asserts a collective as well as an individual right to the maintenance of cultural identity and to self-identification as indigenous.

Part 3 of the draft declaration asserts indigenous peoples' rights to practice their culture and to preserve and utilize sacred and historical sites and archaeological artifacts. It calls for protection of their languages, oral traditions, and philosophies and of their exercise of their religious traditions. Part 4 demands indigenous rights to establish their own educational systems, to develop their own forms of education consistent with their culture, and to utilize their own language as the language of instruction. Part

5 establishes the right of indigenous peoples to participate fully in their own decision-making institutions and in those administrative and legal institutions that make policy affecting them. It also endorses their right to pursue traditional medicine, health practices, and means of subsistence and their own development strategies, while states are obliged to provide immediate improvement of indigenous economic and sanitary conditions.

Part 6 declares indigenous peoples' right to maintain their profound spiritual and material relationship to their total environment, whether traditionally owned or otherwise occupied, and fully recognizes indigenous laws, traditions, and systems of land tenure. Furthermore, Article 27 of Part 6 requires that:

> Indigenous peoples have the right to the restitution of the lands, territories, and resources which they have traditionally owned or otherwise occupied or used, and which have been confiscated, occupied, used or damaged without their free and informed consent. Where this is not possible, they have the right to just and fair compensation. Unless otherwise freely agreed upon by the peoples concerned, compensation shall take the form of lands, territories and resources in equal quality, size and legal status.

Additionally, Article 28 provides that indigenous peoples possess the right to conservation, restoration, and protection of their total environment; state military operations and disposal of hazardous wastes are prohibited on indigenous lands. Article 29 creates a new right by entitling indigenous peoples to ownership, control, and protection of cultural and intellectual property, including genetic resources and medicines.

Article 31 of Part 7 appears to limit indigenous rights to self-determination:

> Indigenous peoples, as a specific form of exercising their right to self-determination, have the right to autonomy or self-government in matters relating to their internal and local affairs, including culture, religion, education, information, media, health, housing, employment, social welfare, economic activities, land and resources management, environment and entry by non-members, as well as ways and means for financing these autonomous functions.

Article 32 provides for the collective right of indigenous peoples to determine their own citizenship without impairing their citizenship in the state of residence. Article 35 allows indigenous people to freely cross state boundaries in the pursuit of traditional spiritual, cultural, political, economic, and social purposes, and it requires states to implement this right. Article 36 addresses treaties and other agreements with indigenous peoples:

> Indigenous peoples have the right to the recognition, observance and enforcement of treaties, agreements and other constructive arrangements con-

cluded with States or their successors, according to their original spirit and intent, and to have States honor and respect such treaties, agreements and other constructive arrangements. Conflicts and disputes which cannot otherwise be settled should be submitted to competent international bodies *agreed upon by all parties concerned.*

Part 8, the final part of the draft declaration, imposes additional obligations on states. Article 37 requires that all the rights in this declaration be included in national legislation and given full effect. Article 38 requires states to provide financial and technical assistance to make it possible for indigenous peoples to enjoy their recognized rights. Article 39 compels states to provide appropriate and accessible procedures for the resolution of conflicts and disputes with states.

The working group's annual reports suggest that many countries are attempting to address the principles of the draft declaration and are encouraging the protection of indigenous rights within their borders. In each annual session, however, the working group continues to receive reports—which they publish anonymously but often identify by region—concerning the dumping of nuclear and toxic wastes on the territories of indigenous peoples; the development of hydroelectric plants damaging to indigenous environments; arbitrary arrests, disappearances, detention, torture, and military harassment of indigenous peoples; forced sterilization of indigenous women; continued state-enforced assimilation and relocation practices and other acts of genocide; and destitution and woefully inadequate health care among indigenous peoples.

RESPONSES TO THE DRAFT DECLARATION ON INDIGENOUS RIGHTS

When the Sub-Commission on Prevention of Discrimination and Protection of Minorities received the working group's completed draft declaration, it passed Resolution 1993/46 of August 26, 1993, stating that it would consider the text only after the working group had heard comments of states and indigenous organizations on the declaration. The working group also received specific instructions from the General Assembly and the Vienna Declaration of 1993 to complete the draft during its 1993 session. Acceding to this demand, the group sought to complete what it preferred to be a "balanced" text, but when addressing the issue of self-determination it arrived at an impasse with indigenous peoples demanding that the declaration express and confirm that right. From then on Chairperson-Rapporteur Daes characterized the draft declaration as representing the "aspirations" of indigenous peoples, but she continues to personally argue that indigenous self-determination represents constitutional reform for adequate democratic representation rather than a right to autonomy or independence.

When the working group adopted Article 3, declaring the indigenous peoples' right to self-determination, despite Daes's misgivings, "the decision was greeted with a standing ovation from indigenous delegations and a conciliatory response from many governments" (Barsh 1994:52–54). But many states are critical: Denmark and New Zealand prefer wording indicating internal self-determination only, while Brazil, India, Sweden, and the United States object to the use of the term *self-determination*. The U.S. representative indicated that self-determination is a principle, not a right. In perhaps the most serious opposition to the internationalization of indigenous issues, Brazil, Canada, Finland, and Sweden object to the proposed right of indigenous peoples to enjoy adequate access to appropriate international forums for adjudication of complaints regarding violations of treaties and other agreements (Barsh 1994:53–56).

The Four Directions Council's assessment of the completion of the draft declaration indicates that not all states are in agreement on the principles enunciated therein (United Nations 1993d). The government of Myanmar, for example, considers the draft to be illegitimate and prefers the application of all existing human rights declarations and conventions instead of the creation of new rights without legal merit. Japan argues that because the declaration is legally nonbinding, "it is inappropriate to call upon States, or to bear legal obligations on States to take effective measures." The Japanese observer, furthermore, comments that the document is vague and wordy and insists that "collective rights" do not appear in other international instruments and are therefore not established. The observer also contends that without a precise definition of *indigenous populations* the declaration is necessarily meaningless (United Nations 1995g:2–3).

Mexico opposes the use of the term *self-determination*, finding this and other provisions in the declaration to be incompatible with existing international law, and suggests that self-identification as *indigenous* should be limited to the right of an ethnic group to remain part of the plural society that makes up the state to which they belong. Mexico insists that the declaration is inconsistent with the Mexican constitution, which indicates that it is the state that transmits title to land, either as private property, or as community property where title is reserved by the state, because "ownership by the Nation is inalienable and imprescriptible" (United Nations 1995g:3–5). Morocco, likewise, finds the internal self-determination clause, Article 31 of the declaration, and the use of the term *indigenous peoples* to be among many provisions and articulations that are incompatible with existing international law and appear to threaten the established principles of territorial integrity and state sovereignty (United Nations 1995g:5–6).

The United States, on the other hand, professes a profound commitment to "promoting and protecting indigenous rights throughout the

United States" and the world and considers itself to be in basic agreement with the principles of the declaration, but "emphasize[s] that a number of provisions in the current draft refer to 'rights' which do not currently exist under international law" (United Nations 1995g:6–9). The U.S. representative explains further that "while certain indigenous communities, such as recognized tribal governments, may be largely self-governing and exercise autonomy over a broad range of issues, as they do in the United States, these powers of self-government are exercised within the overall domestic legal framework of the State in which they reside" (United Nations 1995g:7–8). The United States opposes the use of the word *peoples* because international law applies primarily to the rights of individuals. The principle of self-determination for [recognized] indigenous peoples in the United States implies tribal self-government and limited autonomy, rather than the right to an independent state. The United States is also concerned that articles designed to protect cultural rights may unfortunately and unlawfully impinge upon the human rights of individuals.

The drafters of the declaration did not simply acquiesce to the wishes of the indigenous nations; criticism of the declaration has come not only from states. The Black Hills Teton Sioux contend, contrary to the U.S. position just outlined, that the language appended to Article 36, that treaty disputes could be settled by international bodies "agreed to by all parties concerned," did not appear in the previous draft and is absolutely unacceptable (United Nations 1994d). The representative of the Black Hills Teton Sioux persuasively presents their position:

> Historically, language which has been unclear and open to interpretation has provided the United States with a way to violate our legal treaties. This phrase will completely destroy the positive effect of [article] 36 and preserve the status quo. Nation States have not had to answer for treaty abuses and violations unless they wanted to. The addition of this language will continue this unjust system and maintain Nation-State violations of the sacredness of treaties with the Lakota nation and all indigenous nations. (United Nations 1994d:5)

The Black Hills Teton Sioux Nation demands removal of this phrase from the declaration and restoration of the original wording of the article.

In earlier deliberations, certain indigenous representatives commented that although a limited use of the term *peoples* in the declaration is unacceptable, "fear of indigenous self-determination leading to secession is unfounded because of the general approach and understanding of international legal instruments" (United Nations 1989c:17). The meaning of *peoples* and the explicit affirmation of the principle of self-determination, therefore, imply the internal self-determination that indigenous peoples believe is necessary in order to prevent continuing human rights abuses.

Other indigenous representatives have argued that *self-determination* should not be qualified, and the Mohawk Nation has insisted that the declaration should recognize treaties as having been made between "equals" (United Nations 1991b:9–11).

The Inuit Tapirisat of Canada, in their comment on Article 3, support the inclusion of self-determination as a fundamental and essential right of indigenous peoples because self-determination is correctly regarded as a prerequisite to the complete appreciation of all human rights, including individual rights (United Nations 1994e). The Inuit Tapirisat's argument, representing indigenous positions and cultural conflict between indigenous peoples and states in stark clarity, is well worth presenting at length:

> In a cultural context, the protection of individual rights provides freedom to assimilate for individuals who wish to assimilate, but insufficient protection against assimilation for those who don't. The protection of collective rights can provide freedom at the individual and the collective level to choose assimilation, or not. The draft declaration recognizes this by addressing not just the status of indigenous peoples as individuals, but, just as importantly, the status of indigenous peoples and cultures as equal in dignity, rights and freedoms to other peoples and cultures. Inuit believe in individual and collective rights as complementary aspects of an holistic human rights regime.
>
> . . . The denial of the right to self-determination to indigenous peoples because our peoples and our territories have suffered a form of colonization trapping us within existing States is no less discrimination, is no less an arbitrary and unjust denial of fundamental human rights. . . . The draft declaration on the rights of indigenous peoples is important for its contribution to ensuring the universality of all human rights, and to ensuring the full enjoyment of human rights by all indigenous peoples by securing our inalienable right to self-determination. (United Nations 1994e:1–2)

The Inuit Tapirisat position expressively represented here attempts to forestall states' efforts to further undermine the self-determination clause and supporting clauses of the declaration.

The International Indian Treaty Council, one of the original indigenous organizations engaged in the contemporary struggle for indigenous liberation, refers to the United Nations–sponsored study of self-determination in which Special Rapporteur Cristescu writes that "the principles of equal rights of peoples and that of self-determination are two components of one norm" (United Nations 1995c:2–5). Thus understood, self-determination is the essential privilege of a community of peoples, a right of individuals in profound association, and consequently the violation of this collective right constitutes a violation of their fundamental freedoms. According to Cristescu, the right to self-determination exists "without regard to time." In other words, it is a right existing prior to the United Nations charter that internationally proclaims it. On the basis of this reasoning the International Indian Treaty Council asserts that "no one can deny that indigenous peoples enjoyed the right to self-determination before the colonial conquest, since time immemorial; . . . neither time nor oppression have extinguished it" (United Nations 1995c).

The International Indian Treaty Council presents a revealing interpretive analysis of the relations between indigenous peoples and states, noting that whether or not states legally recognized the sovereignty of indigenous peoples,

> The end result has been the same in all of these cases: indigenous peoples all over the world today are denied the right to self-determination, upon which their very survival depends. . . . Examples abound . . . of how the denial of self-determination leads to every conceivable kind of human rights abuse. To paraphrase [Special Rapporteur] Cristescu, without the right to self-determination, other human rights are devoid of meaning. (United Nations 1995c:3–4)

The role of the United Nations, argues the International Indian Treaty Council, is not to invent rights and freedoms and select to whom they should apply, but to assist peoples to realize fundamental human rights and freedoms and to pursue investigative studies and recommend actions that promote observance of and respect for those rights and liberties. Self-determination for indigenous peoples, the International Indian Treaty Council explains, depends on their right to land, because land is their means of subsistence and is necessary for the continuation of their culture; "without their traditional lands, they are denied their very identity as peoples" (United Nations 1995c:4–5).

The International Indian Treaty Council expresses its awareness of various states' concern that the draft declaration's recognition of the right to indigenous self-determination may ultimately lead to national instability or contribute to the demise of states. It contends, however, that "it is the failure to recognize this basic right of peoples that has contributed to the destruction of States" (United Nations 1995c:5). This denial

> threatens the peace and stability as well as the moral integrity and national honor of States. It is this failure to observe the basic right and fundamental freedom of all peoples that causes massive violations of human rights and fundamental freedoms in all parts of the world today. Until it is resolved, it will continue to be a source of profound division and frequently violent conflict between peoples. (United Nations 1995c:5)

The International Indian Treaty Council also strongly supports the subjective self-identification of indigenous peoples as proposed by Special

Rapporteur Martínez Cobo. Its position is that "the definition of indigenous peoples or persons is the concern of indigenous peoples themselves, not States" (United Nations 1995c:2).

The World Council of Indigenous Peoples, like the International Indian Treaty Council one of the first indigenous nongovernmental organizations to attain consultative status in the United Nations, also seeks to clarify the issue of indigenous self-determination (United Nations 1995c:8–16). It argues that "a failure to recognize indigenous peoples' inherent right, as peoples, to self-determination is not only racist and demeaning, but also violates the fundamental principle of equality and non-discrimination" as defined in the United Nations Charter and other United Nations declarations and conventions (United Nations 1995c:9). The World Council of Indigenous Peoples takes a somewhat more conciliatory tone than the Mohawk Nation, the Inuit Tapirisat, or the International Indian Treaty Council, contending that the conflict between indigenous self-determination and the territorial integrity of states is not inevitable:

> First, indigenous peoples have consistently stated that our aspirations do not include independence or secession, but rather autonomy and control over the direction of our lives and affairs. Second, the Declaration on Principles of International Law Concerning Friendly Relations and Cooperation Among States recognizes that the exercise of the right to self-determination is contextual and includes a range of options in addition to secession and independence. It states that "the establishment of a sovereign and independent State, the free association of integration with an independent State or the emergence into any other political status freely determined by a people constitute modes of implementing the right of self-determination by that people." (United Nations 1995c:9)

The World Council of Indigenous Peoples correctly states that the draft declaration discourages secession in Article 45. It goes on to argue that while Article 3 guarantees the full right of self-determination to indigenous peoples under international law, this article must be read in conjunction with Article 31, which conveys that the preferred expression of indigenous self-determination should be in the forms of autonomy and self-government. The World Council of Indigenous Peoples cautions, however, that these articles indicate "a preference, not a limitation, qualification or the exclusive means of exercising that right" (United Nations 1995c:10).

The World Council of Indigenous Peoples acknowledges Chairperson-Rapporteur Daes's explanatory note accompanying the draft declaration, in which she contends that indigenous peoples should exercise the right to self-determination through the political and legal systems of the state unless these state systems are "so exclusive and non-democratic that

[they] can no longer be said to be representing the whole people" (United Nations 1995c:10). It concludes that this position is consistent with the Declaration on Friendly Relations, which states that

> nothing in the foregoing paragraphs shall be construed as authorizing or en-
> couraging any action which would dismember or impair, totally or in part,
> the territorial integrity or political unity of sovereign and independent States
> conducting themselves in compliance with the principles of equal rights and
> self-determination of peoples as described above and thus . . . representing
> the whole people belonging to the territory without distinction as to race,
> creed or colour. (quoted in United Nations 1995c:10)

It is a state's responsibility, therefore, to comply with international law in order to maintain its legitimate right to sovereignty.

The draft declaration, as understood by the World Council of Indigenous Peoples, thus requires indigenous peoples

> to work within the constitutional and democratic framework of the State,
> through the establishment of effective partnership based on mutual respect
> and good faith. The State has a corresponding duty to accommodate the ex-
> ercise of indigenous peoples' right to self-determination, autonomy, self-
> government and participation through power-sharing and legal constitu-
> tional and democratic reform. . . . The option of secession may only be
> exercised by indigenous peoples should the State fail to accommodate their
> rights and be so abusive and unrepresentative "that the situation is tanta-
> mount to colonialism." (United Nations 1995c:10)

Thus the World Council of Indigenous Peoples asserts indigenous peoples' right to secession as the last recourse in response to relentless, uncompromising, and devastating state-sponsored oppression and tyranny.

The World Council of Indigenous Peoples also emphasizes that indigenous peoples and their land are inseparable; that *terra nullius,* discovery, and conquest are legal fictions that should be immediately and forever repudiated; that indigenous peoples' collective rights are necessary for their survival; and that none of the provisions of the draft declaration should be in any way diminished in future negotiations. Regarding the important issue of treaties, the World Council of Indigenous Peoples argues that:

> Article 36 provides for the "recognition, enforcement and observance of
> treaties, agreements and other constructive arrangements concluded with
> States or their successors, according to the original spirit and intent. . . ." The
> recognition that treaties concluded between indigenous peoples and States
> are valid and legitimate objects of international scrutiny and concern is im-
> portant. To state otherwise would be to perpetuate a distinction based upon

racial and cultural superiority and the notion that the powerful are free to ignore their obligations under international law simply because they have the ability to dominate other peoples.

. . . Despite the important statement noted above, Article 36 needs to be improved if it is to guarantee the recognition and enforcement of treaty rights. The major flaw . . . is that Article 36 does not provide indigenous peoples with independent access to the proposed dispute resolution mechanisms. This compromises the efficacy of the Article as a whole and must be remedied. . . . The draft Declaration does require that all disputes should be submitted to an international body "agreed to by all parties" (Art. 36) and that the procedures used therein be "mutually acceptable and fair" (Art. 39). However, in the absence of some arrangement with States to submit disputes (as provided for in Article 39), indigenous peoples must rely upon the good will of States to submit the dispute. This is especially problematic as it may be against States' interests to do so. (United Nations 1995c:14–15)

The World Council of Indigenous Peoples notes the absence of any international forum that can adequately address indigenous complaints, despite calls for the establishment of a permanent forum for indigenous peoples. Nevertheless, the World Council of Indigenous Peoples endorses the draft declaration, believing it to be a device through which states and indigenous peoples can form alliances based upon reciprocal rights and duties that will enhance democratic unity and prevent violent confrontation between diverse peoples.

THE FUTURE OF THE DECLARATION ON INDIGENOUS RIGHTS

After the Sub-Commission on Prevention of Discrimination and Protection of Minorities heard the states' and indigenous organizations' comments and criticisms, it submitted the draft declaration to the Commission on Human Rights. The declaration will proceed through the Economic and Social Council, then on to the General Assembly.

So far only the Working Group on Indigenous Populations has embraced an open-door policy that allows both indigenous NGOs and indigenous political organizations that lack consultative status to directly participate in its processes, and indigenous insight and experience were crucial to the final outcome of the document. It is possible that succeeding sessions will no longer be accessible to indigenous peoples for such direct and necessary input and negotiation. The Commission on Human Rights, through its Resolution 1995/32 of March 3, 1995, has decided to establish "an open-ended inter-sessional working group . . . to elaborate a draft declaration, as authorized by the Economic and Social Council" (United Nations 1995a:1). Indigenous peoples have expressed their concern that the wording of the resolution could be interpreted to mean that the Commission on Human Rights may prepare an entirely new draft declaration; they urged that "the preservation of the integrity of the draft declaration was essential to indigenous peoples" (United Nations 1995f:12).

Many indigenous organizations state that continued indigenous participation in the process is necessary, and they criticize the complexity of the Economic and Social Council's rules for the participation of indigenous organizations that lack consultative status. Some indigenous organizations, especially those in Asia, have requested adoption of an official definition of *indigenous peoples* so that their governments will not be able to continue to deny their existence and consequently prevent their participation in the process (United Nations 1995f:13). Chairperson-Rapporteur Daes likewise urges the continued open participation of indigenous organizations in the process and requests that governments and the Commission on Human Rights elect an indigenous representative as chairperson-rapporteur of the new working group. She also suggests that governments include indigenous representatives in their delegations to the sessions of the working group and that the Voluntary Fund for Indigenous Populations expand its terms in order to support indigenous representatives desiring to attend the sessions of the new working group (United Nations 1995f:10).

The government of New Zealand expresses its appreciation for the Commission on Human Rights decision to establish an open-ended intergovernmental working group to consider the draft declaration. New Zealand urges governments to maintain the momentum established by the Working Group on Indigenous Populations and to build on the draft, elaborating from it an "appropriate and universally applicable declaration." New Zealand also observes the necessity of continued indigenous participation in the process and encourages the Centre for Human Rights and the secretariat to ensure that all eligible and interested indigenous people's groups may attend the intergovernmental sessions, and it lends support to the broadening of the terms of reference of the Voluntary Fund for Indigenous Populations (United Nations 1995a:10–11, 1995f:12). The government of Australia also acknowledges the necessity of full and open indigenous participation in order to "ensure that the rights and aspirations of indigenous peoples were properly reflected in the draft declaration" (United Nations 1995f:12–13).

In a statement supporting the efforts of the Working Group on Indigenous Populations and the draft declaration, the Indian Law Resource Center, an indigenous NGO, requests that the Sub-Commission on Prevention of Discrimination and Protection of Minorities allow

> the fullest possible attendance and participation of indigenous representatives at the Commission, similar to the rules by which indigenous representatives

participate in meetings of the Working Group on Indigenous Populations. Under present rules, indigenous representatives without consultative status would not be allowed to participate, and this will be a great loss to the Sub-Commission and Commission. Participation by indigenous peoples should be available at all relevant meetings of the Sub-Commission and Commission, including any working group the Commission may set up to study and discuss the draft declaration. (United Nations 1993b:1–2)

The Indian Law Resource Center also requests that indigenous peoples be permitted to utilize the Voluntary Fund for Indigenous Peoples for travel to all United Nations meetings that are of concern to them, such as those of the Commission on Human Rights and the Sub-Commission on Prevention of Discrimination and Protection of Minorities. Travel funds for attendance at these meetings is currently not available to indigenous peoples.

The United States has advanced a position on this issue similar to that outlined by the Indian Law Resource Center; it states in its submission to the Commission on Human Rights that

> The United States fought hard during the fifty-first session of the Commission to ensure that indigenous organizations not in consultative status with the Economic and Social Council, including tribal governments, would also have the opportunity to contribute to the negotiation. It is much appreciated that consensus was achieved on a procedure that will allow "relevant organizations of indigenous people" to apply to participate in the process. (United Nations 1995b:7)

With the obvious logical necessity of continued indigenous participation in the process and with such strong support for it coming from indigenous peoples and state members, it is to be hoped that rules and procedures will be restructured to accommodate indigenous participation.

THE STUDY ON AGREEMENTS BETWEEN STATES AND INDIGENOUS POPULATIONS

In the final volume of his report of his investigation, Special Rapporteur Martínez Cobo recommended that because treaties and other agreements are profoundly important to a large number of indigenous peoples, a thorough study of these agreements should be prepared, including analysis of all points of view on these agreements (United Nations 1991a:2). Indigenous organizations have consistently demanded the international recognition of treaties, and indigenous representatives have expressed the "solemn, spiritual nature of these treaties within their culture and the importance of this study to them" (United Nations 1991b:19). Respect for treaties, human rights activist and Nobel laureate Rigoberta Menchú argues, "could serve as the base for the building of a new alliance" between indigenous peoples and states (Menchú, quoted in Barsh 1994:55).

In Resolution 1989/77 of May 24, 1989, the Economic and Social Council authorized the appointment of a special rapporteur to study treaties, agreements, and other constructive arrangements between states and indigenous peoples (United Nations 1990b:11). Miguel Alfonso Martínez, a member of the Working Group on Indigenous Populations, was appointed to collect all pertinent materials, including scientific and scholarly writings on treaties and other agreements, and to prepare a study on the present and future utility of these agreements, some of which establish indigenous self-determination and collective rights, and some of which are known to have been unfairly negotiated, breached, or left unratified. Commission on Human Rights Resolution 1988/56 of March 9, 1988, mandates the special rapporteur to carry out this study with the "ultimate purpose of ensuring, on a practical level, the promotion and protection of the basic rights and freedoms of 'indigenous populations'" (United Nations 1992e:6, 56). Several indigenous political organizations, such as the International Organization of Indigenous Peoples, a Canadian NGO with consultative status, consider this report to be as important in the long run as the Declaration on the Rights of Indigenous Peoples (United Nations 1993c:2).

Martínez stated in his preliminary report that according to the mandate, the principle objective of his study was one of offering "elements, conclusions and recommendations for the achievement, on a practical level, of the maximum promotion and protection possible, both in domestic and international law, of the rights of indigenous populations and especially of their human rights and fundamental freedoms" (United Nations 1991a:14). In an attempt to promote conciliation, Martínez declared that his recommendations should take "innovative, forward-looking approaches," involving mutual recognition, harmony, and cooperation (United Nations 1991a:15–16). The recommendations should enhance a comprehensive process of juridical "standard setting" in interpretation and resolution of disputes concerning treaties and other agreements, but, Martínez recognizes, such a "comprehensive process" must include the application of anthropological and historical materials and approaches. At the time he made his preliminary report Martínez envisioned his completed study as one made up of three fundamental parts:

> The first is to be dedicated to the origins of the practice of concluding treaties, agreements and other constructive arrangements between indigenous peoples and States; the second will deal with their contemporary significance and the third will discuss their potential value as elements for the regulation of the future relationships between indigenous peoples and States. (United Nations 1991a:21)

At the same time Martínez stated that his final recommendations may include the suggestion that national and international forums assume legal jurisdiction to adjudicate treaty disputes (United Nations 1990a:27). Indigenous representatives have consistently suggested that the International Court of Justice would be the appropriate body to adjudicate treaty disputes between states and indigenous peoples, so many indigenous organizations were critical of Martínez's preliminary report following its publication (United Nations 1993c:2) although they expressed their full support for continuation and completion of the study (United Nations 1992c:31).

In 1999 Martínez finally submitted his study in its final form (United Nations 1999). In it he endorses the general conclusions, judgments, and recommendations of his previous submissions. He had difficulty completing the report because he faced opposition from governments, delays in the return of questionnaires from governments and intergovernmental organizations, and unfulfilled promises of financial resources. At the time of the preliminary report, after he had amassed over four hundred documents pertaining to specific treaties, agreements, and other arrangements, Martínez requested the assistance of specialized research experts. During the 1991 annual meeting of the Working Group on Indigenous Populations, an indigenous representative expressed concern for the length of time the rapporteur's research has already taken and suggested that a treaty conference involving indigenous peoples and other legal experts be held and papers submitted concerning an array of treaty and agreement issues, which would represent an invaluable contribution to the study (United Nations 1991a:19).

In his first progress report, submitted to the working group in 1992, in which he outlined the direction that his research was taking and offered certain conclusions on the basis of the research completed thus far, Martínez criticized both states and indigenous organizations for neglecting to submit completed questionnaires. Martínez stated that the lack of indigenous submissions was particularly regrettable, although he recognized that indigenous oral traditions may not be easily transferred to his predetermined format. One indigenous respondent had criticized the form as overly legalistic and dictatorial in enforcing a certain interpretation that "most Bands are not comfortable with," and commented that if those bands were to complete the form, they would fear undue repercussions from the state, which had violated its treaty obligations (United Nations 1992e:3–5).

In the second chapter of the report, entitled "Some Anthropological and Historical Considerations on Key Issues Relevant to the Study," the special rapporteur recognized that because the negotiating processes that result in treaties and other agreements between states and indigenous peoples often involve cultures, histories, and perceptions that are dissimilar, in order to assess the significance of the instrument, it is absolutely necessary to understand the rationales held by the parties involved when they agreed to the treaty. For this important task the special rapporteur devised a methodological approach that combined cultural relativism, anthropological functionalism, an emerging form of postmodernism, and most importantly ethnohistory. Martínez's team utilized research primarily from the fields of legal and political anthropology in order to comprehend indigenous legal and political systems. Martínez aspired to be especially vigilant in discovering and avoiding the elemental ethnocentrism and Eurocentrism naturally found in these anthropological and historical materials and the treaty documents, and although indigenous histories for the most part remain to be written, he emphasized to as great a degree as possible the indigenous point of view. The special rapporteur determined that the most in-depth review was required of differences in conceptualizations of kinship, of time (especially fidelity to the past) and space, of the individual and the group, of humans' relationship with land and nature, of the role of authority and law, and of protocol in encountering outsiders.

In the third chapter of the report, entitled "The First Encounters: Indigenous Peoples, Euro-Centrism and the Law of Nations," Martínez provided a brief overview of the development of international law, especially with regard to indigenous peoples and territories, and of the origin and evolution of the treaty-making process. His research informed him that when the British and French were struggling to gain supremacy in North America, they enlisted the aid of indigenous nations and established formal legal relations with those nations, which often had superior military forces. He learned that it is absolutely clear that the European nations regarded the indigenous nations with whom they negotiated as independent and sovereign nations possessed of all the associated legal implications in international law, namely "the inherent international personality and legal capacity on the indigenous part for negotiating and entering into treaty relations, resulting from their status as subjects of international law in accordance with the legal doctrines of those times" (United Nations 1992e:23–24). This legal approach of the European powers would later be carried over into Oceania and parts of Asia.

Martínez argued that his conclusions were supported by additional historical facts:

> In the first place, at the time of those first encounters, most indigenous nations in the region had territory, a distinct, permanent population, capacity for international relations and easily identifiable forms of government. These constitute the four key criteria which throughout the history of international law . . . have been required for a political entity to be recognized as having the personality and the capacity to be the subject of international law. (United Nations 1992e:24–25)

The special rapporteur explained that U.S. law continues to recognize indigenous nations as sovereign, independent, self-governed, and even, in *Worcester v. Georgia* (1832), international. It is much the same in Canada. There is no question that the early indigenous nations considered themselves sovereign and independent, with territories, populations, and international political relations. Similar conclusions may hold with respect to Africa, Asia, and Oceania.

The special rapporteur notes that later legal and political actions that unilaterally stripped indigenous nations of their international and sovereign status were clearly intended to divest them of their land rights. This is undeniably the situation with the Indian Removal Act of 1830 and the *Cayuga Indians* (1926) and *Islands of Palmas* (1928) arbitration cases. The outcome of these cases, unquestionably ethnocentric, Eurocentric, and colonialist in character, then influenced the nature of the League of Nations and the United Nations, all the way to the Working Group on Indigenous Populations today. Indigenous peoples have attempted to utilize the League of Nations and the International Court of Justice in order to assert their claims, but by its very nature the international legal system is weighted against them. Special Rapporteur Martínez intends to study more thoroughly the manner in which this striking change occurred.

In the report's fourth chapter, entitled "Diverse Juridical Situations within the Scope of the Study," Martínez identifies five types of situations that require the attention of the United Nations: (1) treaties concluded between states and indigenous peoples; (2) agreements made between states or other entities and indigenous peoples; (3) other constructive arrangements arrived at with the participation of the indigenous peoples concerned; (4) treaties concluded between states containing provisions affecting indigenous peoples as third parties; (5) situations involving indigenous peoples who are neither parties to nor the subject of any of the above-mentioned instruments (United Nations 1992e:30). Due to the overwhelming nature of the task, the special rapporteur has selected a series of cases exemplifying each of the categories.

In the treaty category the special rapporteur cautions that the treaties' context requires comprehensive analysis that includes study of the history of the international relations of the nations involved and of the time-period during which the treaty was concluded, because there was change over time in the treaty-making goals of the successors of the European powers; this change is evident particularly in the 1795 Treaty of Greenville and in the development of the political question doctrine in the United States. The special rapporteur has selected ten representative examples for this study from a wide variety of regions and time periods.

Martínez calls the Great Law of Peace, the Covenant Chain alliances, and the treaties with the Haudenosaunee, or Iroquois Confederacy, the most "enlightening example" of relations between sovereign indigenous and European nations. A second example, which is closely related to the Haudenosaunee situation, are the treaties with the Mikmaq Nation of eastern Canada, especially the Treaty of 1725 between the Mikmaq Nation and the British, which guarantees fishing, hunting, and trading rights for the Mikmaq and takes precedence over the modern Nova Scotia Lands and Forest Act. In response to English-French conflicts in the region in the early 1700s, the Mikmaq had allied themselves with the Passamaquoddy, Malecite, Penobscot, and Abenaki in the Wabanaki Confederacy, and with the assistance of the Ottawas the Wabanaki Confederacy had eventually entered into relations with the Mohawk of the Covenant Chain, their former enemies.

Martínez also examines two important treaties between the United States and the Delaware and other nations east of the Mississippi. The Treaty of Fort Pitt (1788) and the Treaty of Greenville (1795) represent the evolution of treaty-making relationships. On the one hand, the Treaty of Fort Pitt "recognized statehood for a confederation of indigenous peoples to be headed by the Delaware nation, which would have a representative in Congress" (United Nations 1992e:40). This promised statehood never materialized. On the other hand, the Treaty of Greenville between the United States, which was then in a position of nearly overpowering military strength, and the Wyandot (Huron), Delaware, Shawnee, Chippewa, Kickapoo, Potawatomi, Ottawa, and Miami surrendered to the United States the ancestral lands of present-day Ohio and Indiana.

Special Rapporteur Martínez also singles out the history of the Five Civilized Tribes, which include the Creek, the Choctaw, the Chickasaw, the Cherokee, and the Seminole nations. After a long history of political, military, and trade alliances with the Spanish, French, and English, in the early 1800s the five tribes were forced to enter into treaties of allotment and removal with the United States, which, like the Treaty of Greenville, signaled the change in the nature of U.S. treaty making with indigenous nations: "The basic purpose of the policy was to disrupt tribal government and the indigenous communities by offering a fatal—and rather contradictory—choice: either agree to individual allotments (that is, complete assimilation and considerable territorial loss) or move west (that is, segregation). This 'choice' was negotiated by treaties" (United Nations 1992e:44). This series of situations also includes the Indian Removal Act of 1830 and the contradictory cases *Cherokee Nation v. Georgia* (1831) and *Worcester v. Georgia* (1832).

Martínez also examines the relationship between the Maori Nation and the European powers and New Zealand with particular reference to the Declaration of Maori Independence of 1835, the 1840 Treaty of Waitangi and its questions of translation and notions of sovereignty, the Treaty of Waitangi Act of 1975, the Native Land Act of 1909, and the Maori Affairs Act of 1953. He considers treaties of purchase with the indigenous peoples of present-day British Columbia, Canada, entered into by the Hudson Bay Company, representing the British government, which have preserved unextinguished aboriginal title to remaining indigenous land in the region, now settled by European populations.

Martínez also focuses on the 1863 Treaty of Ruby Valley entered into by the Shoshone people of the western United States. The treaty mentions an unceded "Shoshone country" with definite boundaries, and the Shoshone agree to accept a reservation later when they choose to change their way of life. Some Shoshones brought their land claims to the Indian Claims Commission in 1951, and in 1974 their attorneys accepted a compensation award for the Shoshone in the amount of more than $20 million even though the Shoshone people prefer their land rights. Special Rapporteur Martínez questions the right of the Indian Claims Commission to extinguish aboriginal title because the Claims Commission Act does not provide that authority.

Martínez examines the 1868 Treaty of Fort Laramie between the Sioux Nation and the United States, a peace treaty that guarantees the Sioux a large reservation and numerous additional controversial provisions that are still under discussion. Father Peter John Powell indicates that according to the indigenous interpretation of this treaty all lands west of the Missouri River were reserved for the sovereign use of the Sioux in perpetuity.

Finally, Martínez considers two cases in Canada. Treaty No. 6 between the Treaty Six Nations and the British Crown, like the other numbered treaties, guaranteed the indigenous nations party to the treaty lands, gratuities and annuities, schooling, and assistance in times of pestilence and famine. The Cree of Quebec, the Inuit of Quebec, and the Inuit of Port Burwell entered into treaties in 1975 with the Canadian government that allowed them to retain certain rights to traditional lands and to receive compensation for traditional lands they ceded. These agreements resulted from the planned construction of the James Bay hydroelectric complex on traditional indigenous territories; the indigenous peoples were essentially forced to accept the imposition.

Situations in Martínez's second category, "Agreements between States or other entities and indigenous peoples," include treaty-like agreements between the United States and indigenous peoples following the cessation of treaty making in 1871. Some of the other agreements in this category are the 1788 Treaty between Great Britain and the Chiefs of Sierra Leone; the 1791 Agreement between the East India Company of Great Britain and the Mahrattas; the 1818 Treaty of Commercial Alliance between the East India Company and Selangor; the 1922 Agreement between the Government of Canada and the Inuit of the Northwest Territories, otherwise known as the Nunavut Agreement; the 1947 Pangalong Agreement; and the 1989 Agreement between the Federal Minister of Indian Affairs of Canada and the Federation of Saskatchewan

Indian Nations. Instruments in this category vary substantially in their relevance to the purpose of the special rapporteur's study; some are no longer significant.

Under the category "Other Constructive Agreements," the special rapporteur is looking particularly for free and informed consent. The 1979 Greenland Home Rule Act would seem to constitute "the most extensive indigenous self-government arrangement" at the present time (United Nations 1992e:55). Martínez intends "to give very thorough consideration to the specific provisions of the Home Rule Act and to the experiences accumulated under this self-government arrangement, with a view to assessing whether this kind of procedure can be useful for attaining better relations between indigenous and non-indigenous parties" (United Nations 1992e:55–56).

The fourth category, "Situations involving indigenous peoples who are not parties to, or the subject of any of the above-mentioned instruments," covers indigenous peoples of vastly differing historical and political situations. It includes cases of indigenous peoples:

(a) with whom the State has never entered into contractual relations;

(b) who were parties to instruments that in practical terms have been unilaterally abrogated by the State;

(c) who participate in the negotiation and adoption of instruments which were never ratified by the competent State institutions; and

(d) who live in societies in which a deep process of acculturation has taken place and whose legislation does not contain specific provisions guaranteeing distinct protection for their indigenous component, different than the ones recognized for every citizen of the State. (United Nations 1992e:58)

Martínez comments that research in this area remains in the preliminary stage, but that it will include the following case studies: the Australian Aborigines; the Gitskan and Wet'suwet'en of Canada; the Yanomami of Brazil; the Ke Lahui Hawaii, or aboriginal Hawaiians of the United States; the Chittagong Hill tracts of Bangladesh; the Mapuche people of Chile; the indigenous peoples of Guatemala; the Lubicon Cree of Canada; the San of southern Africa; the Ainu of Japan; the California Rancherias of the United States; and the Kuna Nation of Panama.

In the final category, "Treaties between States affecting indigenous peoples as third parties," Special Rapporteur Martínez focuses on the 1494 Treaty of Tordesillas regarding Spanish and Portuguese expansionist claims in the New World, the 1713 Treaty of Utrecht, the 1751 Sweden/Finland-Norway/Denmark Border Treaty, the 1763 Treaty of Paris and the Royal

Proclamation of 1763, the 1794 Jay Treaty, the 1819 Adams-Onis treaty, the 1848 Treaty of Guadalupe-Hidalgo, the 1867 Purchase of Alaska, the 1916 Migratory Birds Convention, and the 1989 ILO Convention Concerning Indigenous and Tribal Peoples in Independent Countries (Convention No. 169). These treaties will possess varying degrees of utility in clarifying or promoting indigenous rights and protection.

At the First Peoples Summit rumors surfaced that the Special Rapporteur Martínez and the subcommission were considering abandoning the project altogether because of governments' and indigenous peoples' uncooperativeness and untimeliness in providing primary sources (United Nations 1993c:2). Nevertheless, the special rapporteur's final report provides tremendous support for the articles in the draft Declaration on the Rights of Indigenous Peoples that cover indigenous self-determination and treaties with indigenous peoples, and it affirms indigenous peoples' expression in their own declarations of their view that their treaties are "sacred," binding international law, entered into between sovereign, independent, and equal nations. In paragraph 315 of his final report, Martínez supports establishment of a permanent forum of indigenous peoples as an international body empowered to decide conflicts based on treaties with indigenous peoples (United Nations 1999).

THE FUTURE ROLE OF THE WORKING GROUP ON INDIGENOUS POPULATIONS

The Working Group on Indigenous Populations continues to carry out its dual mandate of reviewing developments pertaining to the promotion and protection of the human rights and fundamental freedoms of indigenous populations and giving special attention to the evolution of international standards concerning the rights of indigenous populations. In relation to the standard-setting mandate, Chairperson-Rapporteur Daes informed the thirteenth session of the working group that there was growing interest in developing and adopting a definition for the term *indigenous peoples*. Daes is considering designating a specific theme for each forthcoming annual session. The working group also pushes for the continuation of the study on indigenous peoples and transnational corporations, and it has recommended an investigative study of state disposal of toxic waste in indigenous territories. The group will assist in the establishment of a Permanent Forum for Indigenous Peoples, and it plans to continue fulfilling its original directives by overseeing developments in international, regional, and national legislation concerning the protection of the rights of indigenous peoples and by disseminating important historical, legal, and political information regarding indigenous peoples and cultures (United Nations 2000a, 2001a). Also, Daes has completed her studies as special rapporteur of the Sub-Commission on the Protection of Indigenous Cultural Heritage (United Nations 1993a, 1995e; see Appendix) and special rapporteur on indigenous peoples and their relationship to land (United Nations 2001b).

In Resolution 48/163 of December 21, 1993, the United Nations General Assembly invited indigenous organizations and other interested NGOs to "consider the contributions they can make to the success of the International Decade of the World's Indigenous Peoples." The chairperson-rapporteur of the working group drafted a program of activities based on the uncompleted aspects of the International Year for the World's Indigenous People (United Nations 1994a). It was proposed that the activities would be organized according to a yearly thematic structure for the decade:

* 1995 Social Development and the Family

* 1996 Subsistence, Survival, and Health

* 1997 Language, Education, and Cultural Integrity

* 1998 Protecting Spiritual and Cultural Heritage

* 1999 Restoring Relationships with Land and Resources

* 2000 Achieving Environmentally Sound Development

* 2001 Law, Justice, Individual Rights, and Dignity

* 2002 Self-Government and Self-Determination

* 2003 Indigenous Peoples in Peace and Security

* 2004 Partnership in International Governance (United Nations 1994a:2–3)

The chairperson-rapporteur also recommends specific activities that could be undertaken at the international and national levels to publicize the Indigenous Decade, to encourage participation in events, and to fulfill the purpose of the Decade. During the thirteenth session of the working group, indigenous representatives stated that there seemed to be a general lack of awareness of the International Decade of the World's Indigenous Peoples among indigenous communities and the public. Indigenous representatives suggest that because they are the subjects of the International Decade, they should be more involved in the planning, coordination, and implementation of the activities. Several representatives who were present at the session called for the United Nations to sponsor a world conference on indigenous peoples (United Nations 1995a:25–27).

When the World Conference on Human Rights proposed "the establishment of a permanent forum for indigenous peoples in the United Nations system," a proposal was also forwarded suggesting that the Commission on Human Rights should "consider the renewal and updating of the mandate of the Working Group on Indigenous Populations upon completion of the drafting of a declaration on the rights of indigenous peoples." Miguel Alfonso Martínez, member of the working group and author of a working paper on the group's future role, argues that ambiguous wording of the World Conference proposals and recommendations has led to several mistaken conclusions concerning the future of the working group. Martínez challenges these misconceptions. First, the working group does not have a time limit for its existence, such as date of completion of the draft declaration, nor does it require periodic renewal of its mandate, because the broad terms of the original mandate offer a wide "conceptual umbrella" covering most, if not all, pertinent areas of concern to indigenous peoples. Second, no decision to dissolve the working group has been taken by any competent body. Third, the completion of the draft declaration does not imply the end of one of the working group's two mandates (United Nations 1994h).

Martínez believes that the General Assembly and the Commission on Human Rights both intend that there be two permanent United Nations bodies dealing exclusively with indigenous issues: the Permanent Forum for Indigenous Peoples and the Working Group on Indigenous Populations. It is Alfonso Martínez's position that the working group should also play important roles in the implementation and evaluation of the activities of the Indigenous Decade because it has accumulated substantial knowledge and understanding of indigenous issues and because such activity would be consistent with its mandate. Finally, Martínez contends that the working group should not become a forum for formal adjudication of indigenous complaints even though the 1503 Procedure has proven inadequate to deal with the rights of indigenous peoples; the need for a separate and appropriate permanent international forum capable of adjudicating conflicts involving indigenous peoples is increasingly obvious (United Nations 1994h:13–15).

Chapter Six

THE MAORI OF AOTEAROA (NEW ZEALAND) AND THE TREATY OF WAITANGI

✦ Like the Iroquois, the Maori of Aotearoa (New Zealand) claim sovereignty established in both English law and international law by virtue of an authentic, recognizable treaty and other acts and agreements. Prior to the arrival of the English, the Maori tribes existed as separate nations and confederacies with recognizable populations, territories, governments, and political relations between tribes (Best 1924, [1925] 1972; Salmond 1991). After the arrival of the English several Maori tribes united under a single flag through a declaration of independence that was recognizable at the time in English law and international law; they called their new state the United Confederation of Tribes of New Zealand (Ross 1980). Later, representatives of numerous Maori tribes signed the Treaty of Waitangi (1840). According to the Maori version of the text, and as Maori-speaking English missionaries explained to the Maori, Britain recognized Maori independence and sovereignty, and in exchange the Maori granted the British the exclusive right to purchase their lands and recognized the British Crown as the source of ultimate justice and resolution of disputes, like a court of the international law of nations. Several Maori tribes, suspecting British duplicity or preferring to relinquish nothing to the British, refused to sign (Adams 1977; Binney 1989; Buick [1936] 1976; Colenso [1890] 1971; Ross 1972a, 1972b; Rutherford 1949).

When the English, and later the Pakeha (English settlers) of a semi-independent, European New Zealand, failed to uphold or even recognize the Treaty of Waitangi, many tribes united under a Maori king and a constitution. The movement was known as *Kingitanga*, and it was a further expression of their *Mana Motuhake*, or separation and independence from the New Zealand government (Sorrenson 1963). These Maori also engaged in defensive wars to protect both their political independence and their territories (Belich 1986, 1989; Riseborough 1989; Rusden 1888; Sinclair 1961). Other Maori tribes met at the 1860 Conference of Kohimarama to endorse and reconfirm the principles of the Treaty of Waitangi as expressed in its Maori version. This was the origin of a movement known as Kotahitanga (Cox 1993; Orange 1980). The New Zealanders defeated the Maori militarily and continued to dismiss the Treaty of Waitangi as a legal nullity, a position best expressed in the influential case *Wi Pareta v. The Bishop of Wellington and the Attorney General* (1877). They strove to eradicate Maori identity and to alienate and assimilate Maori lands by any means necessary. This led to several unsuccessful attempts by Maori leaders to directly address the British Crown, the arbiter of justice according to the Treaty of Waitangi, and to present their concerns to the League of Nations. The latter half of the twentieth century saw a Maori resurgence, with Maori asserting their legal rights and human rights in New Zealand courts, through political activism, and through involvement in the international indigenous peoples' movement, including active participation in the meetings of the United Nations Working Group on Indigenous Populations (Brookfield 1989, 1990, 1994; Cox 1993; Haughey 1984; Hazlehurst 1995; Henderson 1972; Keith 1990; Kingsbury 1989; R. Walker 1987, 1989, 1990, 1992; D. V. Williams 1989, 1990; Wilson 1990).

THE ORIGINS OF THE MAORI

East Polynesian islanders, physically and culturally similar to the indigenous peoples of Hawaii, the Cook Islands, and Tahiti, sailed in ships capable of carrying one hundred persons with plentiful quantities of supplies and reached the islands of modern-day New Zealand sometime between A.D. 400 and 1000. The approximate date of A.D. 800 for arrival in the North Island, or Aotearoa, is generally accepted by archaeologists (J. Davidson 1983:292; Anderson 1983:7, 1989). The Maori, a name by which they would become known only after 1840 and then by European designation, occupied the South Island roughly one hundred years later. These first inhabitants brought with them several varieties of plants, as well as dogs and rats. There is no evidence, however, that they successfully transferred the pig, a significant food source among East Polynesian peoples (J. Davidson 1983:293–94).

The cold climate of the islands, especially the South Island, was not especially well-suited to early East Polynesian horticultural practice. Fish and seals were abundant, but without other large animals on the islands, the Maori first developed the moa hunter culture known as the Archaic Maori culture. The moa was a large flightless bird like the Australian emu, and along with numerous other birds, including a few other flightless birds, it was particularly abundant in the South Island, but it was eventually hunted to extinction. Europeans at first believed that the moa hunters were a pre-Maori, Melanesian Stone Age people who were later displaced by the Polynesian Maori; this appears not to have been the case (Anderson 1983, 1989; J. Davidson 1983, 1984, 1992).

By the time Captain James Cook arrived in the eighteenth century, the Maori were a horticultural and fishing people. They cultivated crops, particularly *kumara,* and they harvested the sea. According to New Zealand anthropologist Elsdon Best (1924, [1925] 1972) and his successors in the study of Maori culture (Biggs 1960; Firth 1973; Metge 1976; Oppenheim 1973; Salmond 1983; Te Rangi Hiroa 1949; Vayda 1960), the Classic Maori, characterized as a warrior society, engaged in a form of ritualized warfare that included elements of cannibalism and through which occurred the transfer of mana, or power and prestige. The animistic religions of the Classic Maori entail a reverence both for the spirits of natural objects such as rivers, streams, trees, and mountains and for the spirits of the ancestors who coexist with the Maori in daily life. The Classic Maori spiritual world was expressed through wood carving, a semisacred activity carried out by *tohunga,* specialists who were educated in Maori tribal schools (Neich 1983).

The Maori community was composed of subtribes *(hapu),* tribes *(iwi),* and confederations of tribes with political leaders known as *rangatira,* or chiefs, and *ariki,* or paramount chiefs. Property, particularly land, was held in common as tribal property, and decisions concerning the tribe or tribal property required consensus. The land and forests of the islands of New Zealand and its coastal waters and other resources were divided up into the traditional territories of numerous independent tribes. Maori life was regulated at every level by the laws of *tapu,* or sacredness, and mana, or power, authority, and sovereignty (Bowden 1979; Salmond 1989).

EUROPEAN COLONIALISM IN NEW ZEALAND

Through the Treaty of Tordesillas (1494), Pope Alexander VI divided the world in half, allotting all unclaimed territories east of a longitudinal line two thousand kilometers west of the Cape Verde Islands to the Portuguese, all territories west of the line to the Spanish. This principle was later extended to the Pacific through the Treaty of Zaragoza (1529), which established an indeterminate demarcation line and granted the eastern portion to the Spanish and the western to Portugal. With the exception of Spanish colonization of the Philippines and the Marianas islands, where the indigenous Chamorro fell in population from 70,000 to 1,318 in little more than a century as they were "killed in massacres, died of introduced diseases, or were shipped off as slaves and indentured servants to the Philippines," neither Age of Discovery maritime power was able to fully exploit or retain its Pacific possessions (Nile and Clerk 1996:125–26).

In 1609 the Dutch obtained control of the Spice Islands (present-day Indonesia) from Portugal and seized colonial supremacy in the Pacific. The islands were renamed the Dutch East Indies, and the Dutch East India Company was established with a monopoly license over the entire Pacific for the extension of Dutch trade into the region. In 1642, as an employee of the company, Abel Tasman explored Australia's southern coast and "discovered" both Tasmania and New Zealand. With the two ships *Heemskerck* and *Zeehaen,* Tasman sailed into a bay on the northern coast of New Zealand's South Island, where he was greeted by Maori warriors of the Hgati Timata-kokiri tribe in canoes. The Maori sounded a trumpetlike instrument, and a Dutch sailor was instructed to respond with a similar trumpet call. The Maori then attacked the two ships, killing four of Tasman's crew. The Dutch kept the discovery of New Zealand secret and did not pursue any additional ventures there, concentrating instead on exploitation of the Dutch East Indies. The islands of New Zealand remained isolated from European activity until the voyage by Captain James Cook in 1769 and the English and French assumption of colonial supremacy in the Pacific in the second half of the eighteenth century (Nile and Clerk 1996:126–27).

During his first voyage Cook spent six months mapping the New Zealand coastline while scientists and artists explored and recorded the islands' natural features. Cook endured several violent skirmishes with the *tangata maori,* or local people, but with the assistance of the Polynesian interpreter Tupaia he was able to establish trade relations, exchanging European goods for food and water. Demonstrations of European firepower proved useful in restraining Maori hostility. In the reports of his three visits to New Zealand, Cook recommended the islands as suitable for colonization and wrote that he regarded the Maori people, unlike the Australian and Tasmanian Aborigines, as intelligent and capable (Nile and Clerk 1996:130–32; Salmond 1991).

The French quickly followed Cook to the islands. During the first French expedition in 1772 Captain Marion du Fresne and fifteen of his crew were killed by the Maori. The French responded with a violent reprisal, destroying three villages and causing numerous Maori casualties (Dunmore, ed., 1992; Nile and Clerk 1996:133; Tremewan 1990). The first semipermanent and permanent European occupants of the islands included whalers and sealers, escaped convicts from New South Wales, and missionaries. They all located primarily along the northern coasts of the North Island (Salmond 1991; H. Wright 1967).

Introduced to European products, the *iwi,* or Maori tribes, competed with each other for direct trade relations with Britain, and their competition often escalated into large-scale military confrontations. The carnage among a people already distinguished by the ferocity of their warfare was enhanced by the introduction of European weapons. Also, the introduction of the potato had made horticulture far easier, and Maori men were freed to concentrate on other pursuits, generally trade, raiding, and intertribal warfare.

Hongi Hika of the Ngapuhi tribe was the first to seek possession of European arms, which were used to retaliate against and invade enemy Maori tribes in the south. He visited Britain in 1820 under the auspices of the Church Missionary Society and met King George IV, who presented him with a coat of armor. Later, with the aid of large sums of financial assistance resulting from his trip overseas Hongi Hika purchased a cache of guns, and the violence of tribal warfare escalated to an unprecedented level. Other Maori tribes were compelled to compete in weapons purchases so they could defend themselves and retaliate against their attackers (Wilson 1985). Out of the Musket Wars emerged a number of powerful Maori warlords, including Te Rauparaha of the Ngati Toa, who led a devastating campaign against the tribes of the South Island (MacDonald 1990:10; Smith 1910). Other well-known Maori warriors, or military and political leaders, of this period were Te Wherowhero of the Waikato and Te Waharoa of the Ngati Haua.

Depopulated by the violence of the trade wars and by European-introduced diseases, by the 1830s the Maori began to noticeably lose ground to British settlers and land speculators. As economic relations expanded, missionaries settled among the tribes, seeking converts, educating them in European ways, and teaching reading and writing in the Maori language as it was understood by the missionaries. The missionaries established their presence among and importance to many Maori tribes by serving as peacemakers, and the Maori adopted the Christian religion as one of peace and brotherhood. The English missionaries taught the Maori that the British Crown sought a special relation with them in order to protect them, and they joined the Aborigines Protection Society in London in promoting a Maori New Zealand and requesting British protection for the Maori (Binney 1969; Kelsey 1984:22). After Frenchman Charles de Thierry, a purveyor of fraudulent land deals, planned to declare himself "Sovereign Chief of New Zealand," thirteen Maori chiefs, spurred on by perhaps exaggerated fears of a French invasion, petitioned the king of England for protection in 1831 (Orange 1990:6; Tremewan 1992).

THE TREATY OF WAITANGI AND THE ALIENATION OF THE MAORI

In 1833 James Busby arrived in New Zealand as British Resident, an auxiliary of the governor of New South Wales (Australia) authorized by the British government to protect traders and settlers, to protect the Maori tribes from atrocities, to apprehend escaped convicts, and to offer some form of permanent government for the Maori (Orange 1990:7). Busby sought to fulfill the latter obligation in two ways. First, in 1834 he supported the establishment of a flag representing a number of chiefs acting in collective capacity. The resulting rudimentary national government of a sovereign and independent New Zealand was ridiculed by the governor of New South Wales, but the British Crown recognized it, at least in theory, by using it to register New Zealand ships. Second, he supported the formation of the United Confederation of Tribes of New Zealand, which collectively signed the Declaration of the Independence of New Zealand in 1835 (Orange 1987:19–23).

Thirty-four northern Maori chiefs signed the declaration, and the signature of others was sought with promises that the British would recognize Maori sovereignty under British protection (Ross 1980:83). The declaration was written in both English and Maori. In the Maori version *Maori sovereignty* was translated as "mana," and *Maori independence* was translated as "rangatiratanga," or "chiefship." In this document New Zealand was declared to be an "independent state" under the governance and sovereignty of the Maori Confederation (Orange 1987:255–56). Even though Busby persisted in seeking additional signatories and attracted eighteen more between 1836 and 1839, including the important *ariki,* or paramount chief, Te Wherowhero as the final signatory, the proposed annual assemblies of chiefs never took place, primarily because of continued intertribal fighting (Ross 1980).

British authorities considered the possibility of establishing British colonies that would coexist with independent Maori tribes, but despite the declared sovereignty of the Maori Confederation, they eventually decided to found a settler state in New Zealand. This decision was due in large part to the unrelenting pressure of both the New Zealand Company, which preferred to colonize New Zealand via a private enterprise model (Burns 1989), and the Christian Missionary Society, which sought to preserve its position of influence and its land acquisitions in New Zealand (Adams 1977; Binney 1969; Kelsey 1984:23). In 1840 newly appointed Lieutenant Governor William Hobson set out to define the territory over which his jurisdiction should extend. Assisted by his secretaries, several missionaries, and later James Busby, he drew up a treaty document containing his own terms.

Hobson's intent was clearly to achieve an absolute and irreversible transfer of sovereignty from the Maori tribes to the British Crown; this appears in Article 1 of the English version of the treaty. Busby added a provision declaring that the British would protect Maori possession of forests, fisheries, and lands. It appears in Article 2 along with a declaration of the Crown's right of preemption, or right of first refusal, in Maori land sales, which has been erroneously but persistently regarded by the Crown as equivalent to the exclusive right of purchase of Maori lands. Article 3 provided that the Maori would henceforth be regarded as proper British subjects.

William Colenso ([1890] 1971) reports that the Maori were informed of the contents of the treaty through a Maori-language version drawn up by Protestant missionaries, primarily Henry Williams and his son, who were in possession of large quantities of land for which they desired title guaranteed by the British Crown. The account of the signing also indicates that when many Maori chiefs heard the treaty, they were reluctant to sign such a document. The missionaries discussed the treaty further with the chiefs in the Maori language. Many of them returned the following day to sign, and each signatory received blankets and other gifts. Hobson shook the hand of each signer, and proclaimed in Maori to each one "We are now one people."

There was no intertribal consensus on the Treaty of Waitangi. Several tribes did not sign the treaty, and among the tribes with signatories, many important chiefs and *ariki,* such as Te Wherowhero, refused to sign. Several who signed reversed their positions later; when they were apprised of the English interpretation of the treaty, they sought to remove their signatures. Over five hundred signatures were collected beginning with the forty-six on the day of the first signing, but these signatures or marks came mainly from lower ranking chiefs and overwhelmingly from the northern part of the North Island. Nevertheless, Hobson immediately proclaimed Maori cession of and British sovereignty over the North Island via the Treaty of Waitangi, including the territories of those tribes who chose not to enter into the treaty arrangement, and over the less-populated South Island via discovery during the voyages of Captain Cook.

The Treaty of Waitangi was intended to establish British international legal title to New Zealand, thereby fending off the expansionist ventures of the French and the Americans, but the New Zealand Company regarded the treaty as meaningless. The governor of the New Zealand Company, Joseph Somes, wrote to the British colonial secretary in 1843: "We have always had serious doubts whether the Treaty of Waitangi made with naked savages by a Consul invested with no plenipotentiary powers, without ratification by the Crown, could be treated by lawyers as anything but a praiseworthy device for amusing and pacifying savages for the moment" (Somes, quoted in MacDonald 1990:12). The undersecretary to British Colonial Secretary Lord Stanley responded to Somes inquiry: "Lord Stanley entertains a different view of the respect due to the obligations contracted by the Crown of England, and his final answer to the demands of the New Zealand Company must be that, so long as he has the honor of serving the Crown, he will not admit that any person or Government acting in the name of Her Majesty can contract a legal, moral or honorary obligation to despoil others of their lawful and equitable rights" (Stanley, quoted in MacDonald 1990:12).

This vague endorsement of the Treaty of Waitangi by the Crown's representative did not quell the New Zealand Company's operators' desire to cheaply and rapidly acquire Maori land. Because the Treaty of Waitangi, though signed by representatives of the British Crown, was never ratified by the British parliament, its status in international law was apparently never officially established, and the European settlers—the Pakeha—tended to adopt the New Zealand Company's position on the treaty's legal status. The Maori flag and the Declaration of Independence of the United Tribes of New Zealand were already far outside the realm of Pakeha thought and consideration.

LEGAL IMPERIALISM AND THE COLONIZATION OF AOTEAROA

In her article "Legal Imperialism and the Colonization of Aotearoa" (1984), New Zealand law professor Jane Kelsey argues that the British, from the beginning, utilized law as a means of drawing the Maori into an inescapable sphere of British legal sophistry in order to dispossess them of their land and sovereignty peacefully, rather than through conquest, a process which ultimately is as violent as brute force. Kelsey reports that British considerations of establishing a Maori New Zealand were quickly undermined by the goals and actions of the New Zealand Company. The company's requests for a British charter to colonize and settle New Zealand were twice rebuffed in the 1830s, but its mission to New Zealand in 1839 clearly confirmed its operators' determination to colonize New Zealand regardless (Adams 1977; Burns 1989). According to Kelsey,

> The [Church Missionary Society] by this time also supported moves toward full annexation, in part to pre-empt the New Zealand Company, but also to protect their own interests. The threatened encroachment of Catholicism and a clear desire to secure title to their own very large personal and institutional land holdings meant the abandonment of their earlier proposals for a "Maori New Zealand." In 1839 the Colonial Office finally gave way and issued official instructions for the annexation of Aotearoa. The stated goal of all parties was clear—to establish and promote peaceful white settlement in the name of God, the Queen and their own self-interest. Policy toward the Maori people was officially to be that of "amalgamation" or more crudely, the conversion of the Maoris into brown-skinned pakehas. Unofficially, many were unconcerned about the fate of the Maoris and several were already publicly advocating their eventual extermination. (Kelsey 1984:23)

The Aborigines of Australia and Tasmania were already direct witnesses to British colonial policy including extermination of indigenous inhabitants (J. Roberts 1978; L. Ryan 1981).

According to Kelsey, the Treaty of Waitangi was irrelevant to the British annexation of New Zealand, even though the romantic myth of the treaty as a symbol of the unity and amity of two races, two civilizations persists. On June 15, 1839, the commission of the governor of New South Wales was officially extended to include all parts of the islands of New Zealand that would be or were already acquired as sovereign British territory; annexation had by this time become official policy. On January 14, 1840, George Gipps, the governor of New South Wales, swore in Hobson as both consul and lieutenant governor of New Zealand; the latter position demonstrated Britain's assumption of sovereign powers. On January 19, 1840, Gipps issued proclamations declaring the appointment of Hobson and the jurisdiction of the governor of New South Wales over New Zealand. He also proclaimed, in Kelsey's words, that "no title to land in New Zealand purchased after this date would be recognized unless derived from the British crown, and past purchases of 'native land' would be investigated by commissioners appointed by the Crown" (Kelsey 1984:24).

On January 30, 1840, Gipps issued two additional proclamations, announcing that the laws of New South Wales would now be extended to areas of New Zealand already ceded or that may be ceded to the British Crown, and that Hobson would assume his duties on this date. The first marks and signatures were placed on the Treaty of Waitangi on February 6, 1840, and even though their number were few and the signatories were not representative of the majority of Maori tribes, on February 8, 1840, Hobson officially marked the transfer of sovereignty with a twenty-one gun salute. On May 21, 1840, Hobson issued proclamations of British sovereignty, by treaty for the North Island and by discovery for the South Island. Hobson defended his position to the British Colonial Office by falsely claiming that there had been universal tribal agreement to the treaty in the north, and by insisting that the Maori tribes of the South Island were so primitive that they were incapable of agreeing to a treaty. He did not give political or anthropological evidence for his position regarding the South Island, and that position contradicted his orders to Major Thomas Bunbury to collect signatures of the South Island Maori tribes. Kelsey argues that Hobson took this action because he needed "to preempt the impatient New Zealand Company, who were in the process of forming their own government under their own constitution in Wellington" (Kelsey 1984:24–25).

On June 16, 1840, the New South Wales Legislative Council passed an act declaring that "the laws of New South Wales extend to Her Majesty's Dominions in the Island of New Zealand." The act had been introduced there prior to Hobson's proclamations, and it was apparently passed in ignorance of them. On October 2, 1840, Hobson's proclamations received the approval of the British Colonial Office and were published to notify other foreign powers of British claims to sovereignty over New Zealand. On March 30, 1841, Hobson was informed that the Treaty of Waitangi was in the process of formal ratification and therefore had been officially recognized. Hobson had received instructions from the British Colonial Office to treat the Maori with "sincerity, justice and good faith," and Lord Normanby of the British Colonial Office had directly told him that because New Zealand had already been recognized as a free and independent state, no declaration of British sovereignty would be accepted unless the "free and intelligent consent of the natives, expressed according to their established usages, shall be first obtained." Nevertheless, the British viewed annexation and colonization as a foregone conclusion, regardless of the Treaty of Waitangi and the aspirations and independence of the Maori peoples (Kelsey 1984:26; Orange 1987:30–31). According to Kelsey, the treaty served Pakeha settlement strategies, the Pakeha motive of promoting the alienation of Maori land, and the destruction of Maori independence and self-sufficiency (Kelsey 1984:27).

The Treaty of Waitangi was translated into Maori by English missionaries in New Zealand, and it was the Maori-language version to which the overwhelming majority of Maori signatories agreed. Pakeha New Zealanders considered this fact irrelevant, and they eventually forgot about it—until rather late in the twentieth century. In 1972, New Zealand writer Ruth Ross, neither a Maori nor a professional historian, published two seminal articles on the existence and priority of the Maori version of the treaty. Ross emphasizes that in the treaty *sovereignty* was translated as "kawanatanga," an invented word that is a transliteration of *governor* with an appropriate Maori suffix. The word may not have been meaningless to the Maori, but it was well-known that the Maori would recognize the word *mana* as "sovereignty." *Mana* was used by Busby in the declaration of independence, and this concept was communicated among the tribes throughout New Zealand. In the treaty the tribes were also guaranteed their *rangatiratanga,* already understood literally as "chiefship" and, in relation to the British, as "independence." The *kawanatanga* offered to the queen of England, then, appears to be a foreign concept, but the Maori had earlier envisioned it as the acceptance of the authority of an ultimate arbiter to whom tribes could appeal for the determination of justice and protection of rights and powers. The Maori were also guaranteed their *taonga. Taonga* is a Maori concept of broad literal and metaphorical meaning; it includes everything of value to the Maori (Ross 1972a, 1972b). According to the leading scholars of Maori political history, from the time the treaty was signed, the Maori understood the word's significance in this way (Orange 1987, 1990; Walker 1987, 1990).

This Maori understanding of the treaty is confirmed by the presence of another English version of the treaty, this one written by George Gipps, the governor of New South Wales under whose jurisdiction New Zealand was originally placed. In Gipp's version, all sovereignty and right of preemption resided with the British Crown, and not a single Maori would agree to it (Orange 1987:260–61; R. Ross 1972a:145). Later, in June 1843, the New Zealand newspaper *Southern Cross* published one of the English versions of the treaty alongside an English translation of the Maori version. The paper's editors noted the differences, and assuming that the English version was the actual treaty, they claimed that it could not be valid: the Maori could not have understood the treaty—as required by Normanby—because their version did not convey the same meaning as the English version (Orange 1987:103).

In 1842 a dispute erupted between two tribes that were not signatories to the Treaty of Waitangi. The attorney general of the Colonial Office, William Swainson, cautioned Acting Governor Willoughby Shortland about intervening militarily against one of the tribes, claiming that British sovereignty was not absolute: where tribes had not signed the Treaty of Waitangi, no free and intelligent Maori consent had been given. Sovereignty had not been transferred, and these Maori were therefore not British subjects; they were beyond the limits of British law and the Crown's authority. Others countered that Hobson's proclamation extended British sovereignty over the entirety of the islands and over all inhabitants and that the treaty was thus irrelevant. The British Colonial Office, which was responsible for the instructions that Swainson had conveyed, responded: "It was for the Queen, on the advice of her responsible Ministers, to interpret her own pledges;—to say how far a perfectly unanimous consent of the native chiefs was necessary;—and to determine whether the assent actually given was or was not free and intelligent" (quoted in Kelsey 1984:26). The Treaty of Waitangi was sealed, metaphorically, with the queen's personal promise to the Maori to maintain this "sacred" agreement; nevertheless, the Treaty of Waitangi and the promises made to the Maori were quickly declared irrelevant when it was convenient for the British Colonial Office to do so.

THE WHITE MAN'S ANGER AND THE MAORI LAND WARS

The New Zealand Land Claims Bill of 1840, initiated by Gipps, had called for the investigation of all land sales that had occurred prior to the signing of the treaty and allowed the Crown to claim "surplus" Maori lands that had been fraudulently and illegally purchased. This called into question all Maori title and dated British sovereignty from the time of discovery by Cook. Although the bill partially fulfilled Hobson's and Busby's promises to return to the Maori all land unjustly taken from them prior to the signing of the Treaty of Waitangi, the Maori were ultimately afforded only a severely restricted right to the occupancy and use of the confiscated "surplus" land (Orange 1987:94–97). The Maori were greatly alarmed by the new government's stated capacity to take "surplus" land, even though it was being taken from Pakeha only. They consulted a missionary, who guaranteed them that their land was protected by the Treaty of Waitangi.

In order to calm Maori fears, the government established a Maori-language newspaper called the *Maori Messenger* and used the paper to provide information concerning laws and policies and to attempt to communicate its sincerity and its commitment to the just treatment of the Maori people. The Maori-language version of the Treaty of Waitangi was printed in one of the first issues of the *Maori Messenger* (Orange 1987:97–98).

After the treaty was signed, the New Zealand Company brought a flood of settlers. This led to an increase in tensions between the still numerically superior Maori and the Pakeha who were encroaching upon their territories. The settlers lusted after the Maori lands and forests, which were, from the settler's perspective, being allowed to lay in waste. Many Maori tribes, however, were engaged in growing a variety of crops and many Pakeha settlements were dependent on the food they supplied. The Maori were also exporting food to Australia. Financially prosperous, they replaced the missionary schools with their own, and Maori-language literacy among them rose dramatically.

In 1844 Hongi Hika's nephew Hone Heke, in a symbolic gesture of the independence the Maori had never surrendered or given away, cut down the British flag that flew over Russell, the New Zealand Company settlement in Kororeraka. Hone Heke believed that the Pakeha's long-term goal was complete possession of Maori land. With the military and moral support of several Maori tribes, Hone Heke demanded the removal of British authority from Maori regions where Maori had not surrendered their mana to the Crown or had not agreed to the treaty. Three times the settlers raised the flag again, and three times Hone Heke cut it down. During the resulting major military confrontation, Hone Heke's Ngapuhi tribal warriors sacked and burned the settlement. Hone Heke would eventually appeal directly to Queen Victoria in a letter delivered by New Zealand Governor George Grey, asking her to uphold Maori mana as their ancestors had recognized through the 1835 Declaration of Independence of the Confederated Tribes of New Zealand (Orange 1987:118–26; Rutherford 1947; Wilson 1985).

The Crown possessed sole right to the purchase of Maori land, but it was required to first establish that all tribal owners of collectively held Maori land agreed to the sale. Because this was a difficult and lengthy process, land sales proceeded at a pace far too slow for the anxious settlers. The Crown then passed the Land Claims Ordinance of 1841, which declared all "unappropriated" or "waste land" beyond that necessary for the "rightful and necessary occupation of the aboriginal inhabitants of the said Colony" to be in the possession of the Crown. The Native Trusts Ordinance of 1844 followed. It provided for the education of the Maori as a "civilizing" mission, "which object may best be attained by assimilating as speedily as possible the habits and usages of the Native to those of the European population." Governor Fitzroy's Proclamation of 1844 abandoned the Crown's right of preemption in order to facilitate land sales from the Maori to British immigrants. The Native Lands Purchase Ordinance of 1846 restored the Crown's right of preemption in order to raise money for the colony's government through land sales and to circumvent long-term Maori leases of land to Pakeha. The ordinance temporarily slowed the spiraling process of Maori land alienation. The New Zealand Government Act of 1846 required Governor Grey to demarcate all land in the colony and to disallow Maori ownership of any land not actually occupied or in use. Unused land would revert to Crown possession. Because the Maori protested, the Crown repealed the act and replaced it with the New Zealand Company Colonization Act, which was somewhat less obvious in its intentions and methods (Kelsey 1984:32–33). In 1848 the Crown government of New Zealand, under Governor Grey, violated the terms of the Treaty of Waitangi by forcing the Maori to sell to the British nearly half of their territory, three million acres of the North Island and thirty million acres of the South Island (Orange 1987:128–29).

The New Zealand Constitution Act of 1852 granted New Zealand a limited form of self-government, with a constitution, a parliament, and six provincial councils. Voting rights were granted only to those who owned property privately, effectively disfranchising the Maori, who continued to own their property communally. Article 71 of the constitution permits Maori lands to be regarded as existing outside the authority of the colonial government, but no New Zealand governor ever enacted this provision. By 1858 the Pakeha outnumbered the Maori, and the settlers were resentful that a large part of the North Island, including most of the prime agricultural land, remained in Maori hands. The Maori, on the other hand, were disappointed with the constitution and with the lack of governmental or administrative support in Maori regions. They were greatly concerned about the erosion of Maori culture, including the authority of the chiefs, the *tohunga,* and the law of *tapu,* and they were alarmed at the continuing alienation of Maori land. In 1858 several northern Maori tribes met and elected a Maori king, Te Wherowhero, who took the name Potatau I and pledged to remain loyal to the queen but to retain Maori mana, to establish a government that would coexist with but be independent of the New Zealand government, and to halt land sales. The governor of New Zealand regarded his action as treason.

In 1860 the New Zealand government attempted to purchase land from the Waitara, who refused to sell. The settlers especially coveted the area they occupied, so when one Maori chief could be persuaded to sell, the government quickly moved to take possession. Wiremu Kingi, a local chief, resisted, refusing to allow the confiscation. The New Zealand military immediately attacked Kingi's *pa,* or earthen fortress, an act that set off a war. Warriors from Potatau I's Waikato tribe joined Wiremu Kingi's forces over the king's objections. The governor, as a pretext for invading Potatau I's territory, then falsely claimed that the confederated Waikato forces were planning to invade Auckland. Realizing that truth was on the side of the Maori, the British commander, General Duncan Cameron, resigned. The British troops involved in the conflict were later removed, but only after they carried out a scorched-earth campaign under a new commander. New Zealand settlers continued the conflict, which evolved into a deadly guerilla war (Belich 1986; Rusden 1888; Sinclair 1961).

During this conflict with the Maori, the New Zealand parliament passed the Native Lands Act of 1862, sponsored by Minister of War Thomas Russell, who was also a major land speculator. This act once again dispensed with the Crown's right of preemption, and it established a Land Court that was authorized to individualize Maori title to land. The Suppression of Rebellion Act of 1863, also sponsored by Russell, declared that Maori defense of their land was "rebellion against the Crown," the penalty for which was execution as well as confiscation of land. Military courts were established to judge the resistance cases, and habeas corpus was suspended; at the same time Pakeha were granted immunity for crimes committed against the Maori. The New Zealand Settlements Act of 1863 allowed confiscation of land from any Maori tribe believed to have members supporting rebellion. These laws aided in the confiscation of three million acres of Maori land, regardless of whether the Maori tribes in question were at war or at peace with the New Zealand government (Kelsey 1984:33–34; Reynolds 1990:55; Sorrenson 1963; Walker 1990:119–38).

NEW ZEALAND LEGISLATION AND THE ALIENATION OF THE MAORI

The Native Lands Act of 1865 allowed the Land Court to receive petitions from anyone concerning title to land, and it restricted the court to considering only evidence presented. The act's purpose, as stated in its preamble, was "to encourage the extinction of tribal ownership" (Reynolds 1990:57; Walker 1990:136). Pakeha could bring claims against Maori, who would automatically be stripped of their title if they chose not to participate. If the Maori participated in militarily defending their land, they incurred enormous costs that could be paid only through the sale of additional land. Individual Maori were also pressured or induced into petitioning the court for title, and if the other communal owners were unaware of or unable to defend against the petition, ownership would be placed with the Maori petitioner and then that petitioner could sell land that also belonged to others. The Maori Representation Act of 1867 allowed for the election of four Maori representatives to parliament, a move that gave an appearance of Maori participation in government while preventing effective participation because such a small number of Maori in parliament possessed no political power (Kelsey 1984:34; Walker 1990:144–46). The Native Schools Act of 1867 required the abolition of the Maori language as the language of instruction in all schools wherever possible; in 1871 an amendment to this act required that English be the only language of instruction in schools (MacDonald 1990:14; Walker 1990:146–48).

The Maori were now almost completely demoralized. The Maori King and his followers had fled in exile to the King Country hills. Maori turned away from Christianity and the Christian missions, and prophets began to arise among them. One of the first prophets, Te Whiti, established a village at Parihaka and promoted non-violence. Maori warriors joined Te Whiti and attempted to disrupt the efforts of government land surveyors and till areas of Maori land that were in the process of confiscation (Elsmore 1989; Walker 1990:159). Under the terms of the Maori Prisoners Trial Acts of 1879, New Zealand sent an army, which seized Parihaka and, without encountering Maori armed resistance, forcibly sent Te Whiti and his companions to prison in the South Island without trial. The West Coast Peace Preservation Act of 1882 allowed the indefinite imprisonment of Te Whiti and another Maori, Tohu, without trial and made any effort by others to seek their freedom a criminal offence. The Native Lands Administration Act of 1886 placed authority for all Maori lands in the hands of trustees who had the right to sell or lease that land despite Maori objections or communal rights (Kelsey 1984:34; MacDonald 1990:13–14; Walker 1990:159).

In the late nineteenth century, following the land wars, Te Kotahitanga or the Maori unity movement was revived and formed an independent Maori Parliament; King Tawhiao mirrored Kotahitanga by forming Kauhanganui, the King's House of Assembly. In 1894, the Kotahitanga movement, after a long struggle, introduced to the New Zealand parliament a Maori Rights Bill which would guarantee Maori control over their own land, fisheries, oyster beds, shellfish beds, estuaries and other areas vital to Maori wellbeing. The members of parliament, rather than debate the issue, simply walked out and ended the session. In 1896, parliament defeated a second, watered down Native Rights Bill (Cox 1993; MacDonald 1990:15; Orange 1980; Walker 1990:165–71).

MAORI DELEGATIONS TO THE BRITISH CROWN

Faced with the intransigence of the New Zealand government, several Maori made trips to meet with the British Crown in order to discuss serious violations of the sacred agreement, but with no success. The Treaty of Waitangi, despite the Queen's personal guarantee, was now considered to have been a political agreement subject to parliamentary approval rather than a personal or royal agreement for which the Crown held personal responsibility (Brookfield 1994:16). In 1882, chiefs of the Ngapuhi tribe requested to meet with Queen Victoria, but the Colonial Secretary refused them an audience. Their petition sought to inform the Queen that the New Zealand government refused to adhere to the principles of the Treaty, and they asked for a royal commission to investigate illegal land confiscations. In 1884, the Maori King, Tawhiao, the son of Te Wherowhero, traveled to England accompanied by a deputation including Major Wiremu Te Wheoro, a Maori member of parliament who had fought on the side of the government during the Maori wars, in order to address the Queen with their grievances. They, too, were refused permission to speak with the Queen and were instructed to submit their petition to the New Zealand parliament. During the first part of the twentieth century, another Maori King, Te Rata, did meet with King George V and Queen Mary but on the condition that he raise no troubling issues, and again nothing came of the effort. In 1924, the Maori prophet W. T. Ratana led a delegation to London in order to petition the King, but his mission was obstructed by the New Zealand High Commissioner and Ratana failed to meet either the King or the British Prime Minister. Ratana then turned to the League of Nations, requesting its assistance in resolving Maori grievances but once more came away with nothing (Henderson 1972; Sanders 1977:8). Subsequently, Ratana submitted a petition to the New Zealand parliament to have the Treaty of Waitangi ratified. Again, nothing came of rather monumental efforts although in 1945 the Maori Affairs Committee of parliament recommended that copies of the Treaty of Waitangi be published as a "sacred reaffirmation" and placed in all New Zealand schools (MacDonald 1990:15; Walker 1990:196).

In 1928, however, New Zealand's Prime Minister Gordon Coates initiated a royal commission to investigate the grievances of the Maori. The commission found that in Taranaki, the Maori "were treated as rebels and war declared against them before they had engaged in rebellion of any kind, and in the circumstances they had no alternative but to fight in their own self-defence," not in opposition to the Queen or British sovereignty, but in "a struggle for house and home," in "an unjust and unholy war" (quoted in MacDonald 1990:15). The commission believed the claim that the Waikato tribes had threatened to invade Auckland and were, therefore, not blameless, but the commission did regard the confiscations excessive. Payments based on the value of Maori land at the time of confiscation were offered to the Taranaki, Waikato, and other tribes as compensation, but the Waikato tribes refused and insisted on the return of their land. In 1946 a revised offer of payment was accepted by the Waikato tribes. Nonetheless, legislation in New Zealand in the twentieth century continued to alienate the Maori from their enormously diminished landholdings and to destroy their cultural independence and identity.

MAORI DISPOSSESSION AND RESURGENCE IN THE TWENTIETH CENTURY

The Land Settlement Act of 1904 declared that land "not required or suitable for occupation by the Maori owners" be placed in the control of Land Councils, which had no Maori representation. The Suppression of Tohunga Act of 1907 made illegal the tohunga, the spiritual and educational school of traditional Maori society. The Land Laws Amendment Act of 1912 eased the possibility of converting leases of Maori land by Pakeha into Pakeha freeholdings, or ownership. The Maori Social and Economic Advancement Act of 1945 did attempt to return land to Maori following expiration of leases; however, the Maori themselves had no control over the process. The Maori Affairs Act of 1953 enabled a Pakeha Trustee, acting as a Maori Land Purchase Agent, to compulsorily purchase Maori land that could be regarded as uneconomic. The Maori Affairs Amendment Act of 1967 required Maori land owners to individualize their title to land or else have it confiscated by the government (Kelsey 1984:35–36).

During the 1950s and 1960s, Maori people began leaving the rural areas for New Zealand's cities. The Maori became a more visible presence for the Pakeha New Zealander; racial discrimination and Maori poverty were now obvious. During the early 1970s the urban Maori began to develop a new approach to appealing for resolution of land issues and recognition of Maori language and culture: the protest movement. In 1970, urban Maori, mostly students and college graduates, formed the activist organization Nga Tamatoa, which first campaigned for Maori-language schools. In 1971 Nga Tamatoa attempted to disrupt the annual Treaty of Waitangi celebration in Waitangi, largely a Pakeha event, claiming that the Treaty had not protected their land, forests, and fisheries. Following contact with Native Americans in the United States and participation in the "Trail of Broken Treaties" march on Washington, in 1975 Nga Tamatoa helped organize a Maori Land march from the extreme north of the northern island to Wellington at its southern tip, led by eighty-year-old Whina Cooper, which drew the attention of Maori and Pakeha alike to Maori grievances.

The Maori continued to pursue justice in New Zealand courts despite the long history of legal defeats. Eva Rickard, a Maori woman, single-handedly pursued a ten-year battle against the government for return of Maori land on the west coast south of Auckland that had been taken from them by the government, on a temporary basis, during World War II in order to build an airport. The government did not return the property following the conclusion of the war and eventually allowed a golf course to be built on the premises. Despite death threats and legal assaults, Rickard finally won the case in 1983, and the land was returned to the tribe (Mac-Donald 1990:16; Reynolds 1990:60–61).

In 1978, Maori occupied Bastion Point, an area of land rightfully belonging to the Ngati Whatua, who had been violently driven out from it more than thirty years previously. The government refused to return the property even though the Ngati Whatua had always remained loyal to the Crown. The protesters were forcibly removed by six hundred soldiers and police, with the assistance of bulldozers and helicopters (Reynolds 1990:61; Walker 1990:215–19). In 1981 Maori protests at the annual Waitangi Day celebration took an ugly turn when members of the Waitangi Action Committee, an activist organization committed to halting the celebration of the treaty until it is actually honored in practice, were hauled away by police during the ceremony and charged with rioting (Hazlehurst 1995). In 1984 urban Maori and traditional Maori from the rural areas, from all parts of New Zealand, joined forces for the first time in a peace march known as the Hikoi. Under the banner of Te Kotahitanga, the Maori unity movement, they marched from the center of the Maori king's territory to Waitangi in order to call for the governor to honor the Treaty of Waitangi. Police stopped them at a bridge before they could enter the Waitangi grounds during the annual Waitangi Day celebration (MacDonald 1989, 1990:17–18). The depth of Maori frustration led directly to the movement for Maori self-determination and sovereignty, or *Mana Motuhake,* perhaps most popularly expressed in the works of Maori activist Donna Awatere (1982a, 1982b, 1983), who demands the return of New Zealand to Maori control.

THE FORMATION OF THE WORLD COUNCIL OF INDIGENOUS PEOPLES

In 1971 George Manuel, a member of the Shushwao tribe of British Columbia in Canada and head of the National Indian Brotherhood (NIB), traveled to New Zealand and Australia and later Scandinavia, meeting with indigenous peoples and becoming acquainted with their history and political concerns. Manuel attended the United Nations conference on the environment in Stockholm in 1972 as an advisor to the Canadian delegation, then later met with the International Labour Organization and the World Council of Churches in Geneva, the International Work Group for Indigenous Affairs in Copenhagen, and Survival International and the Anti-Slavery Society in London. While he was in Copenhagen, Manuel announced his intention to organize an international conference on indigenous peoples and to establish ties with the National Congress of American Indians in the United States. In 1972 the National Indian Brotherhood endorsed the idea of an international conference that would be organized and controlled by indigenous people and applied for NGO status at the United Nations (Sanders 1977:11–12).

The first preparatory meeting for the conference was held in Georgetown, Guyana, in 1974. With the financial support of religious organizations, such as the World Council of Churches, indigenous representatives from Canada, New Zealand, the United States, Australia, Greenland, Guyana, and Norway attended. At the preparatory meeting the participants approved the proposal for an international conference and offered a definition of *indigenous people:* "The term indigenous people refers to people living in countries which have a population composed of differing ethnic or racial groups which are descendants of the earliest populations living in the area and who do not as a group control the national government of the countries within which they live" (quoted in Sanders 1977:12). This definition was intended to assist in the selection of appropriate delegates to the conference.

The National Indian Brotherhood began laborious preparations for sponsoring the international conference. The NIB was granted NGO status in the United Nations in 1974, with the understanding that the NGO status would then transfer to the organization that would be created as a result of the conference. It was the first indigenous organization to receive that recognition. In 1975 a second preparatory meeting was held in Copenhagen. The members of the conference policy board were George Manuel, Neil Watene of New Zealand, Julio Tumiri Apaza of Bolivia, Trino Morales of Colombia, Charles Trimble of the United States, Aslak Nils Sara of Scandinavia, and Robert Peterson of Greenland. Sam Deloria of the United States and Angmalortok Olsen of Greenland also participated (Sanders 1977:13–14).

The conference was held in Port Alberni, British Columbia, in October 1975, hosted by the Sheshat band of Nootka Indians. The conference was attended by two hundred and sixty people, of whom fifty-two were delegates, and the countries represented included Argentina, Australia, Bolivia, Canada, Colombia, Ecuador, Finland, Greenland, Guatemala, Mexico, New Zealand, Nicaragua, Norway, Panama, Paraguay, Peru, Sweden, the United States (including representatives from Hawaii), and Venezuela. The Maori delegates were members of the New Zealand Maori Council, an organization established by legislation and receiving funding from the government of New Zealand. Other indigenous organizations also received government support. The workshops for the conference covered representation at the United Nations; the charter of the World Council of Indigenous People, the international indigenous organization that would result from the conference; social, economic, and political justice for indigenous peoples; conserving indigenous cultural identity; and preserving indigenous land and natural resources. George Manuel was elected chairman of the World Council of Indigenous Peoples, and Neil Watene of New Zealand was elected a member of the board. Among the conference's resolutions were one asserting council's need to contribute to the United Nations study on discrimination against indigenous populations and another condemning Brazil for policies of genocide and ethnocide carried out against indigenous peoples.

In August 1977 the World Council of Indigenous Peoples held its second assembly in Sweden. The conference was notable for its statement of rights and principles concerning indigenous peoples and especially for its insistence on indigenous peoples' irrevocable right to self-determination and on their right to their land, whether they possess title or not, as the fundamental principle of legal justice. The World Council of Indigenous Peoples' Declaration on Human Rights begins as follows:

> We have surveyed those areas [that] were invaded by the Europeans. To make their intrusion they used various means: direct or indirect violence, fraud and manipulation. These were the methods they used to occupy the land of the indigenous populations and acquire titles to such property which was rightfully owned by the aboriginals. These infamous conditions still prevail as of today, without any consideration to the fundamental declarations of the United Nations on Human Rights. (reprinted in Bodley 1990:219–22)

The declaration is followed by an initial list of principles and an appeal for an immediate end to violence against indigenous peoples.

A third general assembly was held in Australia in 1981. At its fourth general assembly, held in Panama in 1984, the World Council of Indigenous Peoples elaborated on its declaration of principles of indigenous rights:

> Principle 1. All indigenous peoples have the right of self-determination. By virtue of this right they may freely determine their political status and freely pursue their economic, social, religious and cultural development.

> Principle 2. All states within which an indigenous people lives shall recognize the population, territory and institutions of the indigenous people.

> Principle 3. The cultures of the indigenous peoples are part of the cultural heritage of mankind.

> Principle 4. The traditions and customs of indigenous people must be respected by the states, and recognized as a fundamental source of law.

> Principle 5. All indigenous peoples have the right to determine the person or groups of persons who are included within its population.

Principle 6. Each indigenous people has the right to determine the form, structure and authority of its institutions.

Principle 7. The institutions of indigenous peoples and their decisions, like those of states, must be in conformity with internationally accepted human rights both collective and individual.

Principle 8. Indigenous peoples and their members are entitled to participate in the political life of the state.

Principle 9. Indigenous peoples shall have exclusive rights to their traditional lands and its resources; where the lands and resources of the indigenous peoples have been taken away without their free and informed consent such lands and resources shall be returned.

Principle 10. The land rights of an indigenous people include surface and sub-surface rights, full rights to interior and coastal waters and rights to adequate and exclusive coastal economic zones within the limits of international law.

Principle 11. All indigenous peoples may, for their own needs, freely use their natural wealth and resources in accordance with Principles 9 and 10.

Principle 12. No actions or course of conduct may be undertaken which, directly or indirectly, may result in the destruction of land, air, water, sea ice, wildlife, habitat or natural resources without the free and informed consent of the indigenous peoples affected.

Principle 13. The original rights to their material culture, including archaeological sites, artifacts, designs, technology and works of art, lie with the indigenous people.

Principle 14. The indigenous peoples have the right to receive education in their own language or to establish their own educational institutions. The languages of the indigenous peoples are to be respected by the states in all dealings between the indigenous people and the state on the basis of equality and non-discrimination.

Principle 15. The indigenous peoples and their authorities have the right to be previously consulted and to authorize the realization of all technological and scientific investigations to be conducted within their territories and to be informed and have full access to the results of the investigation.

Principle 16. Indigenous peoples have the right, in accordance with their traditions, to move freely and conduct traditional activities and maintain kinship relationships across international boundaries.

Principle 17. Treaties between indigenous nations or peoples and representatives of states freely entered into, shall be given full effect under national and international laws. (reprinted in Bodley 1990:223–24)

The fourth general assembly also addressed the controversial issue of indigenous liberation movements and the question of armed struggle:

The responsibility of violence rests upon the souls of those who deny justice. The resort to arms is justified, but *only* as a last resort, only after an appeal to reason is no longer available. But when a resort to arms becomes necessary, it should be done with pride and not with shame; it should be used with compassion and not with uncontrolled hate; it must be taken up always with a clear understanding that it is justified only for the sake of liberation of our people and not for the purpose of revenge or suppression of another person's right to life and liberty of self-determination. (reprinted in Burger 1987:59)

The World Council of Indigenous Peoples has continued to participate in the annual meetings of the United Nations Working Group on Indigenous Populations, enlightening the members of the working group, educating indigenous people on the issues, and assisting in addressing those issues.

THE WAITANGI TRIBUNAL AND THE TREATY OF WAITANGI

Since the early twentieth century New Zealand's Labour Party has maintained an important alliance with Maori representatives belonging to the Ratana Party and therefore has taken more of an interest in Maori issues and grievances than the Conservative Party has. However, not until after the beginning of Maori activism in the 1970s were any significant steps for redress taken. In 1975 the Labour Party, then in power, passed the Treaty of Waitangi Act, which created an independent Waitangi Tribunal as a commission of inquiry to investigate Maori claims concerning new legislative acts that are in violation of the principles of the Treaty of Waitangi, including both the English and the Maori versions. The act required that all claimants must be of Maori descent and each claim must be brought by an individual. Only cases concerning legislation dating from 1975 forward could be brought before the panel of three judges, which possessed the authority only to recommend courses of action, including invalidating legislation and proposing forms of government restitution. Furthermore, only land owned by the government of New Zealand could be considered; property that had passed into private ownership was beyond the scope of the tribunal, and those claims were nonjusticiable (Waitangi Tribunal Division 1990). Prior to the conclusion of the Waitangi Tribunal's first hearing, the Conservative Party defeated the Labour Party in national elections. The conservatives' victory was due in no small part to their tough rhetoric against Maori activism and their outspoken opposition to the investigation of Maori claims on the basis of the Treaty of Waitangi.

Aila Taylor of the Te Atiawa of Taranaki, a tribe that had lost most of its ancestral land following the Maori Land Wars, brought the first Maori claim before the tribunal. Taylor argued that the virtually landless Te Atiawa tribe had continued to utilize the ancestral sea areas guaranteed by the Treaty of Waitangi as a food supply source. This resource was being threatened by New Zealand's Think Big development program, which was in the process of constructing a major synthetic fuel plant on the Taranaki coast. Taylor argued that this plant, the centerpiece of the Think Big program, would introduce massive amounts of industrial pollutants into the Te Atiawa seabed reefs, rendering them useless and thus violating treaty guarantees. The government argued that the reefs were of little or no benefit to the Te Atiawa and were no longer an important part of the Maori culture. Taylor invited the Waitangi Tribunal to the Te Atiawa *marae*, or meeting house, to enjoy a banquet of seafood from the reef. While the members of the tribunal were there, and despite Maori reluctance to expose their culture and tribal history, Taylor brought before them a number of witnesses, including Te Atiawa elders, who explained the relationship of the Te Atiawa people to those coastal waters and complained of environmental pollution, the desecration of sacred sites, and the destruction of reefs throughout New Zealand's coastal waters. The Waitangi Tribunal decided in favor of the Te Atiawa, but the government, under the Conservative Party, rejected the tribunal's decision. A popular outcry, however, convinced the government to change its position (MacDonald 1990:16–17).

The Treaty of Waitangi Amendment Act of 1985 authorized the Waitangi Tribunal to investigate claims dating from the time the treaty was signed in 1840. The act added more judges to the tribunal to handle the anticipated increase in the number of cases. The tribunal has found in favor of Maori tribes in several additional cases, including the case concerning Bastion Point. But the tribunal's authority remains severely restricted:

Once land goes into private ownership—no matter what race the owner belongs to—there is no way it can be taken away from the present owner and given back to a previous owner. The most the tribunal can do is to suggest that the government could offer to buy especially sacred land, a burial ground for example, from a private owner and then to pass it back to a tribe. . . . On top of that, the tribunal is also limited to the principles of the treaty. That is to say, the tribunal is not to concern itself with narrowly interpreting the exact words of the treaty, but with its underlying ideas, and it is not to seek an ideal application of those principles but must look for practical answers. (Reynolds 1990:68)

The New Zealand government has already announced a limit on the amount of money it will spend to make restitution to the Maori; it is far less than the actual value of the injustices suffered by them.

Conclusion

ANTHROPOLOGY AND THE

LIBERATION OF INDIGENOUS NATIONS

[In 1883] Northern Pacific railroad executives invited Sitting Bull to Bismarck, North Dakota, for ceremonies celebrating the completion of their transcontinental route. Sitting Bull rode at the head of the parade and sat with the dignitaries on the speakers' platform. When it was his turn to speak, he rose and began in Sioux: "I hate all white people. You are thieves and liars. You have taken away our land and made us outcasts." The army officer assigned to translate was stunned but then recovered and told the audience how happy Sitting Bull was to be there and how he looked forward to peace and prosperity between the whites and the Indian people. The audience gave Sitting Bull a standing ovation and the railroad executives invited him to another ceremony in St. Paul. Sitting Bull had great public acceptance and popularity.

—Judith Ries, *Native American History*, 292–93

✦ The twentieth century was witness to the tragic results of a wrongheaded notion of progress: the annihilation of indigenous cultures and the transformation of traditional territories on a global scale as settler movements and military regimes powered by the force of mass production and consumption expanded the limits of their domain through assimilation and genocide of peoples, through environmental destruction and ecocide. Although expansion has occasionally decelerated as a result of indigenous peoples' protests, contemporary emphases on human rights and cultural and environmental preservation, and the theory and practice of sustainable development, it is rarely if ever permanently stopped or reversed. For example, in Brazil talk of building the Xingu River dam continues in government and business circles with little regard for the effect the project will have on the Kayapo Indians of the central part of the country.

Indigenous peoples have attempted to address their tormentors in the past with limited or no success; their words have been dismissed or distorted. Even when indigenous peoples' concerns are seriously addressed, the result is most often a more humane form of assimilation, as with offers of national citizenship, programs for social welfare, and projects for sustainable development that ultimately incorporate indigenous territories economically. The right of all peoples to self-determination as a principle of international law has itself increasingly come under attack with the suggestion that the practice of democracy and equal rights supersedes the principle of self-determination (Barber 1993; Mitchell 1990).

From the beginning of the twentieth century, the English, or Pakeha, New Zealanders glorified themselves through a cultural belief that exalts exceptional and progressive Pakeha racial tolerance and bicultural Pakeha-Maori harmony (Pearson 1990). This belief originated with the signing of the Treaty of Waitangi, when Captain Hobson greeted each Maori signee with the remark, in Maori, that now "We are one people." This utopian myth has been conspicuously denounced by the Maori—at the 1978 Bastion Point protests; during the 1979 Haka Party Incident when Maori physically attacked Pakeha engineering students who were staging a party in the form of a *haka,* or Maori war dance, in disregard of longstanding Maori complaints; and in repeated disruptions of the annual Waitangi Day celebrations, where Maori protestors proclaim that the treaty is a fraud (Hazlehurst 1995; Karetu 1993; Walker 1990:221–25, 233, 236). A 1982 response to these events contrasted with a general Pakeha presumption of Maori intransigence and incorrigibility: New Zealand's race relations conciliator and its Human Rights Commission issued a report on race relations to the government of New Zealand, stating,

> We are at a turning point in regard to harmonious race relations. . . . The myth of New Zealand as a multicultural utopia is foundering on reality. Since Bastion Point, the Haka Party Incident and the recent disturbances at Waitangi, there has been heightened awareness regarding racial conflict. . . . Pakeha New Zealanders cannot understand why, after all these years, ill-feeling is developing and their institutions are under attack. (quoted in Walker 1990:225)

The race relations conciliator recommended that the New Zealand government fulfill its obligations as provided in the *International Convention on the Elimination of All Forms of Racial Discrimination* (1965).

In the mid-1970s a group of New Zealand academics and intellectuals organized to form the Auckland Committee on Racism and Discrimination (ACORD), a group pledged to combat racial discrimination. ACORD defines racism as the domination and oppression of one ethnic group by another. If such domination is part of the established ways of the society it is institutional racism. Institutional racism is insidious; it is not necessarily carried out by bigots, it need not involve obvious discrimination, and it need not be based on explicit distinctions between people of different racial origins. Even if you do not discriminate against other ethnic groups on an individual level you will still be part of the process and reality of institutional racism. . . . New Zealand society is institutionally racist; one group, the Pakeha, holds the power (it controls the decision-making and the means for enforcing compliance with those decisions).

. . . We Pakeha decide how everyone should live, what everyone should learn, and by what criteria people shall be judged and so on. . . . The Pakeha understanding of democracy is summed up in the phrase "majority rule." Of course, consensus is often sought, but when opinion is often divided we fall back on the vote and the majority has its way. (quoted in Walker 1990:278)

Through the efforts of Maori activists and committed individuals such as the members of ACORD, who identify Pakeha democracy as an instrument of institutional racism, the New Zealand government was obliged to directly address Maori grievances. According to Ranginui Walker, New Zealand is being pushed firmly into the postcolonial era with the formation of the Waitangi Tribunal, the implementation of The Treaty of Waitangi (State Enterprises) Act of 1988, and the New Zealand judiciary's present willingness to rule in favor of the Maori despite public and government outcry (Walker 1990:288). The more recent government limitations on the reparations available to the Maori may represent, however, a firm step backward and an anti-Maori backlash in New Zealand.

In contrast to Professor Walker's argument, other indigenous peoples may be less quick to anticipate or acknowledge the dawn of the postcolonial era. When indigenous people attempted to speak to the world about human rights, preservation of the environment, and especially the self-determination of indigenous peoples prior to the advent of the International Year of Indigenous Peoples in December 1992, they addressed an empty chamber at the United Nations. In 1978 Denmark gave the Inuit of Greenland (Kalaallit Nunaat) self-government and jurisdiction over education, health care, social welfare, and economic development, and Greenland represents for many the model for potential indigenous autonomy worldwide. Nonetheless, Lars Johansen, the premier of the Greenland Home Rule Government, lectured the assembly in New York: "The United Nations is, more than any other forum, the place where liberation from colonization was made possible for many peoples whom today are called the Third World. . . . The time has come when this international system must focus itself on establishing equality for us in the so-called Fourth World. We want our rightful place in the new world order (Johansen, in Ewen, ed.

1994:50–51). Self-determination has consistently been recognized by indigenous representatives and spokespersons in international arenas as the fundamental aspiration of indigenous peoples and nations.

AN INDIGENOUS CRITIQUE OF ANTHROPOLOGY

When anthropologists, legal scholars, and government representatives take the claims, aspirations, recommendations, and demands of indigenous peoples seriously, the weight of the intellectual traditions and boundaries of anthropology, law, and politics as exposed in these pages often represent insurmountable barriers. In the context of institutional racism as defined and elaborated by ACORD, the forces at work may remain insidious. Several indigenous scholars, from their unique vantage point, have offered proposals for the future of anthropological research and action.

In "Here Come the Anthros" (1997), a chapter in a collection of essays titled *Indians and Anthropologists: Vine Deloria, Jr., and the Critique of Anthropology,* Cecil King, an Odawa (Ojibwa) who is full professor of comparative education and director of the Ontario Aboriginal Teacher Education Program, proposes that the anthropological conceptual apparatuses in American Indian ethnography and ethnology constitute a form of intellectual violence against American Indians. The damage done by these concepts, King argues, extends far beyond anthropological texts and discussions. He writes:

> In the last twenty years, Indian, Metis, and Inuit peoples have moved from reservations and isolated communities into places of greater visibility, but they are seen through the images built out of anthropological studies of them.
> . . . Now, we as Indians, Metis, and Inuit people want self-determination. We want self-government. When will anthropologists become instrumental to our ambitions, our categories of importance? How helpful is it to be called tribal or primitive when we are trying to negotiate with national and provincial governments as equal nations? Anthropological terms make us and our people invisible. (King 1997:117)

King insists that Indians have become the prisoners of academic classifications while the academics themselves prosper. He demands that Native Americans define themselves in their own languages and in their own terms, that they maintain "the legitimate authority over the integrity of their own intellectual traditions" without constricting the advancement of knowledge, and that they "be consulted and respected not only as human beings, at the very least, but as independent nations with the right to determine what transpires within their boundaries" (King 1997:118).

In the same collection Vine Deloria Jr. writes in his essay "Anthros, Indians, and Planetary Reality" (1997) that despite all protestations to the contrary, anthropologists today still preserve the Social Darwinist ideologies that he criticized in *Custer Died for Your Sins* (1969). He contends that when anthropologists are pressed for an explanation of their methods or the nature of their inquiry, they justify their research on the grounds that tribal people represent earlier stages of human cultural evolution and that by studying them we learn about our own past. Deloria regards anthropology as a "deeply colonial academic discipline" (Deloria 1997:211) with a racist undercurrent that is vividly expressed in anthropologists' positions on the issues of Indian reburial and the historical relationship between the governing principles of the Iroquois and the creation of the U.S. Constitution.

America's state religion is science, but an irrational and inhuman science, Deloria argues, and its society is "structured along a combination of racial and economic class lines that enable people with the proper connections to prosper and condemn the majority to a lifetime of meaningless or demeaning work" (Deloria 1997:211). Environmentalism lauds the indigenous peoples as the guardians of the planet, but it has not stopped the destruction: the "industrial machine grind[s] up both people and habitat in its insatiable need for raw materials." The New World Order, Deloria continues, "looks startlingly similar to medieval feudalism in that the elite of each country has devised ways to keep political and economic power while the mass of humankind is unable to muster any sense of national or planetary will." The relationship between Indians and anthropologists cannot be separated from the world in which we live. Ours is "an era of meltdown, breakdown, and disintegration. . . . The social sciences of academia have been revealed as the hobbies of the affluent class" and may follow the humanities into oblivion as the universities pursue their true function—"molding the personalities capable of accommodating the business world" (Deloria 1997:213–14; see United Nations 1994c, 2000d, 2001c, 2001d, 2001e, 2001f).

Deloria does believe, nevertheless, that anthropology could prove to be of significant value to both tribal peoples and those of the industrial world. Deloria singles out the work of several anthropologists for praise: Barbara Lane's work with the Indian peoples of Washington, in which she provided the ethnological background necessary for their victory in a fishing rights lawsuit; William Sturtevant's assistance to Indian communities seeking federal recognition; Deward Walker and Larry Zimmerman's work regarding Indian reburial issues; and Jack Campisi's assistance to eastern Indians and others seeking federal recognition regarding their claims (Deloria 1997:210). As for the field of anthropology itself, Deloria suggests that the values and organizational structures of tribal societies can help in understanding industrial societies. Festivals and kinship relations might be a way to restore civility to American culture, for example. As Deloria notes, anthropologists have tended to assert that the values of the West were the norm, but "now it is time to reverse the perspective," and employ tribal values to critique western society. Once anthropologists adopt this perspective, "that will be the signal that something of real value is contained within the tribal context" (Deloria 1997: 220–21). Deloria contends that anthropologists have neglected the study of their own societies and the histories of their own peoples and that therefore they are unable to leave behind their colonial mentality and provide the critique of "modern civilization" for which they would otherwise be particularly well-suited.

In "Are Anthropologists Hazardous to Indians' Health?" (1988), Russel Lawrence Barsh criticizes the priority of science over philosophy in anthropology. He links scientific anthropology with the racist evolutionism that inspired the dispossession and destruction of the Indian nations; with the theft of cultural items of invaluable worth; with the participation of anthropologists in the Indian New Deal, the Indian Claims Commission, and other legal proceedings that have continued the destruction of Indian nations and the assimilation of Indian peoples; with development anthropology, which serves scientific colonialism; with the position of information brokers who define indigenous societies inaccurately and in ways detrimental to their quest for self-determination; that is, with cultural and intellectual colonial domination. Through their field research anthropologists, like missionaries, create the conditions for state or nonindigenous expansion into indigenous territories while contaminating the very data they seek to acquire. Barsh reproaches anthropologists for the self-centered self-interest that is demonstrated in their quest for positions of employment in these areas and for the compromises to their integrity that they must make in order to keep these positions or advance within the system of administration. Nevertheless, Barsh recognizes that anthropologists' reflections on their own cultural evolutionary bias and their consequent advocacy of the equal worth of all cultures has helped to stimulate the contemporary American Indian struggle for identity and dominion. Barsh praises both Franz Boas and James Mooney who together "reformed anthropology as a science of the oppressed" and took from the field, from exposure to Indian society, a humanity in opposition to the machine-age notion of organizational efficiency and an "emphasis on the uniqueness of individuals and cultures, the importance of social processes, and the indeterminate nature of human destiny" (Barsh 1988:4–5).

Barsh points out that anthropologists have often documented the effects of colonialism on indigenous societies, but oddly have rarely engaged in study of the colonial system and the ideologies and socioeconomic forces that drive it. He notes the struggle for an appropriate and effective ethics within the anthropological profession that is revealed in the American Anthropological Association's "Principles of Professional Responsibility" (1971), but asserts that a profound ethical question remains: "Should an anthropologist record the death of an entire society without trying to prevent it?" (Barsh 1988:25).

> The principle of self-determination—that is, "peaceful, self-respecting rela-
> tions between peoples and cultures" . . .—should be the foundation for a new
> anthropological ethics. More, perhaps, than any other discipline, anthropol-
> ogists have witnessed first-hand the ill effects of colonialism and paternalism.
> Advocacy of self-determination is the best way anthropology can repay all its
> subjects for many years of hospitality. What is needed, however, is more than
> "mere talk." Anthropologists have more access to powerful institutions than
> the societies they have studied, not only as individual citizens, but also as an
> organized academic discipline. To fail to fully utilize this access might justly
> be considered complicity, albeit tacit, in the continued destruction of tribal
> societies. (Barsh 1988:29)

Barsh suggests that although anthropology has never achieved an integrative scientific insight or paradigm beyond evolutionism, it nonetheless
possesses an integrative moral insight—that is, cultural relativism, the denial of science, and the subversion of acceptance, in opposition to the co-
ercion and control of the planned society (1988:30–31).

TRANSNATIONALISM, INTERNATIONAL LAW, AND HUMAN RIGHTS IN ANTHROPOLOGY

Miguel Alfonso Martínez, the special rapporteur for the "Study on
Treaties, Agreements, and Other Constructive Arrangements between States
and Indigenous Populations," criticized anthropology, with the exception of
ethnohistorical and reflexive or postmodern anthropology, as being rooted
in the ethnocentric and Darwinist social evolutionism that is responsible for
the distorted view of indigenous societies prevalent in social scientific studies and ultimately in international law. Recent research in political and legal
anthropology pursues a far broader and more profound examination of the
international sociocultural forces impacting indigenous societies.

In "Anthropology, Law, and Transnational Processes" (1992), Sally Engle Merry demonstrates that recent anthropological research on legal systems has transcended the focus on isolated local situations and examines
the impact of national and international legal systems on local systems.
According to Merry, contemporary approaches to the anthropology of law
have expanded in four general directions:

> The first is a shift to a national and transnational context. . . . The second is a
> greater interest in cultural analysis: in the ways legal institutions and actors
> create meanings, the impact of those meanings on surrounding social rela-
> tionships, and the effect of the cultural framework on the nature of the legal
> procedures themselves. The third is a renewed interest in legal pluralism,
> freed of its static heritage but used as a way of talking about the multiplicity
> of coexisting legal systems and interconnections.

... The fourth is increased attention to power and to the ways law constructs and deconstructs power relations. Law is no longer only a mode of social control; it is also a constitutive system that creates conceptions of order
and enforces them. (Merry 1992:360)

Merry's political and legal anthropology addresses transnational or globalization issues; the impact of major transnational institutions and policies
on indigenous peoples; and law, arising through state power and transnational processes, as a tool for creating reality.

In "Anthropology and Human Rights" (1993), Ellen Messer examines
the contributions of anthropologists to the human rights regime and
their efforts to incorporate that regime into their research. She counters
the presumption that anthropologists have remained uninvolved in
the formulation of human rights: "The evidence suggests that anthropologists have prevailed in broadening the international discourse on
human rights, which now includes collective and indigenous rights
and details more specific content for social, economic, and cultural
rights. Reciprocally, the human rights perspective has broadened the
terms in which anthropologists construe social transformation and the
anthropology of development" (Messer 1993:222). Anthropologists
contribute to a broadening concept of human rights through ethnographic research, work with collectivities to enhance human rights protection, and examination of the contexts in which human rights
abuses occur. Messer contends that in addition to reporting human
rights abuses and analyzing the contexts in which they appear, anthropologists should actively participate in the prevention of human rights
abuses and in the advocacy of political and economic change that en-
hances human rights regimes and indigenous peoples' self-directed development (Messer 1993:241–42).

Carole Nagengast, in "Violence, Terror, and the Crisis of the State"
(1994), urges anthropologists to analyze the contemporary state and
state violence. She proposes that the fundamental goals of the contemporary state, pursued through its array of institutions and state apparatuses, are "assimilation, homogenization, and conformity within a fairly
narrow ethnic and political range" to form a uniform and compliant cit-
izenry (Nagengast 1994:109). The crisis of the state, Nagengast argues,
results in its monopolization of power versus the desires and demands
of peripheral peoples in opposition to conformity with the state. Only
recently have anthropologists begun to examine "violence and conflict
between groups and the state and among groups within states, especially violence rooted in ethnicity, nationalism, bids for autonomy and
self-determination, and political demands for fundamental change"
(Nagengast 1994:110).

ANTHROPOLOGY AND THE SELF-DETERMINATION OF
INDIGENOUS PEOPLES

In this volume I have sought to identify a tradition within anthropology—
a tradition that has its source in Las Casas and later in Morgan, Cushing,
Boas, Benedict, and others—that has promoted, through adherence to
principles of cultural relativism and the fundamental rights of individuals
and peoples, the preservation and liberation of indigenous peoples and
cultures in opposition to assimilation, state expansion, and most recently,
absorption into the global capitalist system. Informed by the works of
Foucault and Todorov and by recent critiques of the politics and application of anthropological theory, ethnography, scientific anthropology, and
development anthropology (e.g., Bodley 1990; Escobar 1995; Fabian 1983;
Nader 1994, 1996a, 1996b, 1997; Robertson 1984; Schneider 1984;
Thomas 1994), this approach takes the principles outlined by the authors
of the Declaration of Barbados as fundamental to its task. It proposes that
the work of anthropologists in the area of indigenous rights constitutes a
subfield of anthropology that is equal to and separate from development
anthropology, scientific anthropology, ethnography, and humanistic anthropology. As suggested by Deloria and Barsh, the teaching of this subfield should emphasize the historical and ethnohistorical analysis of indigenous nations in relation to colonial and postcolonial forces or
administrations. This includes especially the history, actions, and ideologies of our own sociopolitical systems, as well as indigenous representa-
tions of their own identity and aspirations, in association with the history
and implementation of national and international laws. Upon this basis
we can better understand the contemporary issues that indigenous peoples confront, and enter the field of human rights as knowledgeable and
capable advocates and associates of indigenous self-determination, liberation, and the exercise of human rights.

Appendix

THE "MATAATUA DECLARATION"

✦ From June 12 to 18, 1993, indigenous representatives from Japan (the Ainu), Australia, the Cook Islands, Fiji, India, Panama, Peru, the Philippines, Suriname, the United States, and Aotearoa–New Zealand, and nonindigenous delegates from a total of fourteen countries met in the Bay of Plenty region of Aotearoa for the First Conference on the Cultural and Intellectual Property Rights of Indigenous Peoples, sponsored by the Nine Tribes of Mataatua (Maori). In the preamble of the resulting Mataatua Declaration on Cultural and Intellectual Property Rights of Indigenous Peoples, the plenary endorsed the Indigenous Peoples' Earth Charter and declared the right of indigenous peoples to self-determination and that one aspect of that right is "exclusive ownership of their cultural and intellectual property" (First Conference on the Cultural and Intellectual Property Rights of Indigenous Peoples 1994). The plenary recommended that indigenous peoples define for themselves the content and extent of their own intellectual and cultural property and devise their own regulations concerning the recording and external use of that information. It also recommended that they create their own education, research, and training centers for the promotion of cultural and environmental practices; reacquire indigenous lands for the advancement of indigenous subsistence practices; and appraise current legislation concerning the protection of antiquities. It recommended that they establish indigenous organizations with the capacity to monitor and supervise the commercial use of indigenous cultural properties in the public domain, advise and encourage indigenous peoples on how to protect their cultural heritage, and engage in mandatory consultative processes with respect to new legislation affecting indigenous peoples' cultural and intellectual property rights.

The Mataatua Declaration plenary further recommended that states and international agencies recognize the right of indigenous peoples to ownership and control of their cultural heritage and asserted that current laws are inadequate for the protection of this right. In cooperation with indigenous peoples the appropriate development of these laws should incorporate collective as well as individual ownership and origin, retroactive coverage of historical as well as recent works, protection against debasement of culturally significant items, a cooperative rather than a competitive framework, the recognition that the first beneficiaries should be the direct descendants of the traditional guardians of that knowledge, and a multigenerational scope.

The plenary proclaimed indigenous peoples' traditional guardianship over indigenous flora and fauna in their territories and their consequent right to manage the commercialization of these plants and medicines. This necessitates the immediate cessation of the current commercialization of indigenous medicinal plants and human genetic material until appropriate mechanisms protecting indigenous rights are in place. Additionally, all settlements of land and resource claims with indigenous peoples should be expedited with the purpose of promoting traditional subsistence practices. The plenary called on the United Nations "to incorporate the Mataatua Declaration in its entirety in the United Nations study on cultural and intellectual property of indigenous peoples" and to take action against states with persistent policies that violate the cultural and property rights of indigenous peoples. The plenary also called for the United Nations to immediately end the Human Genome Diversity Project until indigenous peoples are fully appraised of its implications and may then approve its continuation if appropriate (United Nations 1994g:11–15).

In response to indigenous peoples' concerns regarding the protection of indigenous cultural heritage, as expressed in the Mataatua Declaration and in other documents, such as the Temuco-Wallmapuche Declaration (1994), and as authorized by Resolution 1993/44 of August 26, 1993, by the Sub-Commission on Prevention of Discrimination and Protection of Minorities, Special Rapporteur Erica Irene Daes states in the final document, "Principles and Guidelines for the Protection of the Heritage of Indigenous Peoples" (1995), that

> The Temuco-Wallmapuche Declaration of 2 December 1994 underscores the urgency of taking international action to protect the heritage of indigenous peoples from further erosion by commercial interests. The rapid expansion of regional trading blocks in the Americas and South-East Asia and the intellectual property provisions of the Uruguay Round of GATT will facilitate and accelerate the acquisition of patents to indigenous peoples' knowledge by biotechnology firms in the North. (United Nations 1995e:6)

The special rapporteur proclaims that indigenous peoples' ownership of their cultural heritage should remain collective, permanent, and inalienable and that indigenous peoples should exercise control over all research that is conducted within their territories or utilizes their people as subjects. The special rapporteur proposes that the United Nations should draft a convention "to establish international jurisdiction for the recovery of indigenous peoples' heritage across national frontiers, before the end of the International Decade of the World's Indigenous Peoples" (United Nations 1995e:15). The special rapporteur's proposal for a convention protecting the cultural heritage of indigenous peoples has not yet received authorization; however, the Commission on Human Rights sponsored a seminar, with Daes as Chairperson-Rapporteur, that has developed "draft principles and guidelines for the protection of the cultural and intellectual heritage of indigenous peoples" (United Nations 2000b).

WORKS CITED

Major documents—charters, conventions, declarations, and covenants—of the United Nations and regional bodies are listed under the name of the document as it is cited in the text. Minor United Nations documents are listed under United Nations.

Adair, John
  1973   "Clyde Kluckhohn and Indian Administration." In *Culture and Life,* ed. W. W. Taylor, J. L. Fisher, and E. Z. Vogt. Carbondale: Southern Illinois University Press.
Adams, Jill
  1994   "The Indian Child Welfare Act of 1978: Protecting Tribal Interests in a Land of Individual Rights." *American Indian Law Journal* 19 (2): 301–52.
Adams, Peter
  1977   *Fatal Necessity: British Intervention in New Zealand 1830–1847.* Auckland: Auckland University Press.
Adams, Richard N.
  1975   *Energy and Structure: A Theory of Social Power.* Austin: University of Texas Press.
  1981   "Natural Selection, Energetics, and Cultural Materialism." *Current Anthropology* 22 (6): 603–24.
African Charter on Human and Peoples' Rights
  1981   Organization of African Unity. Doc CAB/LEG/67/3/Rev 5.
Akwesasne Notes
  1981   *A Basic Call to Consciousness: The Haudenosaunee Address to the Western World.* 2d ed. Mohawk Nation via Rooseveltown, New York: *Akwesasne Notes.*
Alfred, Gerald R.
  1991   "From Bad to Worse: Internal Politics in the 1990 Crisis at Kahnawake." *Northeast Indian Quarterly* 8 (1): 23–31.
  1995   *Heeding the Voices of Our Ancestors: Kahnawake Mohawk Politics and the Rise of Native Nationalism.* Don Mills, Ont.: Oxford University Press Canada.

Alfredsson, Gudmundur
  1986   "Fourth Session of the Working Group on Indigenous Populations."
          Nordic Journal of International Law 55 (1–2): 22–30.
American Convention on Human Rights.
  1969   Organization of American States Treaty Series. No. 36, Organization of
          American States. Off. Rec. OEA/Ser.L/V/II.23, doc. 21, rev. 6.
Americas Watch
  1983   *Creating a Desolation and Calling It Peace.* New York: Americas Watch Com-
          mittee.
  1984   *Guatemala: A Nation of Prisoners.* New York: Americas Watch Committee.
Anaya, S. James
  1990   "The Rights of Indigenous Peoples and International Law in Historical
          and Contemporary Perspective." *1989 Harvard Indian Law Symposium*
          1:191–225.
  1991   "Indigenous Rights Norms in Contemporary International Law." *Arizona
          Journal of International and Comparative Law* 8 (2): 1–39.
  1994   "The Native Hawaiian People and International Human Rights Law: To-
          ward a Remedy for Past and Continuing Wrongs." *Georgia Law Review* 28
          (2): 309–64.
Anders, Gary
  1990   "The Alaska Native Experience with the Alaska Native Claims Settlement
          Act." Pp. 127–45 in *The Struggle for the Land: Indigenous Insight and Indus-
          trial Empire in the Semiarid World,* ed. P. A. Olson. Lincoln: University of
          Nebraska Press.
Anderson, Atholl J.
  1983   *When All the Moa Ovens Grew Cold: Nine Centuries of Changing Fortune for
          the Southern Maori.* Dunedin, New Zealand: Otago Heritage.
  1989   "The Last Archipelago: 1000 Years of Maori Settlement in New Zealand."
          Pp. 1–19 in *Towards 1990: Seven Leading Historians Examine Significant As-
          pects of New Zealand History,* ed. D. Green. Wellington: Government
          Printer.
Anonymous
  1935   "Anthropologists and the Federal Indian Program." *Science* 81:170–71.
Aquila, Richard
  1983   *The Iroquois Restoration: Iroquois Diplomacy on the Colonial Frontier,
          1701–1754.* Detroit: Wayne State University Press.
Awatere, Donna
  1982a   "Maori Sovereignty, Part One: The Death Machine." *Broadsheet* 6:38–42.
  1982b   "Maori Sovereignty, Part Two: Alliances with Pacific Island People, White
          Women, the Trade Union Movement, and the Left." *Broadsheet* 10:24–29.
  1983   "Maori Sovereignty, Part Three: Beyond the Noble Savage." *Broadsheet*
          1–2:12–19.
Ball, Milner S.
  1987   "Constitution, Court, Indian Tribe." *American Bar Foundation Research Jour-
          nal* 12:1–140.
Barber, Benjamin R.
  1993   "Global Democracy or Global Law: Which Comes First?" *Indiana Journal of
          Global Legal Studies* 1 (1): 119–37.

Barsh, Russel Lawrence

1982a "Monkey See, Monkey Do: Canada's Indian Programs Reflect U.S. Failures." *Indian Truth* 246:4–5, 10–12.

1982b "The Indian Reorganization Act: When Will Tribes Have a Choice?" *Indian Truth* 247:4–5, 10–12.

1982c "Indian Land Claims Policy in the United States." *North Dakota Law Review* 58 (1): 1–81.

1983 "Indigenous North America and Contemporary International Law." *Oregon Law Review* 62 (1): 73–125.

1987a "Revision of ILO Convention No. 107." *American Journal of International Law* 81 (3): 756–62.

1987b "Plains Indian Agrarianism and Class Conflict." *Great Plains Quarterly* 7 (2): 83–90.

1988 "Are Anthropologists Hazardous to Indians' Health?" *The Journal of Ethnic Studies* 15 (4): 1–38.

1989 "United Nations Seminar on Indigenous Peoples and States." *American Journal of International Law* 83 (3): 599–604.

1990 "An Advocate's Guide to the Convention on Indigenous and Tribal Peoples." *Oklahoma City University Law Review* 15 (1): 209–36.

1991 "Progressive-Era Bureaucrats and the Unity of Twentieth-Century Indian Policy." *American Indian Quarterly* 15 (1): 1–17.

1993a "The Challenge of Indigenous Self-Determination." *University of Michigan Journal of Legal Reform* 26 (2): 277–312.

1993b "A 'New Partnership' for Indigenous Peoples: Can the United Nations Make a Difference?" *American Indian Culture and Research Journal* 17 (1): 197–227.

1994 "Indigenous Peoples in the 1990s: From Object to Subject of International Law?" *Harvard Human Rights Journal* 7 (1): 33–86.

Barsh, Russel Lawrence, and James Youngblood Henderson

1979 "The Betrayal: *Oliphant v. Suquamish Tribe* and the Hunting of the Snark." *Minnesota Law Review* 63 (4): 609–40.

1980 *The Road: Indian Tribes and Political Liberty.* Berkeley: University of California Press.

Barsh, Russel Lawrence, and Ronald L. Trosper

1975 "Title I of the Indian Self-Determination and Education Assistance Act of 1975." *American Indian Law Review* 3 (2): 361–95.

Belich, James

1986 *The New Zealand Wars and the Victorian Interpretation of Racial Conflict.* Auckland: Auckland University Press; Oxford: Oxford University Press.

1989 *"I Shall Not Die": Titokowaru's War, New Zealand 1868–1869.* Wellington: Allen and Unwin.

Bell, Leonard

1992 *Colonial Constructs: European Images of the Maori, 1840–1914.* Carlton: Melbourne University Press.

Benedict, Ruth

1934 *Patterns of Culture.* Boston: Houghton Mifflin.

[1940] 1962 *Race: Science and Politics.* 2d ed. New York: Viking Press.

[1942] 1983 *Race and Racism.* London: Routledge and Kegan Paul.

Benedict, Ruth, and Mildred Ellis
1942   *Race and Cultural Relations: America's Answer to the Myth of a Master Race.*
        Washington, D.C.: National Council for the Social Studies, National Asso-
        ciation of Secondary-School Principles, Department of the National Edu-
        cation Association.
Benedict, Ruth, and Gene Weltfish
1943   *The Races of Mankind.* New York: Public Affairs Committee.
Berger, Thomas R.
1995   *Village Journey: The Report of the Alaska Native Review Commission.* 2d ed.
        New York: Hill and Wang.
Berkhofer, Robert C., Jr.
1979   *The White Man's Indian: Images of the American Indian from Columbus to the
        Present.* New York: Vintage Books.
Berman, Howard R.
1978   "The Concept of Aboriginal Rights in the Early History of the United
        States." *Buffalo Law Review* 27 (3): 637–67.
1988   "The International Labour Organization and Indigenous Peoples: Revision
        of ILO Convention No. 107 at the 75th Session of the International
        Labour Conference, 1988." *The Review of the International Commission of
        Jurists* 41:48–57.
Best, Elsdon
1924   *The Maori,* 2 vols. Memoirs of the Polynesian Society, vol. 5. Wellington:
        Board of Maori Ethnological Research.
[1925] 1972   *Tuhoe: Children of the Mist.* Memoirs of the Polynesian Society,
        vol. 6. Wellington: A. H. & A. W. Reed.
Bieder, Robert E.
1986   *Science Encounters the Indian, 1820–1880: The Early Years of American Eth-
        nology.* Norman: University of Oklahoma Press.
Biggs, Bruce
1960   *Maori Marriage.* Wellington: The Polynesian Society.
Binney, Judith
1969   "Christianity and the Maoris to 1840." *The New Zealand Journal of History*
        3 (2): 143–265.
1989   "The Maori and the Signing of the Treaty of Waitangi." Pp. 20–31 in *To-
        wards 1990: Seven Leading Historians Examine Significant Aspects of New
        Zealand History,* ed. D. Green. Wellington: Government Printer.
Blaisdell, Kekuni
1997   *Kanaka Maoli Self-Determination and Reinscription of Ka Pae'Aina (Hawai'i)
        on the U.N. List of Non-Self-Governing Territories.* Available at
        <www.inmotionmagazine.com>.
Boas, Franz
[1911] 1938   *The Mind of Primitive Man.* 2d ed. New York: Macmillan.
1919   "Scientists as Spies." *The Nation* 109:797.
Bodley, John H.
1990   *Victims of Progress.* 3d ed. Mountain View, Calif.: Mayfield Publishing
        Company.
Bowden, Ross
1979   "Tapu and Mana: Ritual Authority and Political Power in Traditional

Maori Society." *Journal of Polynesian History* 14 (1): 50–61.

Bowen, Julia A.
1991   "The Option of Preserving a Heritage: The 1987 Amendments to the Alaska Native Claims Settlement Act." *American Indian Law Review* 15 (3): 391–404.

Boyce, Douglas W.
1987   "'As the Wind Scatters the Smoke': The Tuscaroras in the Eighteenth Century." Pp. 151–63 in *Beyond the Covenant Chain: The Iroquois and Their Neighbors in Indian North America, 1600–1800,* ed. D. Richter and J. Merrell. Syracuse: Syracuse University Press.

Brodeur, Paul
1985   *Restitution: The Land Claims of the Mashpee, Passamaquoddy, and Penobscot Indians of New England.* Boston: Northeastern University Press.

Brookfield, F. M.
1989   "The New Zealand Constitution: The Search for Legitimacy." Pp. 1–24 in *Waitangi,* ed. I. Kawharu. Auckland: Oxford University Press.
1990   "Maori Rights and Two Radical Writers: Review and Response." *New Zealand Law Journal* 11:406–20.
1994   "The Treaty of Waitangi, the Constitution and the Future." Paper presented to the New Zealand Present and Future Conference, University of Edinburgh.

Brown, Dee
1991 (1970)   *Bury My Heart at Wounded Knee: An Indian History of the American West.* New York: Henry Holt.

Brownlie, Ian, ed.
1992   *Basic Documents on Human Rights.* 3d ed. Oxford: Clarendon Press.

Buick, Thomas Lindsay
[1936] 1976   *The Treaty of Waitangi; or How New Zealand Became a British Colony.* 3d ed. Christchurch: Capper Press.

Burger, Julian
1987   *Report from the Frontier: The State of the World's Indigenous Peoples.* London: Zed Books.

Burke, Joseph C.
1969   "The Cherokee Cases: A Study in Law, Politics, and Morality." *Stanford Law Review* 21 (3): 500–31.

Burnett, Donald E.
1972   "An Historical Analysis of the 1968 'Indian Civil Rights' Act." *Harvard Journal of Legislation* 9:557–626.

Burns, Patricia
1989   *Fatal Success: A History of the New Zealand Company.* Edited by Henry Richardson. Auckland: Heinemann Reed.

Campisi, Jack
1984   "National Policy, States' Rights, and Indian Sovereignty: The Case of the New York Iroquois." In *Extending the Rafters,* ed. M. K. Foster, J. Campisi, and M. Mithun. Albany: State University of New York Press.
1988   "From Stanwix to Canandaigua: National Policy, States' Rights, and Indian Land." Pp. 49–65 in *Iroquois Land Claims,* ed. C. Vecsey and W. Starna. Syracuse: Syracuse University Press.

Campisi, Jack, and William A. Starna
1995   "On the Road to Canandaigua: The Treaty of 1794." *American Indian Quarterly* 19 (4): 467–90.
Canby, William C.
1988   *American Indian Law in a Nutshell.* 2d ed. St. Paul, Minn.: West Publishing.
Carter, Samuel, III
1976   *Cherokee Sunset, a Nation Betrayed: A Narrative of Travail and Triumph, Persecution and Exile.* Garden City, N.J.: Doubleday and Company.
Cass, Lewis
1830   "Removal of the Indians." *The North American Review* 30 (1): 72–73.
Charter of the United Nations
1945   59 Stat. 1031, T.S. 993, 3 Bevans 1153.
Churchill, Ward
1992   "The Earth is Our Mother: Struggles for American Indian Land and Liberation in the Contemporary United States." Pp. 139–88 in *The State of Native America,* ed. M. Jaimes. Boston: South End Press.
1993   *Struggle for the Land: Indigenous Resistance to Genocide, Ecocide, and Expropriation in Contemporary North America.* Monroe, Maine: Common Courage Press.
1994   *Indians Are Us? Culture and Genocide in Native North America.* Monroe, Maine: Common Courage Press.
1997   *A Little Question of Genocide: Holocaust and Denial in the Americas, 1492 to the Present.* San Francisco: City Lights Books.
Churchill, Ward, and Glenn T. Morris
1992   "Key Indian Laws and Cases." Pp. 13–22 in *The State of Native America,* ed. M. Jaimes. Boston: South End Press.
Clinebell, John Howard, and Jim Thomson
1978   "Sovereignty and Self-Determination: The Rights of Native Americans under International Law." *Buffalo Law Review* 27 (3): 669–714.
Clinton, Robert N.
1989   "The Proclamation of 1763: Colonial Prelude to Two Centuries of Federal-State Conflict over the Management of Indian Affairs." *Boston University Law Review* 69 (2): 329–85.
1990   "The Rights of Indigenous Peoples as Collective Group Rights." *Arizona Law Review* 32 (4): 739–47.
Clinton, Robert N., and Margaret Tobey Hotopp
1979   "Judicial Enforcement of the Federal Restraints on Alienation of Indian Lands: The Origins of the Eastern Land Claims." *Maine Law Review* 31 (1): 17–42.
Clinton, Robert N., Nell Jessup Newton, and Monroe E. Price
1991   *American Indian Law: Cases and Materials.* 3d ed. Charlottesville: The Michie Company.
Cohen, Felix S.
[1940] 1988   *Handbook of Federal Indian Law.* Buffalo: William S. Hein & Company.
1942   "The Spanish Origin of Indian Rights in the Law of the United States." *Georgetown Law Journal* 31 (1): 1–21.
1960   *The Legal Conscience: Selected Papers of Felix S. Cohen,* ed. Lucy Cohen. New Haven: Yale University Press.

Colenso, William
  [1890] 1971   *The Authentic and Genuine History of the Signing of the Treaty of Waitangi.* Christchurch: Capper Press.

Collier, John
  1945   "United States Indian Administration as a Laboratory of Ethnic Relations." *Social Research* 12:265–303.

Convention No. 169. Convention Concerning Indigenous and Tribal Peoples in Independent Countries
  1989   International Labour Organization. *International Labour Organization Official Bulletin* 72, Series A, No. 2.

Convention on the Prevention and Punishment of the Crime of Genocide
  1948   78 U.N.T.S. 277 (United Nations).

Convention Relating to the Status of Refugees
  1954   189 U.N.T.S. 150. Available at <www.unesco.org/most/rr4ref.htm>.

Coulter, Robert T.
  1971   "Federal Law and Indian Tribal Law: The Right to Civil Counsel and the 1968 Indian Bill of Rights." Pp. 49–93 in *Columbia Survey of Human Rights Law,* vol. 3. Baltimore: Deford and Co.

Covenant of the League of Nations
  1919   Available at
       <www.tufts.edu/departments/fletcher/multi/www/league-covenant.html>.

Cox, Lindsay
  1993   *Kotahitanga: The Search for Maori Political Unity.* Auckland: Oxford University Press.

Cushing, Frank Hamilton
  1882–1883   "My Adventures in Zuñi." *Century Magazine* 25:191–207; 25:500–11; 26:28–47.

Daes, Erica-Irene
  1986   "Native People's Rights (Les Droits des Autochtones)." *Les Cahiers de Droits* 27 (1): 123–33.
  1989   "On the Relations between Indigenous Peoples and States." *Without Prejudice* 2 (2): 41–52.
  1993   "Some Considerations on the Rights of Indigenous Peoples to Self-Determination." *Transnational Law and Contemporary Problems* 3 (1): 1–11.

Davidson, Arnold I.
  1986   "Archaeology, Genealogy, Ethics." Pp. 221–34 in *Foucault: A Critical Reader,* ed. D. C. Hoy. New York: Basil Blackwell.

Davidson, Janet M.
  1983   "Maori Prehistory: The State of the Art." *Journal of the Polynesian Society* 92 (3): 291–307.
  1984   *The Prehistory of New Zealand.* Auckland: Longman Paul.
  1992   "The Polynesian Foundation." Pp. 3–27 in *The Oxford History of New Zealand,* 2d ed., ed. G. Rice. Auckland: Oxford University Press.

Day, Gordon M., and Bruce G. Trigger
  1978   "Algonquin." Pp. 792–97 in *Handbook of North American Indians,* vol. 15, ed. B. Trigger. Washington, D.C.: Smithsonian Institution Press.

Debo, Angie
  1934   *The Rise and Fall of the Choctaw Republic.* Norman: University of Oklahoma Press.
  1940   *And Still the Waters Run: The Betrayal of the Five Civilized Tribes.* Princeton: Princeton University Press.
  1970   `A History of the Indians of the United States.* Norman: University of Oklahoma Press.
  [1979] 1993   *Geronimo: The Man, His Time, His Place.* London: Pimlico.
Declaration of Principles of International Law Concerning Friendly Relations and Co-Operation among States in Accordance with the Charter of the United Nations
  1970   United Nations General Assembly. Resolution 2625/35. Available at <libwww.essex.ac.uk/Human_Rights/ARES2625.htm>.
Declaration on the Elimination of All Forms of Racial Discrimination
  1963   United Nations General Assembly. Resolution 1904, 18 UN GAOR, Supp. (No. 15), UN Doc. A/5515.
Declaration on Race and Racial Prejudice
  1978   Adopted by the General Conference of UNESCO at its twentieth session, Paris, November 27, 1978. Paris: UNESCO. Available at <www.unhchr.ch/html/menu3/b/d_prejud.htm>.
Declaration on the Granting of Independence to Colonial Countries and Peoples
  1960   United Nations General Assembly. Resolution 1514, 15 UN GAOR, Supp. (No. 16), UN Doc. A/4684.
Declaration on the Inadmissibility of Intervention into the Domestic Affairs of States and the Protection of Their Independence and Sovereignty
  1965   Available at <www.un.org/Depts/dhl/resguide/resins.htm>.
Declaration on the Rights of Persons Belonging to National or Ethnic, Religious and Linguistic Minorities
  1992   United Nations General Assembly. Resolution 47/135. Available at <www.unhchr.ch/html/menu3/b/d_minori.htm>.
Declaration Regarding Non-Self-Governing Territories
  1945   Available at <www.selfdetermination.gi/declaration_regarding_nonself.htm>.
Deloria, Vine, Jr.
  1969   *Custer Died For Your Sins: An Indian Manifesto.* New York: Macmillan.
  1985   *Behind the Trail of Broken Treaties: An Indian Declaration of Independence.* 2d ed. Austin: University of Texas Press.
  1989   "Laws Founded in Justice and Humanity: Reflections on the Content and Character of Federal Indian Law." *Arizona Law Review* 31 (2): 203–25.
  1997   "Anthros, Indians, and Planetary Reality." Pp. 209–21 in *Indians and Anthropologists,* ed. T. Biolsi and L. Zimmerman. Tucson: The University of Arizona Press.
Deloria, Vine, Jr., and Raymond J. DeMallie
  1999   *Documents of American Indian Diplomacy: Treaties, Agreements, and Conventions, 1775–1979.* Norman: University of Oklahoma Press.
Deloria, Vine, Jr., and Clifford M. Lytle
  1983   *American Indians, American Justice.* Austin: University of Texas Press.

1984   *The Nations Within: The Past and Future of American Indian Sovereignty.* New York: Pantheon Books.

DeMallie, Raymond J., ed.

1984   *The Sixth Grandfather: Black Elk's Teachings Given to John G. Neihardt.* Lincoln: University of Nebraska Press.

Dostal, Walter, ed.

1972   *The Situation of the Indian in South America: Contributions to the Study of Inter-Ethnic Conflict in Non-Andean Regions of South America.* Translated by W. J. O'Hara. Geneva: World Council of Churches.

Dowd, Gregory Evans

1992   *A Spirited Resistance: The North American Indian Struggle for Unity, 1745–1815.* Baltimore: Johns Hopkins University Press.

Drinnon, Richard

1980   *Facing West: The Metaphysics of Indian-Hating and Empire-Building.* Minneapolis: University of Minnesota Press.

Druke, Mary

1987   "Linking Arms: The Structure of Iroquois Intertribal Diplomacy." Pp. 29–39 in *Beyond the Covenant Chain,* ed. D. Richter and J. Merrell. Syracuse: Syracuse University Press.

Dunmore, John, ed.

1992   *The French and the Maori.* Waikanae, New Zealand: Heritage Press.

Edmunds, R. David

1983   *The Shawnee Prophet.* Lincoln: University of Nebraska Press.

Eggan, Fred

1975   *Essays In Social Anthropology and Ethnology.* Chicago: Department of Anthropology, The University of Chicago.

Eide, Asbjørn

1985   "Indigenous Populations and Human Rights: The United Nations Efforts at Midway." Pp. 196–212 in *Native Power: The Quest for Autonomy and Nationhood of Indigenous Peoples,* ed. J. Brøsted, J. Dahl, A. Gray, H. C. Gulløv, G. Henriksen, J. B. Jørgensen, and I. Kleivan. Oslo: Universitetsforlaget As.

Elsmore, Bronwyn

1989   *Mana from Heaven: A Century of Maori Prophets in New Zealand.* Tauranga, New Zealand: Moana Press.

Emery, Marg

1981   "Indian Grievances Aired at Russell Tribunal IV." *Indian Truth* 237:1, 4.

Escobar, Arturo

1995   *Encountering Development: The Making and Unmaking of the Third World.* Princeton: Princeton University Press.

European Convention for the Protection of Human Rights and Fundamental Freedoms

1950   312 U.N.T.S. 222. Available at <conventions.coe.int/treaty/en/Treaties/Html/005.htm>

Evans-Pritchard, E. E.

1949   *The Sanusi of Cyrenaica.* Oxford: Oxford University Press.

Ewen, Alexander, ed.

1994   *Voice of Indigenous Peoples: Native People Address the United Nations.* Santa Fe: Clear Light Publishers.

Fabian, Johannes
1983   *Time and the Other: How Anthropology Makes Its Object.* New York: Columbia University Press.
Farb, Peter
1968   *Man's Rise to Civilization: As Shown by the Indians of North America from Primeval Times to the Coming of the Industrial State.* New York: Dutton.
Fenton, William N.
1965   "The Iroquois Confederacy in the Twentieth Century: A Case Study in the Theory of Lewis H. Morgan in *Ancient Society*." *Ethnology* 4 (2): 251–65.
1975   "Lore of the Longhouse: Myth, Ritual, and Red Power." *Anthropological Quarterly* 48 (3): 131–47.
1978   "Northern Iroquoian Culture Patterns." Pp. 296–321 in *Handbook of North American Indians,* vol. 15, ed. B. Trigger. Washington, D.C.: Smithsonian Institution Press.
Firth, Raymond
1973   *Economics of the New Zealand Maori.* 2d ed. Wellington: Government Printer.
First Conference on the Cultural and Intellectual Property Rights of Indigenous Peoples
1994   "Mataatua Declaration on Cultural and Intellectual Property Rights of Indigenous Peoples." In United Nations, "Working Group on Indigenous Populations: A Permanent Forum in the United Nations for Indigenous People: Report by the Secretariat." Working Group on Indigenous Populations. E/CN.4/Sub.2/AC.4/1994/11.
Fletcher, Alice, and Francis La Flesche
1911   "The Omaha Tribe." In *27th Annual Report of the Bureau of American Ethnology.* Washington, D.C.: Smithsonian Institution.
Foreman, Grant
1934   *The Five Civilized Tribes.* Norman: University of Oklahoma Press.
Foucault, Michel
1965   *Madness and Civilization: A History of Insanity in the Age of Reason.* Translated by Richard Howard. New York: Pantheon Books.
1972   *The Archaeology of Knowledge.* Translated by A. M. Sheridan Smith. New York: Pantheon Books.
1973   *The Order of Things: An Archaeology of the Human Sciences.* New York: Vintage Books.
1977a   *Discipline and Punish: The Birth of the Prison.* Translated by A. Sheridan. New York: Random House.
1977b   "Nietzsche, Genealogy, History." Pp. 139–64 in *Language, Counter-Memory, Practice: Selected Essays and Interviews by Michel Foucault,* ed. D. F. Bouchard, trans. S. Simon. Ithaca, N.Y.: Cornell University Press.
1984   *The Foucault Reader.* Edited by Paul Rabinow. New York: Pantheon Books.
Foreman, Grant
1934   *The Five Civilized Tribes.* Norman: University of Oklahoma Press.
1953   *Indian Removal: The Emigration of the Five Civilized Tribes.* 2d ed. Norman: University of Oklahoma Press.
Gambill, Jerry (Rarihokwats)
[1969] 1983   "On the Art of Stealing Human Rights." Pp. 160–62 in *Crossing Cul-*

tures, ed. H. Knepler and M. Knepler. New York: Macmillan Publishing Co.

Geertz, Clifford
1988 *Works and Lives: The Anthropologist as Author.* Stanford: Stanford University Press.

Getches, David, Charles F. Wilkinson, and Robert A. Williams Jr.
1993 *Cases and Materials on Federal Indian Law.* 3d ed. St. Paul: West Publishing Co.

Goldberg, Carole E.
1975 "Public Law 280: The Limits of State Jurisdiction over Reservation Indians." *UCLA Law Review* 22:535–94.

Gould, Stephen Jay
[1981] 1992 *The Mismeasure of Man.* New York: Penguin Books.

Grabowski, Jan
1991 "Mohawk Crisis at Kanasetake and Kahnawake." *European Review of Native American Studies* 5 (1): 11–14.

Graymont, Barbara
1972 *The Iroquois in the American Revolution.* Syracuse: Syracuse University Press.

Green, L. C.
1989 "Claims to Territory in Colonial America." Pp. 1–139 in *The Law of Nations and the New World,* ed. L. C. Green and Olive P. Dickason. Edmonton: University of Alberta Press.

Guerrero, Manuel
1979 "Indian Child Welfare Act of 1978: A Response to the Threat to Indian Culture Caused by Foster and Adoptive Placements of Indian Children." *American Indian Law Review* 7 (1): 51–77.

Haan, Richard
1987 "Covenant and Consensus: Iroquois and English, 1676–1760." Pp. 41–57 in *Beyond the Covenant Chain: The Iroquois and Their Neighbors in Indian North America, 1600–1800,* ed. D. Richter and J. Merrell. Syracuse: Syracuse University Press.

Hall, William Edward
1924 *A Treatise on International Law.* 8th ed. Oxford: Clarendon.

Hannum, Hurst
1988 "New Developments in Indigenous Rights." *Virginia Journal of International Law* 28 (3): 649–78.

Harring, Sidney L.
1989 "The Incorporation of Alaskan Natives under American Law: United States and Tlingit Sovereignty, 1867–1900." *Arizona Law Review* 31 (2): 279–327.
1994 *Crow Dog's Case: American Indian Sovereignty, Tribal Law, and United States Law in the Nineteenth Century.* Cambridge: Cambridge University Press.

Harris, Marvin
1991 "Depopulation and Cultural Evolution: A Cultural Materialist Perspective." Pp. 581–86 in *The Spanish Borderlands in Pan-American Perspective,* ed. D. Hurst-Thomas. Vol. 3 in Columbian Consequences. Washington, D.C.: Smithsonian Institution Press.

Harvey, Irene K.
1982 "Constitutional Law: Congressional Plenary Power over Indian Affairs—A Doctrine Rooted in Prejudice." *American Indian Law Review* 10 (1): 117–50.

Hasager, Ulla, and Jonathan Friedman, eds.

1994   *Hawai'i: Return to Nationhood.* Document No. 75. Copenhagen: International Work Group for Indigenous Affairs.

Haughey, E. J.
1984   "The Treaty of Waitangi: Its Legal Status." *New Zealand Law Journal* 12:392.

Hauptman, Laurence M.
1981   *The Iroquois and the New Deal.* Syracuse: Syracuse University Press.
1986a   *The Iroquois Struggle for Survival: World War II to Red Power.* Syracuse: Syracuse University Press.
1986b   "The Senecas-Cayugas Reject Termination." Pp. 184–204 in *Between Two Worlds,* ed. A. Gibson. Oklahoma City: Oklahoma Historical Society.
1988a   "Iroquois Land Issues: At Odds with the 'Family of New York.'" Pp. 67–86 in *Iroquois Land Claims,* ed. C. Vecsey and W. Starna. Syracuse: Syracuse University Press.
1988b   "The Historical Background to the Present-Day Seneca Nation–Salamanca Lease Controversy." Pp. 101–22 in *Iroquois Land Claims,* ed. C. Vecsey and W. Starna. Syracuse: Syracuse University Press.
1993   *The Iroquois in the Civil War: From Battlefield to Reservation.* Syracuse: Syracuse University Press.

Hazlehurst, Kayleen M.
1995   "Ethnicity, Ideology, and Social Drama: The Waitangi Day Incident 1981." Pp. 81–115 in *The Urban Context: Ethnicity, Social Networks, and Situational Analysis,* ed. A. Rogers and S. Vertovec. Oxford: Berg Publishers.

Henderson, J. M.
1972   *Ratana: The Man, the Church, the Political Movement.* Wellington: A. H. & A. W. Reed.

Henderson, James Youngblood
1977   "Unraveling the Riddle of Aboriginal Title." *American Indian Law Review* 5 (1): 75–137.

Henkin, Louis, Richard Pugh, Oscar Schechter, and Hans Smit
1987   *International Law: Cases and Materials.* 2d ed. St. Paul: West Publishing Company.

Hietala, Thomas R.
1990   *Manifest Design: Anxious Aggrandizement in Late Jacksonian America.* Ithaca, N.Y.: Cornell University Press.

Higgins, Rosalyn
1992   "Admissibility under the Optional Protocol to the International Covenant on Civil and Political Rights." *Canadian Human Rights Yearbook* 1991–1992:57–67.

Hinsley, Curtis M., Jr.
[1981] 1994   *The Smithsonian and the American Indian: Making of a Moral Anthropology in Victorian America.* Washington, D.C.: Smithsonian Institution Press.

Hoebel, E. Adamson
1978   *The Cheyennes: Indians of the Great Plains.* 2d ed. Fort Worth: Harcourt Brace Jovanovich.

Hornung, Rick
1992   *One Nation Under the Gun: Inside the Mohawk Civil War.* New York: Pantheon Books.

Horsman, Reginald
  1967   *Expansion and American Indian Policy 1783–1812*. East Lansing: Michigan
          State University Press.
Howard, Bradley Reed
  1993   "Human Rights and Indigenous People: On the Relevance of International
          Law for Indigenous Liberation." *German Yearbook of International Law*
          35:105–56.
Hoxie, Frederick
  1984   *A Final Promise: The Campaign to Assimilate the Indians, 1880–1920*. Lin-
          coln: University of Nebraska Press.
Hyde, Charles Cheney
  1922   *International Law Chiefly as Interpreted and Applied by the United States.*
          Boston: Little, Brown and Company.
ICIHI (Independent Commission on International Humanitarian Issues)
  1987   *Indigenous Peoples: A Global Quest for Justice*. London: Zed Books.
Inda, Jonathan Xavier, and Renato Rosaldo, eds.
  2001   *Anthropology of Globalization: A Reader*. London: Blackwell.
Indian Law Resource Center
  1984   *Indian Rights—Human Rights: Handbook for Indians on International Human
          Rights Complaint Procedures.* Washington, D.C.: Indian Law Resource Cen-
          ter.
Indigenous Peoples' Caucus
  1999   *Indigenous Peoples' Seattle Declaration on the Occasion of the Third Ministerial
          Meeting of the World Trade Organization.* November 30–December 3, 1999.
          Available at <www.citizen.org>.
International Convention on the Elimination of All Forms of Racial Discrimination
  1965   660 U.N.T.S. 195. Available at
          <www.unhchr.ch/html/menu3/b/d_icerd.htm>.
International Convention on the Suppression and Punishment of the Crime of
          Apartheid
  1973   United Nations General Assembly. Resolution 3068/28, 28 UN GAOR,
          Supp. (No. 30), UN Doc. A/9030.
International Covenant on Civil and Political Rights
  1966   999 U.N.T.S. 171. Available at
          <tuner1.dc1.sonixtream.com/solon/media/tuner/Tuner?aff=wdrv&type=IE>.
International Covenant on Economic, Social, and Cultural Rights
  1966   Available at <www.unhchr.ch/html/menu3/b/a_cescr.htm>.
International Indian Treaty Council
  1977   "International NGO Conference on Discrimination against Indigenous
          Populations in the Americas, September 20–23, Palais des Nations,
          Geneva, Switzerland." *Treaty Council News* 1 (7): 1–35.
Ismaellilo and Robin Wright, eds.
  1982   *Native Peoples in Struggle: Cases from the Fourth Russell Tribunal and Other
          International Forums.* New York: Anthropology Resource Center and Emer-
          gency Response International Network Publications.
Jeffrey, Robert C., Jr.
  1990   "The Indian Civil Rights Act and the *Martínez* Decision: A Reconsidera-
          tion." *South Dakota Law Review* 35 (3): 355–71.

Jennings, Francis
1975   *The Invasion of America: Indians, Colonialism, and the Cant of Conquest.* Chapel Hill: University of North Carolina Press.
1984   *The Ambiguous Iroquois Empire: The Covenant Chain Confederation of Indian Tribes with English Colonies from Its Beginnings to the Lancaster Treaty of 1744.* New York: W. W. Norton & Company.
1988   *Empire of Fortune: Crowns, Colonies, and Tribes in the Seven Years' War in America.* New York: W. W. Norton & Company.

Jennings, Francis, William N. Fenton, Mary A. Druke, and David R. Miller, eds.
1985   *The History and Culture of Iroquois Diplomacy: An Interdisciplinary Guide to the Treaties of the Six Nations and Their League.* Syracuse: Syracuse University Press, D'Arcy McNickle Center for the History of the American Indian.

Johansen, Bruce E.
1993   *Life and Death in Mohawk Country.* Golden, Colo.: North American Press.

Jonas, Susanne, Ed McCaughan, and Elizabeth S. Martínez, eds. and trans.
1984   *Guatemala: Tyranny on Trial: Testimony of the Permanent People's Tribunal.* San Francisco: Synthesis Publications.

Jones, Dorothy V.
1982   *License for Empire: Colonialism by Treaty in Early America.* Chicago: University of Chicago Press.
1988   "British Colonial Indian Treaties." Pp. 185–94 in *Handbook of North American Indians,* vol. 4, ed. W. Washburn. Washington, D.C.: Smithsonian Institution Press.

Josephy, Alvin, Jr., ed.
1971   *Red Power: The American Indian's Fight for Freedom.* New York: McGraw-Hill Publishers.

Karetu, T. S.
1993   *Haka! The Dance of a Noble People; Te Tohu O Te Whenua Rangatira.* Auckland: Reed.

Katchongva, Dan.
1981   "The United States Government Does Not Want to Recognize the Aboriginal Leaders of this Land." *Indian Truth* 240:5.

Kehoe, Alice Beck
1989   *The Ghost Dance: Ethnohistory and Revitalization.* Fort Worth: Holt, Rinehart and Winston.

Keith, Kenneth
1990   "The Treaty of Waitangi in the Courts." *New Zealand Law Journal* 1:37–61.

Kelsey, Jane
1984   "Legal Imperialism and the Colonization of Aotearoa." Pp. 15–43 in *Tauiwi: Racism and Ethnicity in New Zealand,* ed. P. Spoonley, C. MacPherson, D. Pearson, and C. Sedgwick. Palmerston North, New Zealand: Dunmore Press.

Kent, Jay
1982   *Abnaki: The Native People of Maine.* Boulder, Colo.: Centre Films. Film.

Kickingbird, Kirke, Lynn Kickingbird, Alexander Tallchief Skibine, and Charles Chibitty
1980   *Indian Treaties.* Indian Legal Curriculum and Training Program of the In-

stitute for the Development of Indian Law. Washington, D.C.: Institute for the Development of Indian Law.

King, Cecil
1997   "Here Come the Anthros." Pp. 115–19 in *Indians and Anthropologists,* ed. T. Biolsi and L. Zimmerman. Tucson: University of Arizona Press.

Kingsbury, Benedict
1989   "The Treaty of Waitangi: Some International Law Aspects." Pp. 121–57 in *Waitangi,* ed. I. Kawharu. Auckland: Oxford University Press.

Kluckhohn, Clyde
1943   "Covert Culture and Administrative Problems." *American Anthropologist* 45 (1): 213–29.

Kosok, Paul, ed.
1951   "An Unknown Letter from Lewis Henry Morgan to Abraham Lincoln." *University of Rochester Library Bulletin* 6:34–40.

Landsman, Gail H.
1988   *Sovereignty and Symbol: Indian-White Conflict at Ganienkeh.* Albuquerque: University of New Mexico Press.

Landy, David
1978   "Tuscarora among the Iroquois." Pp. 518–24 in *Handbook of North American Indians,* vol. 15, ed. B. Trigger. Washington, D.C.: Smithsonian Institution Press.

Langton, Marcia
1988   "The United Nations and Indigenous Minorities: A Report on the United Nations Working Group on Indigenous Populations." Pp. 83–92 in *International Law and Aboriginal Human Rights,* ed. B. Hocking. Sydney: Law Book Company.

Las Casas, Bartolomé de
[1552] 1992   *A Short Account of the Destruction of the Indies.* Edited and Translated by Nigel Griffin. London: Penguin Books.

Laurence, Robert
1988a   "Learning to Live with the Plenary Power of Congress over the American Indians." *Arizona Law Review* 30 (3): 413–38.
1988b   "On Eurocentric Myopia, the Designated Hitter Rule and 'The Actual State of Things.'" *Arizona Law Review* 30 (3): 459–66.
1990   "The Enforcement of Judgments across Indian Reservation Boundaries: Full Faith and Credit, Comity, and the Indian Civil Rights Act." *Oregon Law Review* 69 (3): 589–687.

Lévi-Strauss, Claude
1952   *Race and History.* Paris: UNESCO.
1955   *Tristes Tropiques.* Paris: Gallimard.

Lewellen, Ted C.
2002   *Anthropology and Globalization: Anthropology in the 21st Century.* Westport, Conn.: Greenwood.

Lewis, Diane
1973   "Anthropology and Colonialism." *Current Anthropology* 14 (3): 581–602.

Lewis, Norman
1969   "Genocide: From Fire and Sword to Arsenic and Bullets—Civilisation Has Sent Six Million Indians to Extinction." *The Sunday Times Magazine* (February 23):34–59.

Locklear, Arlinda F.
1988   "The Oneida Land Claims: An Overview." Pp. 141–54 in *Iroquois Land Claims,* ed. C. Vecsey and W. Starna. Syracuse: Syracuse University Press.

Lurie, Nancy Oestreich
1955   "Problems, Opportunities, and Recommendations." *Ethnohistory* 2 (4): 357–73.
1961   "The Voice of the American Indian: Report on the American Indian Chicago Conference." *Current Anthropology* 2 (5): 478–500.
1966a   "Women in Early Anthropology." Pp. 43–54 in *Pioneers of American Anthropology,* ed. J. Helm. Seattle: University of Washington Press.
1966b   "The Lady from Boston and the Omaha Indians." *American West* 3 (3): 31–33, 80–85.
1978   "The Indian Claims Commission." *Annals of the American Academy of Political and Social Science* 436:97–110.
1988   "Relations between Indians and Anthropologists." Pp. 548–56 in *Handbook of North American Indians,* vol. 4, ed. W. Washburn. Washington, D.C.: Smithsonian Institution Press.

Lyons, Oren R.
1992   "The American Indian in the Past." Pp. 13–42 in *Exiled in the Land of the Free,* ed. O. Lyons and J. Mohawk. Santa Fe: Clear Light Publishers.

MacDonald, Robert
1989   "The Hikoi." *Metro* 6:131–51.
1990   *The Maori of New Zealand.* 2d ed. Report No. 70. London: Minority Rights Group.

MacNeish, Richard S.
1952   *Iroquois Pottery Types: A Technique for the Study of Iroquois Prehistory.* National Museum of Canada, Bulletin 124, Anthropological Series 31.
1976   "The *In Situ* Iroquois Revisited and Rethought." In *Culture Change and Continuity: Essays in Honor of James Bennett Griffin.* Edited by C. E. Cleland. New York: Academic Press.

Mark, Joan
1980   *Four Anthropologists: An American Science in Its Early Years.* New York: Science History Publications.
1988   *A Stranger in Her Native Land: Alice Fletcher and the American Indians.* Lincoln: University of Nebraska Press.

Martínez Cobo, José R.
1986–1987   *Study of the Problem of Discrimination against Indigenous Populations.* 4 vols. Economic and Social Council. E/CN.4/Sub.2/1986/7/Add.1. New York: United Nations.

Matthiessen, Peter
1991   *In the Spirit of Crazy Horse.* 2d ed. New York: Viking Press.

McDonnell, Janet A.
1991   *The Dispossession of the American Indian, 1887–1934.* Bloomington: Indiana University Press.

Mead, Margaret
1932   *The Changing Culture of an Indian Tribe.* New York: Columbia University Press.

Means, Russell
  1983   "The Same Old Song." Pp. 19–34 in *Marxism and Native Americans*, ed. W.
          Churchill. Boston: South End Press.
Mekeel, H. Scudder
  1944   "An Appraisal of the Indian Reorganization Act." *American Anthropologist*
          46(1):209–17.
Menchú, Rigoberta
  1984   *I, Rigoberta Menchú, An Indian Woman in Guatemala*. Edited by Elisabeth
          Burgos-DeBray, translated by Ann Wright. London: Verso.
Meriam, Lewis, and Herbert Work
  1928   *The Problem of Indian Administration: Summary of Findings and Recommenda-
          tions*. Washington, D.C.: The Institute for Government Research.
Merry, Sally Engle
  1992   "Anthropology, Law, and Transnational Processes." *Annual Review of An-
          thropology* 21:357–79.
Messer, Ellen
  1993   "Anthropology and Human Rights." *Annual Review of Anthropology*
          22:221–49.
Metge, Joan
  1976   *The Maoris of New Zealand, Rauthi*. 2d ed. London: Routledge & Kegan
          Paul.
Michigan Law Review
  1976   "Implication of Civil Remedies under the Indian Civil Rights Act." *Michi-
          gan Law Review* 75 (1): 210–27.
Mitchell, Robin
  1990   *The Treaty and the Act*. Christchurch: Cadsonbury.
Mohr, Walter H.
  1933   *Federal Indian Relations, 1774–1788*. Philadelphia: University of Pennsylva-
          nia Press.
Montagu, Ashley
  [1942] 1997   *Our Most Dangerous Myth: The Fallacy of Race*. 6th ed. Walnut
          Creek: AltaMira Press.
Montagu, Ashley, and Floyd Matson
  1983   *The Dehumanization of Man*. New York: McGraw-Hill.
Moody, Roger, ed.
  1993   *The Indigenous Voice: Visions and Realities*. 2d ed. Utrecht, The Netherlands:
          International Books.
Mooney, James
  1896   *The Ghost-Dance Religion and the Sioux Outbreak of 1890*. Washington, D.C.:
          Fourteenth Annual Report of the Bureau of Ethnology.
Morgan, Lewis Henry
  1851   *League of the Ho-de-no-sau-nee, or Iroquois*. Rochester: Sage and Brothers.
  1869   "Indian Migrations, part 1." *North American Review* 109 (10): 391–442.
  1870a   "Indian Migrations, part 2." *North American Review* 110 (1): 32–82.
  1870b   *Systems of Consanguinity and Affinity of the Human Family*. Smithsonian Con-
          tributions to Knowledge, vol. 17. Washington, D.C.: Smithsonian Institution.
  1877   *Ancient Society, or Researches in the Lines of Human Progress from Savagery
          through Barbarism to Civilization*. New York: Henry Holt and Company.

Morris, Glenn T.
1987   "In Support of the Right of Self-Determination for Indigenous Peoples under International Law." *German Yearbook of International Law* 29:277–316.

Moses, L. G.
1984   *The Indian Man: A Biography of James Mooney.* Urbana: University of Illinois Press.

Nader, Laura
1994   "'Solidarity,' Paternalism, and Historical Injustice: Perspectives on the Development of Indian Peoples of Mexico." *PoLAR* 17 (2): 99–104.
1996a   "Anthropological Inquiries into Boundaries, Power, Knowledge." Pp. 1–28 in *Naked Science,* ed. L. Nader. New York: Routledge.
1996b   "The Three-Cornered Constellation: Magic, Science, and Religion Revisited." Pp. 259–78 in *Naked Science,* ed. L. Nader. New York: Routledge.
1997   "The Phantom Factor: Impact of the Cold War on Anthropology." Pp. 107–46 in *The Cold War and the University: Toward an Intellectual History of the Postwar Years,* ed. Noam Chomsky. New York: New Press.

Nagengast, Carole
1994   "Violence, Terror, and the State." *Annual Review of Anthropology* 23:109–36.

Namibia
1971   International Court of Justice. Advisory Opinion. *International Court of Justice* 16.

Nash, June C.
2001   *Mayan Visions: The Quest for Autonomy in an Age of Globalization.* New York and London: Routledge.

Nehamas, Alexander
1993   "Subject and Abject: The Examined Life of Michel Foucault." *The New Republic* 208 (7): 27–36.

Neich, Roger
1983   "The Veil of Orthodoxy: Rotorua Ngati Tarawhai Woodcarving in a Changing Context." Pp. 245–65 in *Art and Artists of Oceania,* ed. S. Mead and B. Kernot. Wellington: Dunmore Press.

Newton, Nell Jessup
1980   "At the Whim of the Sovereign: Aboriginal Title Reconsidered." *Hastings Law Journal* 31 (1): 1215–85.
1984   "Federal Power over Indians: Its Sources, Scope, and Limitations." *University of Pennsylvania Law Review* 132 (2): 195–288.

Nile, Richard, and Christian Clerk
1996   *Cultural Atlas of Australia, New Zealand and the South Pacific.* Oxfordshire, England: Andromeda Oxford.

Opekokew, Delia
1987   "International Law, International Institutions, and Indigenous Issues." Pp. 1–10 in *The Rights of Indigenous Peoples in International Law,* ed. R. Thompson. Saskatoon: University of Saskatchewan, Native Law Centre.

Oppenheim, Lassa
1920   *International Law: A Treatise.* London: Longmans, Green and Co.

Oppenheim, R. S.
1973   *Maori Death Customs.* Wellington: A. H. and A. W. Reed.

Orange, Claudia
1980   "The Covenant of Kohimarama: A Ratification of the Treaty of Waitangi."
         The New Zealand Journal of History 14 (1): 61–79.
1987   *The Treaty of Waitangi.* Wellington: Allen and Unwin New Zealand.
1990   *An Illustrated History of the Treaty of Waitangi.* Wellington and Winchester:
         Allen and Unwin.

Ostrom, Vincent, and Theodore Stern
1959   "A Case Study of Termination of Federal Responsibilities over the Klamath
         Reservation (Report to the Commission on the Rights, Liberties, and Re-
         sponsibilities of the American Indian)." Mimeo.

Oswalt, Wendell H.
1973   *This Land Was Theirs: A Study of the North American Indian.* 2d ed. New
         York: John Wiley & Sons.

Otis, Delos Sackett
1973   *The Dawes Act and the Allotment of Indian Lands.* Edited by Francis Paul
         Prucha. Norman: University of Oklahoma Press.

Parkman, Francis
1851   *History of the Conspiracy of Pontiac, and the War of the North American Tribes
         against the English Colonies after the Conquest of Canada.* Boston: C. C. Lit-
         tle and J. Brown.

Pearson, David
1990   *A Dream Deferred: The Origins of Ethnic Conflict in New Zealand.* Wellington:
         Allen & Unwin Port Nicholson Press.

Pertusati, Linda
1997   *In Defense of Mohawk Land: Ethnopolitical Conflict in Native North America.*
         New York: State University of New York Press.

Philp, Kenneth R.
1977   *John Collier's Crusade for Indian Reform, 1920–1954.* Tucson: University of
         Arizona Press.

Powell, John Wesley
1888   *Truth and Error.* Chicago: Open Court.

Proclamation of Teheran
1968   Proclaimed by the International Conference on Human Rights at Teheran
         on May 13, 1968. Geneva: Office of the United Nations High Commis-
         sioner for Human Rights. Available at
         <www.unhchr.ch/html/menu3/b/b_tehern.htm>

Prucha, Francis Paul
[1962] 1970   *American Indian Policy in the Formative Years: The Indian Trade and
                Intercourse Acts, 1780–1834.* Lincoln: University of Nebraska Press.
1967   *Lewis Cass and American Indian Policy.* Detroit: Wayne State University Press.
1969   "Andrew Jackson's Indian Policy: A Reassessment." *Journal of American
         History* 56 (4): 527–39.
1984   *The Great Father: The United States Government and the American Indian.* 2
         vols. Lincoln: University of Nebraska Press.
1994   *American Indian Treaties: The History of a Political Anomaly.* Berkeley: Uni-
         versity of California Press.

Rappaport, Roy
1977   "Maladaptation in Social Systems." Pp. 79–87 in *The Evolution of Social*

Systems, ed. J. Friedman and M. J. Rowlands. London: Duckworth.

1984   *Pigs for the Ancestors.* 2d ed. New Haven: Yale University Press.

Reynolds, Ted

1990   "The Treaty—What Went Wrong and What Are We Doing About It?" *New Zealand Geographic* 5 (1): 32–71.

Richter, Daniel K.

1987   "Ordeals of the Longhouse: The Five Nations in Early American History." Pp. 11–27 in *Beyond the Covenant Chain: The Iroquois and Their Neighbors in Indian North America, 1600–1800,* ed. D. Richter and J. Merrell. Syracuse: Syracuse University Press.

1992   *The Ordeal of the Longhouse: The Peoples of the Iroquois League in the Era of European Colonization.* Published for the Institute of Early American History and Culture. Chapel Hill: University of North Carolina Press.

Richter, Daniel K., and James H. Merrell, eds.

1987   *Beyond the Covenant Chain: The Iroquois and Their Neighbors in Indian North America, 1600–1800.* Syracuse: Syracuse University Press.

Rickard, Clinton

1973   *Fighting Tuscarora: An Autobiography of Chief Clinton Rickard.* Edited by Barbara Graymont. Syracuse: Syracuse University Press.

Ries, Judith

1996   *Native American History: A Chronology of the Vast Achievements of a Culture and Their Links to World Events.* New York: Ballantine Books.

Right to Be Mohawk

1989   New York: New Day Films.

Riseborough, Hazel

1989   *Days of Darkness: Taranaki 1878–1884.* Wellington: Allen and Unwin Historical Branch.

Roberts, J.

1978   *From Massacres to Mining: The Colonization of Aboriginal Australia.* London: CIMRA.

Robertson, A. F.

1984   *People and the State: An Anthropology of Planned Development.* Cambridge Studies in Social Anthropology, no. 52. Cambridge: Cambridge University Press.

Ross, John O.

1980   "Busby and the Declaration of Independence." *The New Zealand Journal of History* 14 (1): 83–89.

Ross, Ruth M.

1972a   "Te Tiriti o Waitangi: Texts and Translations." *The New Zealand Journal of History* 6 (2): 129–57.

1972b   "The Treaty on the Ground." Pp. 16–34 in *The Treaty of Waitangi,* ed. W. Parker. Wellington: Victoria University of Wellington, Department of University Extension.

Rouse, Irving

1992   *The Tainos: Rise and Decline of the People Who Greeted Columbus.* New Haven: Yale University Press.

Royce, Charles C.

1899   "Indian Land Cessions in the United States." In *18th Annual Report of the Bureau of American Ethnology, 1896–97.* Washington, D.C.: Smithsonian Institution.

Rusden, G. W.
1888   *Aureretanga: Groans of the Maoris.* London: William Ridgeway.

Russell Tribunal
1980   *Report of the Fourth Russell Tribunal on the Rights of the Indians of the Americas: Conclusions.* Amsterdam: Workgroup Indian Project.

Rutherford, James
1947   *Hone Heke's Rebellion, 1844–1846: An Episode in the Establishment of British Rule in New Zealand.* Auckland.

1949   *The Treaty of Waitangi and the Acquisition of British Sovereignty in New Zealand.* Auckland, New Zealand: Aukland University College.

Ryan, Lyndall
1981   *The Aboriginal Tasmanians.* Vancouver: University of British Columbia Press.

Said, Edward W.
1979   *Orientalism.* New York: Vintage Books.

1986   "Foucault and the Imagination of Power." Pp. 149–55 in *Foucault: A Critical Reader,* ed. D. C. Hoy. New York: Basil Blackwell.

1989   "Representing the Colonized: Anthropology's Interlocutors." *Critical Inquiry* 15 (2): 205–25.

Sale, Kirkpatrick
1990   *The Conquest of Paradise: Christopher Columbus and the Columbian Legacy.* New York: Alfred A. Knopf.

Salisbury, Neal
1987   "Toward the Covenant Chain: Iroquois and Southern New England Algonquians, 1637–1684." Pp. 61–73 in *Beyond the Covenant Chain: The Iroquois and Their Neighbors in Indian North America, 1600–1800,* ed. D. Richter and J. Merrell. Syracuse: Syracuse University Press.

Salmond, Anne
1983   "The Study of Traditional Maori Society: State of the Art." *Journal of the Polynesian Society* 92 (3): 309–31.

1989   "Tribal Words, Tribal Worlds: The Translatability of *tapu* and *mana.*" Pp. 55–78 in *Culture, Kin, and Cognition in Oceania: Essays in Honor of Ward Goodenough,* ed. M. Marshall and J. L. Caughey. Washington, D.C.: American Anthropological Association.

1991   *Two Worlds: First Meetings between Maori and Europeans, 1642–1772.* Auckland: Viking Press.

Sanders, Douglas E.
1977   *The Formation of the World Council of Indigenous Peoples.* Document No. 29. Copenhagen: International Work Group for Indigenous Affairs.

1983   "The Re-Emergence of Indigenous Questions in International Law." *Canadian Human Rights Yearbook* 1 (1983): 3–30.

1989a   "The United Nations Working Group on Indigenous Populations." *Human Rights Quarterly* 11 (3): 406–33.

1989b   "Another Step: The United Nations Seminar on Relations between Indigenous Peoples and States." *Canadian Native Law Reporter* 4 (1989): 37–43.

Satz, Ronald N.
1975   *American Indian Policy in the Jacksonian Era.* Lincoln: University of Nebraska Press.

Schneider, David M.
1984   *A Critique of the Study of Kinship.* Ann Arbor: University of Michigan Press.

Schoolcraft, Henry Rowe
1844   "Our Indian Policy." *Democratic Review* 14:169–84.

Segraves, Barbara
1982   "Central Elements in the Construction of a General Theory of the Evolution of Societal Complexity." In *Theory and Explanation in Archaeology: The Southampton Conference,* ed. C. Renfrew, M. J. Rowlands, and B. A. Segraves. New York: Academic Press.

Sinclair, Keith
1961   *The Origins of the Maori Wars.* 2d ed. Auckland: Auckland University Press.

Slavery Convention
1926   *League of Nations Treaty Series* 253. Available at <www1.umn.edu/humanrts/instree/f1sc.htm>.

Smith, S. Percy
1910   *Maori Wars of the Nineteenth Century.* Wellington: Whitcombe and Tombs.

Snow, Alpheus Henry
1921   *The Question of Aborigines in the Law and Practice of Nations.* New York: G. P. Putnam's Sons.

Snow, Dean R.
1984   "Iroquois Prehistory." Pp. 241–49 in *Extending the Rafters,* ed. M. K. Foster, J. Campisi, and M. Mithun. Albany: State University of New York Press for the Newberry Library.
1994   *The Iroquois.* Oxford and Cambridge: Blackwell Press.

Snow, Dean R., and Kim M. Lanphear
1988   "European Contact and Indian Depopulation in the Northeast: The Timing of the First Epidemics." *Ethnohistory* 35:15–33.

Snow, Dean R., and William A. Starna
1989   "Seventeenth-Century Depopulation: A View from the Mohawk Valley." *American Anthropologist* 91 (1): 142–49.

Sorrenson, M. P. K.
1963   "The Maori King Movement, 1858–1885." Pp. 33–55 in *Studies of a Small Democracy,* ed. R. Chapman and K. Sinclair. Hamilton: University of Auckland.

Spicer, Edward H.
1962   *Cycles of Conquest: The Impact of Spain, Mexico, and the United States on the Indians of the Southwest, 1533–1960.* Tucson: University of Arizona Press.

Stamatopoulou, Elsa
1994   "Indigenous Peoples and the United Nations: Human Rights as a Developing Dynamic." *Human Rights Quarterly* 16 (1): 58–81.

Stannard, David E.
1992   *American Holocaust: The Conquest of the New World.* New York: Oxford University Press.

Stanton, William
1960   *The Leopard's Spots: Scientific Attitudes toward Race in America 1815–59.* Chicago: University of Chicago Press.
Starna, William A.
1988   "Aboriginal Title and Traditional Iroquois Land Use: An Anthropological Perspective." Pp. 31–48 in *Iroquois Land Claims,* ed. C. Vecsey and W. Starna. Syracuse: Syracuse University Press.
1994   "The Repeal of Article 8: Law, Government, and Cultural Politics at Akwesasne." *American Indian Law Review* 18 (2): 297–311.
Statute of the International Court of Justice
1945   59 Stat. 1055, T.S. 993, 3 Bevans 1179. Available at <www.un.org/Overview/Statute/contents.html>.
Stephanson, Anders
1995   *Manifest Destiny: American Expansion and the Empire of Right.* New York: Hill and Wang.
Stewart, Omer C.
1948   "Indians Today: History in the Making." Program #438, November 13. Department of Radio Production, University of Colorado, Boulder. Mimeo.
Stocking, George W., Jr.
1968   *Race, Culture, and Evolution: Essays in the History of Anthropology.* New York: Free Press.
———, ed.
1974   *The Shaping of American Anthropology 1883–1911: A Franz Boas Reader.* New York: Basic Books.
Strickland, Rennard
1975   *Fire and the Spirits: Cherokee Law from Clan to Court.* Norman: University of Oklahoma Press.
1986   "Genocide-at-Law: An Historic and Contemporary View of the Native American Experience." *University of Kansas Law Review* 34 (4): 713–55.
Sturtevant, William C.
1954   Statement of William C. Sturtevant Regarding S 2747 and H.R. 7321. In Joint Hearing before the Subcommittee on Interior and Insular Affairs . . . 83rd Congress 2d Session on S 2747 and H.R. 7321. Pt. 8, Seminole Indians, Florida, March 1 and 2. Pp. 1136–37. Washington, D.C.
Swepston, Lee
1990   "A New Step in the International Law on Indigenous and Tribal Peoples: ILO Convention No. 169 of 1989." *Oklahoma City University Law Review* 15 (3): 677–714.
1992   "Human Rights Complaint Procedures of the International Labour Organization." Pp. 99–116 in *Guide to International Human Rights Practice,* 2d ed., ed. H. Hannum. Philadelphia: University of Pennsylvania Press.
Swepston, Lee, and Roger Plant
1985   "International Standards and the Protection of the Land Rights of Indigenous and Tribal Populations." *International Labor Review* 124 (1): 91–106.
Tax, Sol
1957   "Termination versus the Needs of Positive Policy for American Indians." *Congressional Record* 103 (July 3): 116.

Taylor, Graham D.
1980   *The New Deal and American Indian Tribalism: The Administration of the In-dian Reorganization Act, 1934–1945.* Lincoln: University of Nebraska Press.
Te Rangi Hiroa (Peter H. Buck)
1949   *The Coming of the Maori.* Wellington: Whitcombe and Tombs; Maori Pur-poses Fund Board.
Thomas, Nicholas
1994   *Colonialism's Culture: Anthropology, Travel, and Government.* Princeton: Princeton University Press.
Thornton, Russell
1987   *American Indian Holocaust and Survival: A Population History since 1492.* Norman: University of Oklahoma Press.
Todorov, Tzvetan
1984   *The Conquest of America: The Question of the Other.* Translated by Richard Howard. New York: Harper Torchbooks.
Tooker, Elisabeth J.
1971   "Clans and Moieties in North America." *Current Anthropology* 12:357–376.
1978a   "The League of the Iroquois: Its History, Politics, and Ritual." Pp. 418–41 in *Handbook of North American Indians,* vol. 15, ed. B. Trigger. Washington, D.C.: Smithsonian Institution Press.
1978b   "Iroquois since 1820." Pp. 449–65 in *Handbook of North American Indians,* vol. 15, ed. B. Trigger. Washington, D.C.: Smithsonian Institution Press.
1992   "Lewis H. Morgan and His Contemporaries." *American Anthropologist* 94 (2): 357–75.
———, ed.
1985   *Political and Social Organization.* Vol. 1 of *An Iroquois Sourcebook.* Introduc-tion by Elisabeth J. Tooker. New York and London: Garland Publishing.
Trask, Mililani B.
1991   "Historical and Contemporary Hawaiian Self-Determination: A Native Hawaiian Perspective." *Arizona Journal of International and Comparative Law* 8 (2): 77–95.
1994   "The Politics of Oppression." Pp. 91–105 in *Hawai'i,* ed. U. Hasager and J. Friedman. Copenhagen: International Work Group for Indigenous Affairs.
Tremewan, Peter
1990   *French Akaroa: An Attempt to Colonise Southern New Zealand.* Christchurch: University of Canterbury Press.
1992   "French Land Purchases." Pp. 107–21 in *The French and the Maori,* ed. J. Dunmore. Waikanae, New Zealand: Heritage Press.
Trigger, Bruce G.
1976   *The Children of Aataentsic.* 2 vols. Montreal: McGill-Queens University Press.
1978   "Early Iroquoian Contact with Europeans." Pp. 344–56 in *Handbook of North American Indians,* vol. 15, ed. B. Trigger. Washington, D.C.: Smith-sonian Institution Press.
Trigger, Bruce G., and James F. Pendergast
1978   "Saint Lawrence Iroquoians." Pp. 357–61 in *Handbook of North American Indians,* vol. 15, ed. B. Trigger. Washington, D.C.: Smithsonian Institution Press.

Tuck, James A.
1978   "Northern Iroquoian Prehistory." Pp. 322–33 in *Handbook of North American Indians*, vol. 15, ed. B. Trigger. Washington, D.C.: Smithsonian Institution Press.

Tullberg, Steven, and Robert T. Coulter
1991   "The Failure of Indian Rights Advocacy: Are Lawyers to Blame?" Pp. 51–64 in *Rethinking Indian Law*, ed. Committee for Native American Struggles. New Haven: National Lawyers Guild.

Turpel, Mary Ellen
1992   "Indigenous Peoples' Rights of Political Participation and Self-Determination: Recent International Legal Developments and the Continuing Struggle for Recognition." *Cornell International Law Journal* 25 (2): 579–602.

United Nations
1980   Sub-Commission on the Prevention of Discrimination and Protection of Minorities. "The Right to Self-Determination: Implementation of United Nations Resolutions." By Héctor Gros Espiell, special rapporteur. E/CN.4/Sub.2/405/Rev.1.

1981   Sub-Commission on Prevention of Discrimination and Protection of Minorities. "The Right to Self-Determination: Historical and Current Development on the Basis of United Nations Instruments." By Aureliu Cristescu, special rapporteur. E/CN.4/Sub.2/404/Rev.1.

1985   Sub-Commission on Prevention of Discrimination and Protection of Minorities. "Discrimination against Indigenous Peoples: Report of the Working Group on Indigenous Populations on Its Third Session."

1986   Economic and Social Council. "Study of the Problem of Discrimination against Indigenous Populations." Vols. 1–4. By José R. Martínez Cobo, special rapporteur. E/CN.4/Sub.2/1986/7/Add.1.

1987   Economic and Social Council. "Study of the Problem of Discrimination against Indigenous Populations: Conclusions, Proposals, and Recommendations." Vol. 5. By José R. Martínez Cobo, special rapporteur. E/CN.4/Sub.2/1986/7/Add.4.

1989a   Centre for Human Rights. "Communications Procedures." Fact Sheet No. 7. Geneva: United Nations.

1989b   Centre for Human Rights. "The Effects of Racism and Racial Discrimination on the Social and Economic Relations between Indigenous Peoples and States: Report of a Seminar." Geneva, January 16–20, 1989. HR/PUB/89/5. New York: United Nations.

1989c   Sub-Commission on Prevention of Discrimination and Protection of Minorities. "Discrimination against Indigenous Peoples: Report of the Working Group on Indigenous Populations on Its Seventh Session." E/CN.4/Sub.2/1989/36.

1990a   Centre for Human Rights. "The Rights of Indigenous Peoples." Human Rights Fact Sheet No. 9. Geneva: United Nations.

1990b   Sub-Commission on Prevention of Discrimination and Protection of Minorities. "Discrimination against Indigenous Peoples: Report of the Working Group on Indigenous Populations on Its Eighth Session." E/CN.4/Sub.2/1990/42.

1991a   Commission on Human Rights. "Discrimination against Indigenous Populations: Study on Treaties, Agreements, and Other Constructive Arrangements between States and Indigenous Populations: Preliminary Report." Submitted by Miguel Alfonso Martínez, special rapporteur. E/CN.4/Sub.2/1991/33.

1991b Sub-Commission on Prevention of Discrimination and Protection of Minorities. "Discrimination against Indigenous Peoples: Report of the Working Group on Indigenous Populations on Its Ninth Session." E/CN.4/Sub.2/1991/.

1992a Economic and Social Council. "Technical Meeting on the International Year for the World's Indigenous People Convened in Accordance with General Assembly Resolution 46/128." Geneva, March 9–11, 1992. E/CN.4/1992/AC.4/TM/8.

1992b Sub-Commission on Prevention of Discrimination and Protection of Minorities. "Discrimination against Indigenous Peoples: Report of the United Nations Technical Conference on Practical Experience in the Realization of Sustainable and Environmentally Sound Self-Development of Indigenous Peoples." Santiago, Chile, May 18–22, 1992. E/CN.4/Sub.2/1992/31.

1992c Sub-Commission on Prevention of Discrimination and Protection of Minorities. "Discrimination against Indigenous Peoples: Report of the Working Group on Indigenous Populations on Its Tenth Session." E/CN.4/Sub.2/1992/33.

1992d Sub-Commission on Prevention of Discrimination and Protection of Minorities. "Discrimination against Indigenous Peoples: Report of the Working Group on Indigenous Populations on Its Tenth Session: Addendum." E/CN.4/Sub.2/1992/33/Add.1.

1992e Sub-Commission on Prevention of Discrimination and Protection of Minorities. "Discrimination against Indigenous Peoples: Study on Treaties, Agreements and Other Constructive Arrangements between States and Indigenous Populations: First Progress Report." Submitted by Miguel Alfonso Martínez, special rapporteur. E/CN.4/Sub.2/1992/32.

1993a Centre for Human Rights. "Human Rights: A Compilation of International Instruments." Vol. 1 (Parts 1 and 2), Universal Instruments. New York: United Nations. ST/HR/1/Rev.4.

1993b Sub-Commission on Prevention of Discrimination and Protection of Minorities. "Discrimination against Indigenous Peoples: Report of the Working Group on Indigenous Populations on Its Eleventh Session." E/CN.4/Sub.2/1993/29.

1993c Sub-Commission on Prevention of Discrimination and Protection of Minorities. "Discrimination against Indigenous Peoples: Study on the Protection of the Cultural and Intellectual Property of Indigenous Peoples." By Erica-Irene Daes, special rapporteur of the Sub-Commission on Prevention of Discrimination and Protection of Minorities and chairperson of the Working Group on Indigenous Populations. E/CN.4/Sub.2/1993/28.

1993d Sub-Commission on Prevention of Discrimination and Protection of Minorities. "Discrimination against Indigenous Peoples: Written Statement." Submitted by the International Organization of Indigenous Peoples, a nongovernmental organization in consultative status (Category 2). E/CN.4/Sub.2/1993/NGO/21.

1994a Commission on Human Rights. "Discrimination against Indigenous Peoples: Note." By Erica-Irene Daes, chairperson-rapporteur of the Working Group on Indigenous Populations. International Decade of the World's Indigenous People. E/CN.4/Sub.2/1994/52.

1994b Commission on Human Rights. "Evaluation of the International Year: Interim Report of the Coordinator of the International Year of the World's Indigenous People: Note by the Secretariat." Technical Meeting on the International Year and the International Decade of the World's Indigenous People. E/CN.4/1994/AC.4/TM.4/2.

1994c Sub-Commission on Prevention of Discrimination and Protection of Minorities. "Discrimination against Indigenous Peoples: Transnational Investments and Operations on the Lands Of Indigenous Peoples: Report of the United Nations Centre on Transnational Corporations." Pursuant to Sub-Commission Resolution 1990/26. E/CN.4/Sub.2/1994/40.

1994d Working Group on Indigenous Populations. "Standard-Setting Activities: Evolution of Standards Concerning the Rights of Indigenous Populations: Information Received from Indigenous Peoples' and Non-Governmental Organizations: The Black Hills Teton Sioux Nation." E/CN.4/Sub.2/AC.4/1994/4.

1994e Working Group on Indigenous Populations. "Standard-Setting Activities: Evolution of Standards Concerning the Rights of Indigenous Populations: Information Received from Indigenous Peoples' and Non-Governmental Organizations: The Inuit Tapirisat of Canada." E/CN.4/Sub.2/AC.4/1994/4/Add.1.

1994f Working Group on Indigenous Populations. "Working Group on Indigenous Populations: A Permanent Forum in the United Nations for Indigenous People: Information Received from Governments and Indigenous Organizations." E/CN.4/Sub.2/AC.4/1994/11/Add.2.

1994g Working Group on Indigenous Populations. "Working Group on Indigenous Populations: A Permanent Forum in the United Nations for Indigenous People: Report by the Secretariat." E/CN.4/Sub.2/AC.4/1994/11.

1994h Working Group on Indigenous Populations. "Working Group on Indigenous Populations: Future Role of the Working Group." Working paper submitted by Miguel Alfonso Martínez, member of the working group. E/CN.4/Sub.2/AC.4/1994/10.

1995a Commission on Human Rights. "Consideration of a Draft United Nations Declaration on the Rights of Indigenous Peoples: Information Received from Governments." E/CN.4/1995/WG.15/2.

1995b Commission on Human Rights. "Consideration of a Draft United Nations Declaration on the Rights of Indigenous Peoples: Information Received from Governments: Addendum." E/CN.4/1995/WG.15/2/Add.1.

1995c Commission on Human Rights. "Consideration of a Draft United Nations Declaration on the Rights of Indigenous Peoples: Information Received from Non-Governmental and Indigenous Organizations." E/CN.4/1995/WG.15/4.

1995d Commission on Human Rights. "Organization of the Work of the Session: Technical Meeting on the International Year and the International Decade of the World's Indigenous People." Geneva, July 20–22, 1994. E/CN.4/1995/18.

1995e Sub-Commission on Prevention of Discrimination and Protection of Minorities. "Discrimination against Indigenous Peoples: Protection of the Heritage of Indigenous People: Final Report of the Special Rapporteur." By Erica-Irene Daes, in conformity with Sub-Commission Resolution 1993/44 and Commission on Human Rights Decision 1994/105. E/CN.4/Sub.2/1995/26.

1995f   Sub-Commission on Prevention of Discrimination and Protection of Minorities. "Discrimination against Indigenous Peoples: Report of the Working Group on Indigenous Populations on Its Thirteenth Session." E/CN.4/Sub.2/1995/24.

1995g   Working Group on Indigenous Populations. "Consideration of a Permanent Forum for Indigenous People: Report of the Workshop Held in Accordance with Commission Resolution 1995/30." Copenhagen, June 26–28, 1995. E/CN.4/Sub.2/AC.4/1995/7.

1995h   Working Group on Indigenous Populations. "International Decade of the World's Indigenous People: Report of the Technical Meeting on the International Decade of the World's Indigenous People." E/CN.4/Sub.2/AC.4/1995/5.

1999a   Sub-Commission on Prevention of Discrimination and Protection of Minorities. "Human Rights of Indigenous Peoples: Study on Treaties, Agreements and Other Constructive Arrangements between States and Indigenous Populations." Final Report by Miguel Alfonso Martínez, special rapporteur. E/CN.4/Sub.2/1999/20.

2000a   Sub-Commission on Prevention of Discrimination and Protection of Minorities. "Human Rights of Indigenous Peoples: Report of the Working Group on Indigenous Populations on Its Eighteenth Session." E/CN.4/Sub.2/2000/24.

2000b   Commission on Human Rights. "Human Rights of Indigenous Peoples: Report of the Seminar on the Draft Principles and Guidelines for the Protection of the Heritage of Indigenous Peoples." E/CN.4/Sub.2/2000/26.

2000c   Commission on Human Rights. "Prevention of Discrimination against and the Protection of Minorities: Working paper on the relationship and distinction between the rights of persons belonging to minorities and those of indigenous peoples." E/CN.4/Sub.2/2000/10.

2000d   Commission on Human Rights. "Economic, Social and Cultural Rights: Joint Report by the Independent Expert on Structural Adjustment." E/CN.4/2000/51.

2001a   Sub-Commission on Prevention of Discrimination and Protection of Minorities. "Human Rights of Indigenous Peoples: Report of the Working Group on Indigenous Populations on Its Nineteenth Session." E/CN.4/Sub.2/2001/17.

2001b   Commission on Human Rights. "Prevention of Discrimination and Protection of Indigenous Peoples and Minorities: Indigenous Peoples and Their Relationship to Land." Final working paper by Erica-Irene Daes, special rapporteur. E/CN.4/Sub.2/2001/21.

2001c   Economic and Social Council. "Globalization and its impact on the full enjoyment of all human rights." Commission on Human Rights Resolution 2001/32. E/CN.4/RES/2001/32.

2001d   Commission on Human Rights. "Economic, Social and Cultural Rights: The Highly Indebted Poor Countries (HIPC) Initiative: A Human Rights Assessment of the Poverty Reduction Strategy Papers (PRSP): Report submitted by Mr. Fantu Cheru, independent expert on the effects of structural adjustment policies and foreign debt on the full enjoyment of all human rights, particularly economic, social and cultural rights." E/CN.4/2001/56.

2001e   Commission on Human Rights. "Economic, Social and Cultural Rights: The Impact of Structural Adjustment Programs: Written statement submitted by Indian Movement 'Tupaj Amaru,' a non-governmental organization in special consultative status." E/CN.4/2001/NGO/82.

2001f   Economic and Social Council. "Effects of structural adjustment policies and foreign debt on the full enjoyment of all human rights, particularly economic, social and cultural rights." Commission on Human Rights Resolution 2001/27. E/CN.4/RES/2001/27.

Universal Declaration of Human Rights
1948   United Nations General Assembly. Resolution 217A (III), UN Doc. A/810 at 71.

Utley, Robert M.
1963   *The Last Days of the Sioux Nation.* New Haven: Yale University Press.

van Vree, Frank, ed.
1980   *Fourth Russell Tribunal: The Rights of the Indians of the Amerikas: Handbook.* Amsterdam: Workgroup Indian Project.

Vance, John T.
1969   "The Congressional Mandate and the Indian Claims Commission." *North Dakota Law Review* 45 (3): 325–36.

Vayda, Andrew P.
1960   *Maori Warfare.* Polynesian Society Maori Monographs, No. 2. Wellington: Reed.

Veatch, Richard
1975   *Canada and the League of Nations.* Toronto: University of Toronto Press.

Vecsey, Christopher, and William A. Starna, eds.
1988   *Iroquois Land Claims.* Syracuse: Syracuse University Press.

Venne, Sharon
1989   "The New Language of Assimilation: A Brief Analysis of ILO Convention 169." *Without Prejudice* 2 (2): 53–67.

Vollman, Tim
1979   "A Survey of Eastern Indian Land Claims: 1970–1979." *Maine Law Review* 31 (1): 5–16.

Wagley, Charles
1977   *Welcome of Tears: The Tapirapé Indians of Central Brazil.* New York: Oxford University Press.

Wagley, Charles, and Marvin Harris
1958   *Minorities in the New World: Six Case Studies.* New York: Columbia University Press.

Waitangi Tribunal Division
1990   *The Treaty of Waitangi and the Waitangi Tribunal: Te Roopu Whakamana i te Tiriti o Waitangi.* Auckland: Waitangi Tribunal Division, Department of Justice.

Walker, Ranginui J.
1987   *Nga Tau Tohetohe, Years of Anger.* Edited by Jacqueline Amoamo. Auckland: Penguin Books.

1989   "The Treaty of Waitangi as a Focus of Maori Protest." Pp. 263–99 in *Waitangi,* ed. I. Kawharu. Auckland: Oxford University Press.

1990   *Ka Whawhai Tonu Matou: Struggle Without End.* Auckland: Penguin.

1992   "Maori People Since 1950." Pp. 498–519 in *The Oxford History of New*

Zealand, 2d ed., ed. G. Rice. Auckland: Oxford University Press.

Wallace, Anthony F. C.

1958 "Dreams and the Wishes of the Soul: A Type of Psychoanalytic Theory among the Seventeenth Century Iroquois." *American Anthropologist* 60 (2): 234–48.

1978 "Origins of the Longhouse Religion." Pp. 442–49 in *Handbook of North American Indians,* vol. 15, ed. B. Trigger. Washington, D.C.: Smithsonian Institution Press.

1993 *The Long, Bitter Trail: Andrew Jackson and the Indians.* New York: Hill and Wang.

Ward, Alan

1988 "The Treaty and the Purchase of Maori Land." *The New Zealand Journal of History* 22 (2): 169–74.

Wards, Ian

1968 *The Shadow of the Land: A Study of British Policy and Racial Conflict in New Zealand, 1832–1852.* Wellington: Government Printer.

Washburn, Wilcomb E.

1965 "Indian Removal Policy: Administrative, Historical and Moral Criteria for Judging Its Success or Failure." *Ethnohistory* 12 (2): 274–78.

1981 "The Russell Tribunal—Who Speaks for Indian Tribes?" *Indian Truth* 240:8, 14.

1984 "A Fifty-Year Perspective on the Indian Reorganization Act." *American Anthropologist* 86 (2): 279–89.

1995 *Red Man's Land/White Man's Law: The Past and Present Status of the American Indian.* 2d ed. Norman: University of Oklahoma Press.

———, ed.

1973 *The American Indian and the United States: A Documentary History.* 4 vols. New York: Random House.

Weaver, Sally M.

1978 "Six Nations of the Grand River, Ontario." Pp. 525–36 in *Handbook of North American Indians,* vol. 15. ed. B. Trigger. Washington, D.C.: Smithsonian Institution Press.

Western Sahara

1975 International Court of Justice. Advisory Opinion. *International Court of Justice* 12.

Westlake, John

1894 *Chapters on the Principles of International Law.* Cambridge: Cambridge University Press.

Weyler, Rex

1992 *Blood of the Land: The Government and Corporate War against the American Indian Movement.* 2d ed. New York: Everest House.

Wilkinson, Charles F.

1987 *American Indians, Time and the Law: Native Societies in a Modern Constitutional Democracy.* New Haven: Yale University Press.

Wilkinson, Charles F., and Eric R. Biggs

1977 "The Evolution of the Termination Policy." *American Indian Law Review* 5 (1): 139–84.

Wilkinson, Charles F., and John M. Volkman

1975 "Judicial Review of Treaty Abrogation: 'As Long As the Water Flows, or

Grass Grows Upon the Earth'—How Long a Time Is That?" *California Law Review* 63 (3): 601–61.

Williams, David V.

1989   "Te Tiriti o Waitangi—Unique Relationship between Crown and Tangata Whenua?" Pp. 64–91 in *Waitangi,* ed. I. Kawharu. Auckland: Oxford University Press.

1990   "The Constitutional Status of the Treaty of Waitangi: An Historical Perspective." *New Zealand Universities Law Review* 14 (1): 9–36.

Williams, Robert A., Jr.

1988   "Learning Not to Live with Eurocentric Myopia: A Reply to Professor Laurence's 'Learning to Live with the Plenary Power of Congress over the Indian Nations.'" *Arizona Law Review* 30 (3): 439–57.

1990a   *The American Indian in Western Legal Thought: The Discourses of Conquest.* New York: Oxford University Press.

1990b   "Encounters on the Frontiers of International Human Rights Law: Redefining the Terms of Indigenous Peoples' Survival in the World." *Duke Law Journal* 1990 (4): 660–704.

1991   "Columbus's Legacy: Law as an Instrument of Racial Discrimination against Indigenous Peoples' Rights of Self-Determination." *Arizona Journal of International and Comparative Law* 8 (2): 51–75.

1997   *Linking Arms Together: American Indian Treaty Visions of Law and Peace, 1600–1800.* New York: Oxford University Press.

Wilson, James

1986   *The Original Americans: U.S. Indians.* 3d ed. Report No. 31. London: Minority Rights Group.

Wilson, John

1990   "The Maori Struggle for Mana Motuhake." *New Zealand Historic Places* 30:26–30.

Wilson, Ormond

1985   *From Hongi Hika to Hone Heke: A Quarter Century of Upheaval.* Dunedin: John McIndoe.

Winfrey, Robert H., Jr.

1986   "The Indian Civil Rights Act." Pp. 105–37 in *Between Two Worlds,* ed. A. Gibson. Oklahoma City: Oklahoma Historical Society.

Winger, Otho

1935   *The Last of the Miamis: Me Shin Go Me Sia, the Last Tribal Chief of the Miamis.* North Manchester: Otho Winger.

Wright, Harrison M.

1967   *New Zealand, 1769–1840: Early Years of Western Contact.* 2d ed. Cambridge: Harvard University Press.

York, Geoffrey, and Loreen Pindera

1991   *People of the Pines: The Warriors and the Legacy of Oka.* Boston: Little, Brown and Company

Zannis, Mark

1992   "Acts of Defiance." New York: First Run/Icarus. Film.

INDEX